KIDNAPPED
FROM THAT LAND

KIDNAPPED FROM THAT LAND

THE GOVERNMENT RAIDS ON THE SHORT CREEK POLYGAMISTS

Martha Sonntag Bradley

University of Utah Press
Salt Lake City

Volume Nine, Publications in Mormon Studies
Linda King Newell, editor

 The Defiance House Man colophon is a registered trademark
of the University of Utah Press. It is based upon a four-foot-tall,
ancient Puebloan pictograph (late PIII) near Glen Canyon, Utah.

First paperback printing 1996
ISBN-10: 0-87480-528-7   ISBN-13: 978-0-87480-528-4

Library of Congress Cataloging-in-Publication Data

Bradley, Martha Sonntag.
Kidnapped from that land : the government raids on the polygamists
of Short Creek / Martha Sonntag Bradley.
    p.   cm.—(Publications in Mormon studies ; v. 9)
Includes bibliographical references (p.   ) and index.
ISBN-10: 0-87480-415-9   ISBN-13: 978-0-87480-415-7
  1. Mormon Fundamentalism—Arizona—Colorado City—History.
2. Mormon Fundamentalism—Utah—Hildale—History.   3. Polygamy—
Utah—Hildale—History.   4. Polygamy—Arizona—Colorado City—
History.   5. Persecution—Arizona—Colorado City—History—20th
century.   6. Persecution—Utah—Hildale—History—20th century.
7. Colorado City (Ariz.)—Church history.   8. Hildale (Utah)—Church
history. I. Title. II. Series.
BX8680.M534C63   1993
289.3'79159—dc20   93-8293

By the rivers of Babylon, there we sat down,
yea, we wept, when we remembered Zion.
We hanged down our harps upon the willows in
the midst thereof.
For there they that carried us away captive
required of us a song;
and they that wasted us
required of us mirth, saying,
Sing us one of the songs of Zion.
How shall we sing the Lord's song in a strange land?

Psalm 137

Contents

Preface

At 4:00 A.M. on 26 July 1953, a night of an eclipsed moon, Arizona state officials and police officers moved through the darkness to begin an armed invasion of the tiny village of Short Creek in the isolated area north of the Grand Canyon. The village was inhabited by a group of people, nearly all of them of Mormon antecedents but repudiated and excommunicated by their church. The crime of these American citizens? They were living plural marriage.

At 9:00 A.M. that same morning, Arizona's Governor Howard Pyle intoned solemnly over KTAR radio:

> Before dawn today the State of Arizona began and now has substantially concluded a momentous police action against insurrection within its own borders.
>
> Arizona has mobilized and used its total police power to protect the lives and future of 263 children. They are the product and the victims of the foulest conspiracy you could possibly imagine.
>
> More than 1500 peace officers moved into Short Creek.... They arrested almost the entire population of a community dedicated to the production of white slaves who are without hope of escaping this degrading slavery from the moment of their birth.[1]

As Governor Pyle pushed away from the microphone, he must have pondered the significance of what he had just begun and felt the weighty burden of the raid, knowing full well if someone was hurt, if anything went wrong, it would be his responsiblity.

More than four hundred miles to the north, in the warmth of the morning sun in the dusty yard of Short Creek's school, women sat with babies on their laps or stood and paced along with her sister wives and neighbors, wondering what was about to happen, whether or not they would be able to keep their children, and what would happen to the men already being assembled to be taken to the jail in Kingman. Predictably, their thoughts often wandered from the immediate crisis at hand to what the many children would eat for breakfast, who would feed the animals, who would hang out the wash.

Children darted in and out of the milkweed branches along the sides of the dusty road oblivious to the fact that their fathers had been arrested by the government of Arizona, accused of statutory rape, cohabitation, and other violations of the law. A boy not quite old enough to pose a pernicious threat to the morality of American society, yet not young enough to be taken into the custody of the state child welfare services, circled the schoolyard wanting to be a part of the unfolding drama yet fearful, expecting the worst.

A Mormon Relief Society sister in Mesa, Arizona punched air into a pillow for the bed in the spare room wondering how many fundamentalists she would be welcoming into her home, a foster home for those who would be taken from Short Creek that week.

This 1953 raid was the third of three, launched not simply against alleged offending individuals but against the entire community. The first had come in 1935, and the second in 1944. What was it about the men and women of fundamentalist Mormonism that threatened the "moral fiber" of America? Why did the state of Arizona find it necessary to launch a crusade to "protect" the women and children of an entire community? Why was their communal lifestyle seen as un-American?

The story of plural marriage in Short Creek, of its complex relationship to the Mormon Church, and of the government's reaction to both, weave together like triple strands of a braid. Both the mainstream Mormons and the "fundamentalist" Mormons of Short Creek resisted this weaving. Although both acknowledged a common tradition and asserted the all-important principle of prophetic revelation, each denied its manifestations in the other and defined boundaries that were barbed and defiant.

Limitations on the Research

For this study, I used a variety of source materials: newspapers, legislative and governmental records, correspondence, court records, and personal collections. Between 1986 and 1991 I conducted more than eighty interviews with members of the fundamentalist community. The informants included males and females, farmers and businessmen, ecclesiastical and secular leaders, teachers and housewives, married and single individuals. They were selected to give a cross-section of the community. A significant portion of the book is based on the notes and transcripts of these interviews. However, unfortunately, many of the individuals are not cited by name. Due to the complicated legal situation surrounding the issue of polygamy, they are reluctant to be directly quoted in this text. Still, the fundamentalists have generously supported my research by opening their community to my study, arranging numerous interviews, and providing editorial comments on the manuscript. I acknowledge this vote of support and the risk they take in doing so. The fundamentalists do not try to advertise their cause. They are a private people. The manner in which they opened up to my research reflects an extraordinary effort to be understood.

Many of the fundamentalists involved in the three raids have died. Others have left fundamentalism. This story is in large measure the story of those who chose to stay in Short Creek, a choice that reflects their general satisfaction with the lifestyle.

In addition to interviews with the fundamentalists themselves, numerous outsiders who relate to the group have been consulted—these include former governors of both Arizona and Utah, local ecclesiastical leaders, and other contemporaries of the events.

Much of the story of the three raids on the fundamentalists will remain untold. Because public records are protected by the constitutional right to privacy, many of the records that might add further detail to this narrative are unavailable. In 1991 the use of public records was regulated by the Government Access and Management Act (63–2–101) which seals public documents such as juvenile court records for a period of seventy-five years after their creation. Therefore, many records of the highway patrol, juvenile court, social services and other relevant public records that might have been useful for this study have not been consulted despite my repeated efforts to gain access to them. The directors of the archives of the Church of Jesus Christ of Latter-day Saints for their own reasons have also restricted the use of materials about the fundamentalists, Short Creek and the raids. This history thus should be viewed as the story as essentially told by the fundamentalists themselves, reflected in contemporary news accounts.

Although I sympathize with what happened to the fundamentalists during the raids, I am not myself a polygamist nor do I believe the tenets of the fundamentalist faith even though I have roots in the practice that stretch back into the nineteenth century. Nevertheless, my enduring interest in Short Creek has been based on the spirit of historical inquiry rather than a search for religious truth.

Because I have worked on this project for so long it will feel strange to have it come to an end. My family has been long-suffering in their willingness to support my work. I undoubtedly have the best-informed children (outside the world of fundamentalism) on the subject of the principle of plural marriage. And I think that they have benefitted from this search. We have all learned that the bridges we can identify between ourselves and those who seem different are far more valuable than the walls we may erect. And so I thank Richard, Jason, Elizabeth, Rachael, Emily, Katelyn, and Patrick for sharing me with this subject.

I have enormous respect and affection for the three women who helped me polish this manuscript. Lavina Anderson, Marti Dickey Esplin and Linda Newell have helped me shape this book into something better than it was. Lowell Durham's and Jessie Embry's comments on different stages of this project have likewise strengthened my efforts. The careful editing of Richard Firmage and Glenda Cotter has likewise greatly improved this manuscript.

Finally, it is important that I acknowledge the lifetime support of my parents, Luonna Graff Sonntag and George Tadje Sonntag. And, although I am sure my father still thinks of me as a painter and my mother dreams of me as a dancer, perhaps this is some small proof that writing history is a good thing for their only daughter to do.

Mormon Polygamy:
A Historical Overview

1830–1890

Mormonism emerged from the emotional fever of American religious revivalism during the period which historians have called the Second Great Awakening, beginning in the late eighteenth century and continuing in some locations into the 1840s. When Joseph Smith, Jr. organized the Church of Jesus Christ of Latter-day Saints on 6 April 1830, he had gone further than the hope of the Jacksonian era that a youth of humble origins could become a president: Joseph Smith claimed to be a prophet of God.

Only a few years after the organization of the new church, members of which soon became known as Mormons due to their belief in the scriptural authenticity of the *Book of Mormon*, Joseph Smith had carefully considered the idea of a plurality of wives as a part of the sweeping plan for the restoration of the true order of the ancient Church of Christ.[1] The principle fit into Smith's framework for a new and radical reinterpretation of the marriage role in the Mormon plan of salvation. Plural marriage enhanced the patriarchal foundation of Mormon marriage and extended the prestige of the exclusively male priesthood through a new type of family network created by plural unions.[2]

Joseph Smith's vision of the "new and everlasting covenant of marriage" was embodied in Mormon scripture when on 12 July 1843 he dictated the 132nd section of the *Doctrine and Covenants*. It

outlined the peculiar Mormon interpretation of the sacred and binding nature of the marriage relationship. Through his claim to revelation Smith called for the complete restoration of the marriage patterns of Abraham, Isaac, and Jacob. More importantly, "celestial
marriage" for time and all eternity bound men and women together
in an endless union. The "sealing" of couples in the temples of the
Lord through priesthood authority was the final means through
which the most faithful could reach the ultimate status: glory in the
highest of the three kingdoms of God—what Mormons call the
"celestial" kingdom. Smith interpreted plural marriage as a uniquely
exalted form of "celestial marriage"—the "further order" of the patriarchal order of marriage mentioned in *Doctrine and Covenants*
section 132.[3]

During the early 1840s in Nauvoo, the Mormon city on the Illinois bank of the Mississippi River, Smith cautiously introduced the
most trusted of the upper echelon of leaders and friends to both the
idea and the actual practice of plural marriage.[4] It quickly became a
loyalty test for those around the Mormon prophet. Sifting the wheat
from the chaff, plural marriage both confused and divided the members of the fledgling church into two camps: those who were willing
to follow Joseph in all things, and those who were not. Ultimately,
the issue of polygamy helped lead to Smith's death.[5] Thereafter the
future of plural marriage lay in the hands of yet another Mormon
prophet—Brigham Young.

It would take two years for the Council of Twelve Apostles to decide which man to follow among those who claimed to succeed Joseph Smith. The Utah Mormons believe that the "mantle of the
prophet" fell upon Brigham Young—that he was, in other words, the
Lord's choice. During that time those unable to accept the doctrine of
plural marriage often took different paths and chose to separate from
the main body of the Church. By the time those Mormons who chose
to follow Young's leadership had successfully completed the trek
west and established colonies throughout the Great Basin region, the
"Principle" as it came to be referred to was an accepted part of their
tradition and was characterized by a pragmatic, matter-of-fact set of
assumptions about both the responsibilities and limits of the practice.[6]

Although Church leaders had privately lived plural marriage for
nearly a decade, it was not until 1852 that the Mormons publicly acknowledged the practice. By that time the Mormon Church had be-

gun to secure its hold on the territory of the Great Basin and made a successful initial attempt at colonization as well as an unsuccessful attempt at statehood. Rather than President Brigham Young, however, it was Church apostle and intellectual Orson Pratt who stood before an audience of Saints on 29 August 1852 beneath the shade of the old bowery to articulate the Church's position on the Principle. What Pratt would say became the standard message on the plurality for the next forty years. Nothing substantive would be added later beyond this initial justification of the doctrine. According to Pratt, the *Doctrine and Covenants* "contains a doctrine, a small portion of the world is opposed to; but I can deliver a prophecy upon it. . . . It will sail over, and ride triumphantly above all the prejudice and priest-craft of the day; it will be fostered and believed in by the more intelligent portions of the world, as one of the best doctrines ever proclaimed to any people."[7]

Like much of the rhetoric about "celestial marriage" almost 100 years later in the 1940s, Pratt described plural marriage as a sacred and binding contract for time and all eternity. By means of the Principle faithful men and women could insure a bountiful righteous posterity, a "glorious, eternal increase." Essentially, the purpose of plural marriage was the creation of earthly tabernacles (bodies) for the countless number of spirits waiting to come to this earth. The purpose of the Principle was, according to Pratt, procreation. This was also about the closest the Church would come to providing a guideline for living and practicing plural marriage. Mormons, as free agents, were left to find out for themselves how to conduct their affairs.

Regardless of Mormon efforts to legitimize polygamy, public sentiment so opposed the practice that in 1856 the Republican party coupled polygamy and slavery as the "Twin Relics of Barbarism." To them and many other Americans, plural marriage seemed to threaten the very foundation of American traditions.[8]

Seven years after the government sent federal troops to the area to suppress a supposed rebellion of the Latter-day Saints—an action later called the "Utah War"—the first piece of anti-bigamy legislation was passed by the United States Congress. However, the Morrill Anti-Bigamy Act of 1862 failed to cause any change in the way Utah Mormons lived their lives. Within months, the heat of the anti-polygamy campaign was diffused and attention focused instead on the Civil War, and then later on Reconstruction. During this period

of calm before the storm, the Principle became more firmly en-
trenched in the lifestyle of the Mormon people, although it has been
estimated by Stanley Ivins that only between fifteen and twenty percent of all Mormons practiced plural marriage.[9]

In 1875, *Reynolds* v. *United States* tested the constitutionality of
certain anti-polygamy bills.[10] When the Supreme Court qualified the
right to religious freedom it opened the door for decades to cases test-
ing the limits of religious practice.[11]

It was inevitable that a plurality of wives would come under the
perusal of reform-minded American men and women of the 1880s.
Plural marriage, like alcohol or crime, seemed to pose a threat to the
basic moral fiber of America. The very existence of polygamy in Utah
Territory was seen as a threat to the sanctity of the monogamous Vic-
torian family.

A series of strengthened anti-polygamy bills in the 1880s reflected the anxiety caused by the increased attention given to the
Mormons by the government. The reformers whose efforts had
turned the temperance movement into a virtual religion and the
movement for female suffrage into a passion that came to include every issue that appeared to threaten the role of women in society also
turned their attention to plural marriage. The moral reformers of the
1880s believed passionately in the ideal of a homogeneous society yet
saw threats to it everywhere, and nowhere did the threat appear
more bold than in the face of the Mormon polygamous male.

At the same time, the Edmunds Act of 1882 sought to pull the
Mormons into line with mainstream American values by setting in
place severe penalties for polygamists and those accused of the lesser
charge, unlawful cohabitation. It was a classic example of nativist re-
actionary legislation and it struck at the political power of the Mormon leadership in the Utah Territory. John Higham's definition of
nativism as the "intense opposition to an internal minority on the
grounds of its foreign (i.e., un-American) connections"[12] illuminates
one source of the anti-polygamy sentiment of the 1880s.

To the reformer or to the nativist already convinced that the
Mormon polygamist had a total disregard for the law, the Mormon
idea of a political kingdom of God was decidedly un-American. The
closed corporate nature of the entire Mormon colonization effort of
the Great Basin ran counter to American settlement traditions. Mormonism like Catholicism constituted an empire of competing loyal-

ties—church versus country—and was coupled with sectarian mysteries that seemed to threaten American society at its roots.

Nativism led to few major changes in legislation during the 1880s that affected minority populations; however, the Edmunds Act was a prominent exception. The judicial crusade against polygamy was focused, and it resulted in legislation that empowered federal officials to attack the Mormon Church and disrupt the family life of its people.

The Edmunds Act of 1882 strengthened anti-polygamy provisions of the Morrill Anti-Bigamy Act of 1862, the Poland Act of 1874, and, most significantly, the U.S. Supreme Court's 1879 affirmation of the constitutionality of the Morrill Act. The Edmunds Act prohibited both polygamy and unlawful cohabitation, making consecutive prison sentences possible for each and barring from public service or voting anyone practicing polygamy.[13]

This act ushered in the period known to the Mormons as "the raid." Men who were liable to arrest went into hiding on what was called "the underground." Frequently, so did plural wives, moving from place to place with their infants to avoid testifying against their husbands. Between 1884 and 1893, "more than a thousand judgments were secured for unlawful cohabitation and thirty-one for polygamy," each bearing penitentiary sentences and often fines as well.[14] In 1885, John Taylor, who became Mormon Church president after Brigham Young's death in 1877, advised Arizona polygamists to flee to another country when, due to overcrowded Arizona penitentiaries, the court shipped Mormon felons 2,000 miles away to Detroit to serve their sentences.[15]

President Taylor went into hiding in January 1885 and died on the underground two years later in July 1887. Most of the general authorities were also in hiding. Wilford Woodruff, Taylor's successor, appeared at the October 1887 conference to the applause of the audience, but went into hiding after the meeting.[16]

That same year, when the Edmunds-Tucker Act passed, tightening the trap for the Saints, Wilford Woodruff was in hiding either in St. George, Utah or in the nearby settlement of Atkinville.[17]

By 1890, more than 12,000 Utah Mormons had been deprived of their right to vote; and the United States Supreme Court upheld an even more stringent measure in Idaho in February 1890.[18] Early in September 1890, President Woodruff met in California with key political and business leaders. When he returned, he was prepared to take the step to end polygamy that John Taylor had refused to take at his death.[19]

The Demise of Authorized Polygamy, 1890–1933

THE FIRST MANIFESTO, 1890

The practice of polygamy among the Mormons officially ended when Church President and Prophet Wilford W. Woodruff, speaking under the dome of the Tabernacle at the semiannual general conference of the Church in October 1890, presented the "Manifesto." The immediate threat to the continued existence of the Church itself, particularly the Church temples, drove Woodruff to this position.

The Manifesto was essentially a press announcement which had been released a few days earlier after hurried consultation with his two counselors and four of the twelve apostles.[20] Now included as part of the *Doctrine and Covenants*, it denies the accuracy of "press dispatches" asserting the continuation of plural marriage and affirms:

> We are not teaching polygamy or plural marriage, nor permitting any person to enter into its practice. . . .
> Inasmuch as laws have been enacted by Congress forbidding plural marriages, which laws have been pronounced constitutional by the court of last resort, I hereby declare my intention to submit to those laws, and to use my influence with the members of the Church over which I preside to have them do likewise. . . . I now publicly declare that my advice to the Latter-day Saints is to refrain from contracting any marriage forbidden by the law of the land.[21]

Although it was bewildering for many Saints, the Manifesto formally ended the period of civil disobedience sanctioned by John Taylor. The number of prosecutions for practicing polygamy or unlawful cohabitation dropped off dramatically. Many Mormons and non-Mormons alike were uncertain about the future. Also, the Manifesto created the first breach between the official Church body and the polygamist; by the mid-twentieth century that division would be both broad and deep.

The document raised almost as many questions as it answered. Many Mormons stubbornly refused to accept it as a revelation from

God; it confused others by its vague and ambiguous instructions for the future. The Manifesto's omission of commentary concerning the status of existing plural marriages threw many families into cruel dilemmas. Also, secretly authorized polygamous marriages continued to be performed by Church authorities between 1890 and 1904, though in greatly reduced numbers.[22]

Byron Harvey Allred attended the October 1890 conference with his parents and his wife. He wrote: "My father and mother, accompanied by an estimable woman, who had consented to join them in the living of that higher law, had made the long journey to Salt Lake City, primarily for the purpose of having that plural marriage solemnized in the Temple. The adoption of that manifesto placed them in a very unpleasant situation, to say the least."[23] To resolve his own confusion concerning the language and implications of the Manifesto, Allred's father met with the Church First Presidency and questioned President Wilford Woodruff, George Q. Cannon, and Joseph F. Smith about the meaning of the document. Woodruff told him that no plural marriages would be sanctioned or solemnized in the United States because of the tenuous relationship between the Church and the government. According to Allred, "inasmuch as that agreement had reference to no other lands where the practice of plural marriage was not prohibited by law, if father wished to obey the law now he would have to go where it could be done without violating the law."[24] Smith told him that colonization was already under way in Mexico for that purpose. Despite the possibility of continuing in plural marriage outside the United States, Allred and his family were profoundly upset by the Manifesto. We were "bewildered, and thrown into the whirlpool of argument, contention, and division relative to the purpose and effect of that manifesto. We had been deceived. Someone had been mistaken, or (could such a thought be permitted to enter our minds) someone had lied."[25]

Regardless of the confusion among the Mormons themselves about the Manifesto, it did appease the government. In 1891 the First Presidency and Council of the Twelve Apostles sent a petition endorsed by a number of Gentiles,[26] including Territorial Governor Arthur L. Thomas and Judge Charles S. Zane, to the President of the United States seeking amnesty for all violators of federal antipolygamy legislation. On 4 January 1893 President Benjamin Harrison granted amnesty to all Mormons who had been in compliance with the law since the Manifesto was issued.

The period that followed was a carefully qualified truce between the government and the Mormon Church rather than a glorified era of good will, although the celebration of statehood in 1896 turned away from the past conflicts. It would continue to be a crime either to marry polygamously or to cohabit with more than one woman, despite efforts by the Utah State Legislature in 1901 to repeal the territorial cohabitation law, which had been codified into state statute.

THE SECOND MANIFESTO, 1904

Polygamy again became the subject of heated debate during the Reed Smoot hearings of 1904 to 1907. When Church Apostle Reed Smoot announced his candidacy for the United States Senate in 1902, the announcement stimulated renewed anti-polygamy activity. Locally, the Salt Lake Ministerial Association led the resistance, maintaining that a Mormon apostle would never be able to clearly separate church and state. Within weeks, national attention was focused on Smoot, on his connections with the Mormon hierarchy, and on the doctrine of plural marriage. Thirty months later, after thousands of pages of testimony from witnesses and careful scrutiny by the Senate Committee on Privileges and Elections as well as a recommendation for expulsion (a decision the full Senate rejected), Apostle Reed Smoot became a United States Senator—a position he continued to hold for the next thirty years.

In response to the pressure generated by the publicity surrounding the hearings and to clarify continuing confusion among his followers, in April 1904 Church President Joseph F. Smith issued what has been called the Second Manifesto. This document denied allegations that new polygamous marriages had occurred "with the sanction, consent or knowledge of the Church," and warned that known transgressors would be excommunicated.[27] Thus, the Second Manifesto rested on coercive power, the threat of excommunication, rather than on the persuasive power of divine revelation.

In his address at that same April 1904 conference, President Smith described at length the Church's patriotism and claimed the constitutional right of freedom of religion as the justification for polygamy rather than the traditional reason that it was a revelation: "What our people did in disregard of the law and the decisions of the Supreme Court affecting plural marriages," he said, "was in the spirit of maintaining religious rights under constitutional guarantees, and not in any spirit of defiance or disloyalty to the government." There-

fore, Mormon civil disobedience ended when "every means of constitutional defense had been exhausted."[28] Then "the Church abandoned the controversy and announced its intention to be obedient to
the laws of the land."[29] Citing the Mormon twelfth Article of Faith,
he pledged personal loyalty to the American system and, by implica-
tion, also pledged the loyalty of the Mormon people.

As polygamists themselves, Joseph F. Smith and other general authorities felt particularly strong pressure to prove their willingness to
enforce the prohibition against plural marriage. Both Smith and
Francis M. Lyman of the Council of the Twelve were chided on the
witness stand at the Smoot hearings for not being sufficiently firm
with offenders, and Smith was interrogated about how he planned to
provide for his families in the future.

Historian Michael Quinn sees Smith as shielding apostles John
W. Taylor and Matthias F. Cowley, both of whom had been active in
preaching and authorizing post-Manifesto plural marriages, from either ecclesiastical discipline or from being available to testify during
the Smoot hearings.[30] But other historians maintain that "repeated
demands for some kind of action against Taylor and Cowley ultimately pushed the First Presidency and Quorum of the Twelve into
an agonizing series of meetings in October 1905 at which no official
minutes were kept. At their conclusion, Taylor and Cowley signed
resignations from the Quorum of the Twelve Apostles. They were
not immediately made public, and everyone but Reed Smoot regarded them as contingencies of last resort."[31] Six months later, in
April 1906, the men were dropped from the quorum for "being out
of harmony," and successors were appointed.[32]

Although the official relationship between plural marriage and
the Latter-day Saints had been severed, the Principle was still a major
concern of Church leaders. Also the Second Manifesto was not the
end of ambiguity. Quinn points out that "by the way he orchestrated
the sustaining of the Second Manifesto, Joseph F. Smith sent unspoken but public reassurance to those who had conscientiously entered
plural marriage after the Manifesto."[33]

Plural marriages continued to be performed without the official
sanction of the president of the Church; they were performed by certain apostles, stake presidents, and other local leaders who were either honestly or conveniently confused about the Church's stance.
However, a hardening of official policy was apparent in public addresses such as the general conference talks of the First Presidency, as

Church leaders slowly moved from advising against the practice to actively using excommunication against offenders. By 1910, President Smith seems to have felt that the disadvantages to the Church of continued plural marriages were genuinely threatening. He put teeth in the prohibitions that had been pronounced. A letter of 5 October 1910 from the First Presidency to stake presidencies directed them to actively search out those performing plural marriages who had so far evaded detection.[34]

This effort was primarily directed against those who were performing marriages or bringing others into plural marriage, although it also prescribed punishment for those who would "advise" or "counsel" those entering into such marriages. At this point, continued adherence to the doctrine was no longer a matter of personal discretion—it had become an issue of disloyalty to the Church and rebellion against the direction of the president of the Church. The letter described noncompliance as "not only an individual transgression, but a dishonor to the Church as well."[35]

In 1911 the First Presidency repeated these instructions to stake presidents and further urged them to bring offenders—both individuals performing plural marriages and those entering such unions—before Church courts. Future instructions and policies came out as precepts, regulations, and rules rather than as doctrine or updated revelation. (These policy letters were the precursors of the *Handbook of Instructions*, first circulated in the 1910s to Church leaders.) By the time of his death in November 1918, Smith had made nine public statements denouncing new polygamous unions.[36]

A series of Church leaders took on the assignment of spearheading the Church's anti-polygamy efforts. The first, Francis M. Lyman, then president of the Quorum of the Twelve Apostles, undertook to eradicate the practice of plural marriage during the 1910s through the application of ecclesiastical pressure as well as by threats of criminal prosecution in the civil courts.

Lyman, with fellow apostles John Henry Smith and Heber J. Grant, served on a committee formed in 1909 to investigate new polygamous marriages and "call into council" suspected polygamists. During one such confrontation Lyman remarked that the subject "answers just like the other brethren who are in the same position. ... One would think these brethren had rehearsed their pieces."[37]

Apostle Lyman publicly declared war against the polygamists before a gathering of Latter-day Saints in Logan in October 1910. Although the polygamists felt some pressure from these efforts, the *Salt Lake Tribune* doubted his sincerity: "Apostle Lyman's recent little splurge of indignation was no more and no less than a bluff—which fooled nobody in particular, and least of all the *Tribune*."[38]

Lyman was a vigorous and hearty sixty-year-old whose single-minded pursuit of polygamists led to the excommunication of fellow apostle John W. Taylor in 1911. According to an article published by the fundamentalists much later, on his deathbed four years later, Taylor raised himself up and swore that God would avenge him on Lyman: "Brethren, I am called home and will soon leave you. When I get there I am going to demand that Francis M. Lyman be brought before God and my Redeemer, and I am going to be vindicated."[39] One month later Lyman also died, having failed to reduce in any significant way the practice of plural marriage.

Church intellectual and apostle (from 1911 to 1933) James E. Talmage next inherited the charge. He envisioned a sweeping program that would lead to the eventual elimination of plural marriage and which included an elaborate system of sleuthing by hired detectives and Church members "called" to the work. This approach would eventually materialize under the direction of J. Reuben Clark, Jr.[40]

In his October 1918 conference address Charles W. Penrose, soon to be a counselor in the First Presidency, went beyond what had become the approach typical of the Smith era—using threats against the polygamists and making declarations of good faith to the Church. Instead, he tried to explain more fully the doctrine of plural marriage to a new generation that was less familiar with the Principle.

Before the Manifesto was issued, the Principle had been central to Mormon doctrine, identity, and solidarity. In the thirty years that had passed, a new generation of younger Mormons had matured and had little feeling for either the social or the sacred nature of the practice. The Penrose discourse served as a reminder of both. Divided into two main sections, it clearly delineated the issues that would have enduring significance in the Church's future attitude toward the doctrine.

The doctrine of plural marriage as articulated by Joseph Smith, Jr., Penrose summarized, continued to be taught after the discontinuance of the practice of plural marriage. Penrose portrayed Mormon marriage (celestial marriage and its patriarchal order), as a rite that sealed men and women together by the holy order of God. The purpose of celestial marriage was an abundant and faithful progeny: "They shall increase, worlds without end, in their prosperity, in knowledge, in wisdom, in understanding, in dominion, in glory."[41]

Celestial marriage, Penrose explained, is detailed in the 132nd section of the *Doctrine and Covenants* and is therefore sanctioned as a commandment from the Lord. This scripture defines celestial marriage as marriage for "time and all eternity and a necessary prerequisite for the attainment of the highest degree of glory in the celestial world."[42] He then referred to another portion of that revelation which mentioned "further orders" of the holy order of marriage that were under "special direction." The power, authority, and keys to perform celestial marriages were located only in the hands of the president of the Church. "Read it carefully," he urged. "The keys of that power are given to one man at a time on the earth, and you will see sometime, if you cannot now, the wisdom of that law." After pausing to emphasize the importance of his next sentence, he continued: "He holds the keys of that power, and when he turns it, as Brother Woodruff did, it closes the door."[43]

The "further order" to which Penrose referred was plural marriage. In the nineteenth century, the concept of plural marriage was inextricably linked with that of celestial marriage or the patriarchal order. The ideal was still the same in 1918 although the practice of plural marriage had been suspended.

The issue in contention between the official Church leadership and those living plural marriage independently was the location of the power or "keys" to perform such marriages. Penrose reemphasized this point by saying, "I want to refer to this as clearly as possible, and I find it necessary to do it because of some recent occurrences—when men go around and whisper in the ears of the people that this thing is all right if you can keep it secret." He exclaimed: "Keep it [secret] from the man that holds the keys—think of it."[44] Penrose then reiterated the position of Church presidents Lorenzo Snow and Joseph F. Smith, both of whom had affirmed that no other man could authorize plural marriages on the earth.

Obviously, the purpose of Penrose's message was to combat rumors about alternate priesthood authority and to undercut the credibility of those claiming authority to continue performing plural marriages. Recognizing the new generation's vulnerability to these claims, he said, "Do not believe these stories that men who are seeking to indulge their own lust are circulating among the people." Penrose urged members to "try to guard the purity of our innocent girls, many of whom have never heard of such things, and these things are whispered in their ears by some designing person who is a rebel against the Church of Christ."[45]

The Grant Position

In 1921 Church President Heber J. Grant, himself a polygamist,[46] directly addressed the subject of priesthood authority, making it absolutely clear that the official Latter-day Saint position was that the "keys" remained in sole possession of the prophet of the Church. "I brand as plain simple liars those who undertake to say that anybody, aside from the President of the Church, had any right to give revelations to this people.[47]

In an impassioned 1925 ruling on the issue of excommunicated Mormon John Woolley continuing to perform plural marriages, Grant claimed that the very integrity of the Church was being impugned. Woolley, Grant argued, had been "excommunicated from the Church for a similar unlawful and disloyal act some years ago" and consequently was not a member of the Church and held no authority to officiate in "any way whatsoever."[48] On at least three other occasions during his administration President Grant issued equally candid warnings about the punishment for performing plural marriages in an attempt to make his attitude so "clear, definitive, and unequivocal as to leave no possible doubt."[49]

Grant's second counselor between 1921 and 1925, Anthony W. Ivins, became Talmage's successor in the extirpation campaign.[50] Paradoxically, Ivins had performed numerous post-Manifesto plural marriages in the United States and Mexico, and was himself confused by the ambiguous messages of other Church leaders.[51] Ivins, a former sheriff, set to work more quietly but also more effectively, using standard methods of detection and surveillance. The fundamentalist publication *Truth* published a statement by Ivins that foretold the coming partnership of the Church with civil prosecution in the pursuit of polygamists: "I expect the time to come when the civil law will enter into the question, making the lives of these people more miserable than they already are, for that appears to be the only manner in which the system can be stayed."[52]

Ivins explained to another Mormon audience that the new

methods reflected the Church's desire to create a distinction between itself and the fundamentalists. "We are willing to go to such limits...because we wish to do everything humanly possible to make our attitude toward this matter so clear, definite, and unequivocal as to leave no possible doubt of it in the mind of any person."[53]

Ivins assembled the evidence used in a number of excommunication cases that centered on the issue of polygamous living, including those of Heber Cleveland and Joseph Musser.[54] His work, like that of his predecessors Talmage and Lyman, was abruptly ended by his death in 1934. Thereafter, as one polygamist described it, the "mantle" fell upon President J. Reuben Clark, Jr.

As early as 1931 Clark and Grant had adopted a new approach that would become standard procedure by 1950—namely, sidestepping the subject to avoid unnecessary publicity. "We have hesitated somewhat to make public statements or denials to charges and false assertions published in literature sent out by these enemies of the Church and its administration," he said at the April conference that year, "because we have felt that added publicity to their pernicious statements would be gratifying to these and probably useless in stemming their activity."[55]

Another important change in the dialogue of the 1930s reflected a new development in the nature of the enemy. During that decade, the Church faced organized fundamentalist polygamists who now began to make claims to priesthood authority to perform plural marriages in opposition to the priesthood claims of the Church. Church leaders' future statements about the Principle in public discourse now usually dealt with fundamentalists who were actively recruiting new members, encouraging others to ignore the Manifesto, and criticizing the Church position as "fallen" in their own discourses and publications.

In 1933, two years after Grant's 1931 stand, J. Reuben Clark, Jr., Grant's indefatigable counselor, drafted an "Official Statement" published over the signatures of the First Presidency in the "Church News" section of the *Deseret News*. It censured the renewed interest in the "corrupt, adulterous practices of the members of this secret, oathbound organization," gave a careful accounting of the history of the controversy which had raged since the 1890 Manifesto, summarized the legal action that had been taken against the Church by the federal government, catalogued doctrinal support of the Principle, and described the continued practice of polygamy outside Mormonism. An attorney, Clark stressed the contractual nature of the marriage union and the legal discontinuation of the Principle, rather than the fact that it had once been claimed to be a revelation.[56] Featuring Clark's typically erudite candor, the document virtually eliminated the possibility of further misrepresentations of the Church's policy.

The "Official Statement" also clarified the LDS doctrine of celestial marriage. The document carefully distinguished between celestial marriage and plural marriage: "Monogamous marriages for time and eternity, solemnized in our temples in accordance with the word of the Lord and the laws of the Church are Celestial marriages."[57] This flat statement dismantled the fundamentalists' logic for continuing plural marriages because only they were celestial marriages. But although the statement pacified mainstream Mormons, it served as a catalyst for helping to unify various groups of fundamentalists.

To try to determine the motives that impelled past public figures to act as they did is always difficult. Why, for instance, did Grant and Clark intensify their attack on new polygamists? At least three factors seem to be important. First, Church leaders must have tired of the continued government and media harassment, with their repeated accusations of either the Church's bad faith or impotence in stopping the practice. Second, they wanted to resolve the confrontation with fundamentalists whose strident claim to priesthood authority hit directly at the position of the Church president who according to official Church policy and doctrine had sole possession of the "keys of the sealing." And third, these men must surely have been affected personally as relatives and friends continued on a path that seemed to lead them from the fold.

Heber J. Grant was a polygamist but had children by only one wife after 1890. He pled guilty to a charge of unlawful cohabitation in 1899 and paid a fine of one hundred dollars.[58] The highly publicized excommunication of Alpha Higgs, who was President Grant's personal friend and colleague as well as the general secretary of the Church's Young Men's Mutual Improvement Association and assistant manager of the Church's publication, *The Improvement Era*, must have particularly grieved and upset Grant.

His rebellious friends and relatives embarrassed J. Reuben Clark, Jr. One of John W. Taylor's wives was Clark's cousin, while another cousin became the plural wife of a Salt Lake City Mormon after 1890. Heber J. Grant had courted Clark's aunt, Fanny Woolley, after the Manifesto; but Joseph F. Smith denied Grant permission to

marry her, and Matthias Cowley officiated at her wedding to a stake
president in Colorado in 1902. Clark's bishop in Grantsville had
married a plural wife in 1900 and continued to advocate plural marriages as late as 1909. And finally, the Church in 1914 excommunicated his eighty-two-year-old uncle, John W. Woolley, a patriarch
and temple worker, for performing plural marriages—an event which
both saddened Clark and caused him some embarrassment in his
public career in the East.[59]

Clark's work in the State Department during the 1910s and
1920s had led him into a world of outsiders who constantly questioned, undoubtedly mocked, and probed the issue that festered
within Clark like an unattended thorn. Immediately after issuing the
1933 statement, Clark explained to a nonmember associate that it
was necessary because some "carnally minded old birds are saying
the Church is not earnest about the matter, and were winking at the
subject."[60]

Clark came to the assignment equipped with a legal background
and what seems to have been a personal repugnance for polygamists
that made his actions something of a crusade. Under Clark, pursuit
of polygamists became vigorous and heated. During World War I, in
the United States Justice Department, Clark had directed the surveillance of suspected subversives. He used similar covert techniques of
observation against suspected polygamists. He urged a Church-wide
loyalty oath that would weed out offenders, and he oversaw the excommunication of scores of polygamists during the three decades in
which he was actively involved in working against them.[61]

Clark, Grant, Penrose, and Lyman, all key players in the effort to
quash plural marriage, had roots in the practice. Grant had himself
lived the Principle for decades. They were bound by blood and tradition to those both in and out of the Church because of their positions
on the issue. And the continued presence of plural wives in their communities greatly complicated the situation.

Four significant events relating to polygamy occurred in 1935.
First, the Mormon Church excommunicated a group of polygamists
including Price W. Johnson, Edner Allred, and Carling Spencer, who
had gathered in Short Creek, Arizona. Second, Arizona arrested six
polygamists on charges of cohabitation. Third, Joseph Musser
printed the first issue of *Truth*; and fourth, the Utah Legislature increased the penalty for cohabitation on 14 March 1935 with an act
"Making Unlawful Cohabitation a Felony, and Providing That All

Persons Except the Defendant Must Testify in Proceedings There-of."[62] The bill, drafted by lawyer and Church Apostle Hugh B. Brown, himself the child of polygamous parents, received over-whelming support in the LDS-dominated legislature.

Evidence of the prevailing influence of the Mormon Church in the passage of this bill dismayed Musser. The bill was, according to Musser, "fathered in the House by Lyle B. Nicholes, an officer in the Mormon Church, enacted by a legislative assembly, the majority of whom were Mormons, and signed by Governor Henry H. Blood, a Mormon Stake President, and later President of the California Mis-sion. A steering committee comprised of leading Church officials guided the bill through the legislature."[63] This bill made cohabitation a felony punishable by one to five years in the state penitentiary. Similar penalties imposed upon nineteenth-century Mormons had aroused the cry of injustice. Now a new generation of Mormons themselves attacked, prosecuted, and punished the fundamentalists of their generation. Nothing could have indicated more clearly how decisively the mainstream Church had turned from this now embar-rassing and unsettling part of its past.

The Roots of Modern-Day Fundamentalism, 1896–1935

Who were the new polygamists, and why did they actively challenge the authority of the Church from which they sprang? Most were long-term members of the Church and children of polygamous parents who chose to remain loyal to this basic long-standing tenet of their Mormon heritage; and many were unwavering in their adherence to the Principle as the Church position gradually hardened into active prosecution. But as was true in the nineteenth century, opposition separated out the fainthearted, strengthened the strong, and found willing martyrs. The assumption that God required great sacrifices from the faithful provided meaning to their hardships.

Even after the issuance of the Manifesto, the Church's need to deal humanely with the plural wives and their children (who could not be deprived of financial and emotional support) meant that the strands of polygamous lives continued unbroken through the fabric of the Church. No doubt the popular assumption among Americans at large was that those double and triple strands would within a generation smoothly revert to single strands as death took care of residual polygamists and as their descendants contracted monogamous marriages. However, mixed signals from the Church itself—first, its covert authorization of continued new marriages and then, after 1910, its harsh disassociation not only from new marriages but from its authorized post-1890 marriages—provided much of the impetus for the question to remain painfully open in the minds of many faithful Latter-day Saints.

The fundamentalists based their claim to continual priesthood authority on a purported vision President John Taylor received in September 1886 at the home of John W. Woolley in Centerville, Utah where he was in hiding. Taylor's son, Apostle John W. Taylor, told friends that his father had left among his papers a "revelation... that the principle of plural marriage would never be overcome." The more the Church insisted on polygamy's non-authorized status, the more important this link to divine authority became. Accounts of Taylor's vision circulated orally for many years although it was written down by a few different individuals.[1]

The fundamentalist version of that crucial experience developed in several stages. In 1912, Lorin C. Woolley, the son of John W. Woolley, reported that John Taylor said he had visited "all night with the Prophet Joseph" and would "suffer my right hand to be cut off" before he would sign a proposed document that would abandon plural marriage. In 1922, excommunicated polygamist Joseph W. Musser recorded several oral accounts from Lorin Woolley and Daniel Bateman, who had reportedly also been present in the Woolley home in 1886. Musser consolidated these accounts and circulated this version in 1929.[2] It specifies the date as 26–27 September, adds that Jesus Christ also visited John Taylor, and reports an eight-hour meeting during the day of 27 September in which John Taylor put the attendees "under covenant" to continue the practice of plural marriage. Those present were George Q. Cannon, L. John Nuttall, John W. Woolley, Samuel Bateman, Daniel R. Bateman, Charles H. Wilkins, Charles Birrell, George Earl, and Lorin C. Woolley, as well as two women, Julia E. Woolley and Amy Woolley. The Musser account also states that Taylor gave five of them—Cannon, Wilkins, Samuel Bateman, John W. Woolley, and Lorin C. Woolley—authority to perform plural marriages and to ordain others to do the same.[3]

Woolley's 1912 account received limited attention; however, Musser's 1929 redaction had a more profound effect on those Mormons who had not reconciled their feelings about plural marriage, the two manifestos, the Church's increasingly severe separation from the principle of plural marriage, and the overriding issue of whether the "priesthood keys" to perform plural marriages were still on the earth.[4]

Byron Harvey Allred expressed the feeling of many fundamentalists that the leaders of the Mormon Church had begun a dangerous path toward apostasy:

> A careful and prayerful study of the gospel as contained in those sacred documents, when compared with the teachings, practice, and gifts of the Latter Day Saint Church of today, has convinced me beyond the shadow of a doubt that this Church has apostatized, or turned away from many of the saving truths taught in those holy writings, and that the leaders of this Church have perverted the doctrines, changed the ordinances, rejected the fullness of the gospel, and broken the new and everlasting covenant.[5]

Allred clearly thought that the Church was flawed in almost every way imaginable. Thus, something more potent than a "mere belief in the divinity of the doctrine" was provided for the Principle to continue among the faithful, and to help produce a rebellious new generation of polygamous leaders.[6] Joseph White Musser emerged as one of these leaders.

As a youth, Musser's life conformed to the predictable life course of nineteenth-century Mormon men until as an adult he deviated from the norm to assume a posture of dissent. Yet it is striking that no matter how far he moved from the center his life patterns generally continued to resemble those of a Church member.

Mormon scriptures are replete with references to the correct "path to eternal life." In a sociological sense, the notion of "path" represents a series of culturally determined events that serve to identify and define a group with common beliefs, traditions, and way of life. This series is marked informally through customs and beliefs, and is marked formally through ceremonies and celebrations.

By the end of the nineteenth century, the Mormon life course rigidly followed a set of events determined by age. A series of priesthood ordinations—rites of passage for the Latter-day Saints—connected Mormon youths to the body of the Church, identified their willingness to serve (or at least the influence over them of their parents), as well as their faithfulness, and marked their progression toward salvation.

Another image common to Mormon rhetoric is that of a house as a representation of the Kingdom of God—a mansion containing rooms filled with the believing faithful. Musser was truly at home in that house, steeped in the doctrines, traditions, and beliefs that bound the members together. He was an insider—one of the elect. When Musser married his first plural wife in 1894, he was still an insider, a faithful member of the Church. Others among the faithful, including apostles of the Church, continued the subterranean practice of polygamy despite the Manifesto publicly declaring the end of the Principle in 1890. But by the mid-1920s the practice was under heavy attack by Church leaders, and those men and women who continued to teach and practice a plurality of wives were no longer welcome in the metaphorical house of the Lord. Instead, the Church excommunicated them for their failure to yield to the authority of the president of the Church.

Therefore, an examination of Joseph W. Musser's life reveals much about fundamentalist Mormons who did not choose to move with the mainstream Church but instead moved parallel to the Church as both insiders and outsiders.

Joseph Musser began a lifetime of Church service with his baptism at the age of eight. Soon after being baptized, Musser served as secretary in his ward Primary presidency. At the age of twelve, Joseph was ordained to the office of a deacon in the Aaronic priesthood by his father, Amos Musser. He then followed the predictable sequence of priesthood ordination: when he was fourteen, his father once again ordained Joseph to the office of a teacher, and two years later, a priest. As a young adult, he served as president of his ward Young Men's Mutual Improvement Association (YMMIA), as superintendent of the Sunday School, as a ward missionary, as a member of the stake superintendency of the YMMIA, and as a stake tithing clerk. While in his early twenties, Joseph was a branch president of the Uintah Branch of the Church of Jesus Christ of Latter-day Saints and was also an assistant in the Uintah mission office.

The path from being an insider to becoming one persecuted by the Church began in his own home. Musser was born 8 March 1872 in a home on the southeast corner of Motor Avenue in Salt Lake City. His parents, Amos Milton Musser and Mary Elizabeth White, had left Nauvoo with the main body of Saints for the journey west. They were faithful sacrificing members of the Church.

Musser described his father's lifestyle as "patriarchal"—one that included four wives and thirty-five children. Credited by his son as a "defender of the faith,"[7] Amos Musser, as assistant Church historian, received a special commission from the First Presidency to keep a record of all acts of persecution and the "names of the persecutors of those acts against the Church of Jesus Christ of Latter-day Saints."[8] The senior Musser also wrote propaganda material for the Church, including articles in *The Palantic*, a monthly magazine. Among the essay titles were "Fruits of Mormonism," "Mormonism Exposed,"

"Race Suicide vs. Children" (an early anti–birth-control tract), and the "Utah Farmer." The court prosecuted Amos Musser under the provisions of the Edmunds Act and imprisoned him for six months for, in his son's words, "acknowledging his wives and caring for the mothers of his children."[9]

A time of great confusion began with the establishment of the undergound when family members went into hiding to avoid federal prosecution. Joseph Musser wrote in his journal: "At the age of twelve I was frequently called upon to take plural wives with their babies from one place to another, to hide them from the law.... A very sad incident occurred when I was called upon to take a mother with her dead baby to the city cemetery at midnight, where the child was buried away from the sneaking and sensual eyes of the officers."[10]

It was in this environment of persecution for religious beliefs that Joseph's religious worldview evolved. "Coming from such an ancestry and being raised in a polygamous atmosphere, by parents devoted to their religious conception, I naturally inherited and imbibed a strong spiritual nature. From early youth I devoted my time to the Church. I believed intensely in the mission of Joseph Smith, and were it possible to become fanatically religious, but not obdurate toward the religion and actions of others nor offensively dogmatic."[11] Even at a young age he often felt compelled to defend his faith:

> At the tender age of seven or eight I found myself defending my father in his plural life. Two of my older brothers, one his step-son, were making light of his life when I, a mere stripling, took his part and shamed the older boys. Of course, I could at that time know nothing concerning the principle, its social status, or its biological importance, but the fact that my father and mother, noble and grand creatures, were living it was sufficient justification for my endorsement.[12]

Musser had not yet married when Wilford Woodruff presented the Manifesto to the Church in September 1890. Yet within the week his stake president promised him in the name of the Lord that he would enter that covenant of plural marriage. He wrote: "I believed it. And later, while courting my young lady, I told her I expected to enter that law of marriage; that when the time came I would take it up with her and we would make the selection of other wives together. Although I was taking her out of a plural family, she took the matter quite coolly, but she was true to her promise on that occasion."[13]

Joseph married his first wife, Rose Selms Borquist, in the Logan Temple on 29 June 1892. The couple set up house in two rented rooms in Amos Musser's home with a few articles of furniture and a cookstove. They lived on Joseph's $40.00 a month salary. Their first son, Joseph B., was born while his father was away on a mission to the southern states.

On 1 March 1894 Joseph and Rose moved to Forest Dale, Utah and for $950 bought a small two-room home with a tiny kitchen attached to the back. Here the couple had three more children before 1902, when they moved to Heber City, Utah to serve in the Wasatch Mission. In February 1907 they returned to Forest Dale and eventually they bought a home on Seventh East between Simpson and Ashton avenues.

In 1899, when Rose and Joseph had been married for seven years, they received a written invitation from President Lorenzo Snow to go to the temple to receive "Higher Anointings." The Mussers went with four other couples to the Salt Lake Temple on Thanksgiving morning "where the most glorious blessings known to man were sealed upon us. We literally spent a few hours as in heaven mid the glorious calm and quiet of our holy surroundings. We were near the Lord and Oh! how happy!" wrote Musser.[14] At the time, the twenty-seven-year-old Musser was a monogamist and the father of two. He wondered at being so favored, "for we were being sealed with the "Holy Spirit of Promise."[15]

Lorenzo Snow, Church president from 1898 to 1901, introduced Joseph Musser through an unnamed intermediary to the idea of entering the Principle. "In the course of a few weeks," Musser recorded in his journal, "word came from President Snow that I had been chosen to take more wives, and help keep the law of Celestial marriage alive among the Saints. This was a distinct shock to me, as we had been given to understand that to attempt such a move would mean excommunication from the Church. The Manifesto forbade it."[16] After telling his wife about the visit, the two knelt in prayer asking for guidance. "I was placed in a peculiar situation. God's Prophet told me to accept the law and keep it alive. His subordinates said if I did so, they would cut me off from the Church. I could not argue with them and divulge the source of my authority. It was a time when every man was in honor bound to carry his own burdens and yet live every law of the Gospel."[17]

Although he had already planned to enter plural marriage,

Musser was quite shaken by the message. However, after he considered its source, the prophet of the Church, he felt compelled to obey. "I did so," he wrote, "by marrying Mary Caroline Hill, a most beautiful daughter of Bishop William Hood Hill, of Mill Creek Ward." Mary was twenty-five years old and had refused a series of marriage proposals. Her father had served time in the state penitentiary alongside Amos Musser. Despite that fact, when Joseph approached Hill about marrying his daughter he received a flat refusal. "I was greatly taken back. I had been at his home, with other Stake and General Officers of the Church on numerous occasions and eaten at his table. I rather took it for granted that he knew my hidden motive in being there so often and thought he was in harmony with it."[18] Hill eventually approved the match after having discussed the matter with Church apostles John Henry Smith and Matthias F. Cowley. The two married on 13 March 1902. Joseph and Mary had six children, five daughters and a son Guy who would follow in his father's path of teaching the principle of plural marriage. Musser eventually married five women and had children with four of them.

On 16 February 1903 Patriarch John M. Murdock ordained Musser to the office of high priest. He was then the husband to two women; both marriages were post-Manifesto. Four years later, the members of Granite Stake sustained him, as an alternate member of their high council. Joseph F. Smith, Church president after Snow's death, similarly blessed him, saying: "God bless you Brother Joseph. I am glad you are here and that you are in the harness. I hope they will always keep you working."[19]

In the next year, under the ominous shadow of the Second Manifesto issued by President Smith, Musser married his third wife, Ellis R. Shipp, daughter of the prominent local physician Ellis Shipp. The Church called Ellis, an education graduate from the University of Utah, to introduce kindergarten work to the Wasatch Stake.

On 22 July 1909, Francis M. Lyman requested that Musser attend a meeting of the Quorum of the Twelve in the Salt Lake Temple. Musser was invited into the apostles' room where Lyman, John Henry Smith, Heber J. Grant, Rudger Clawson, Orson F. Whitney, David O. McKay, George F. Richards, and Anthony W. Ivins were questioning a number of suspected dissidents. They also questioned Musser for two hours about his feelings concerning plural marriage, about known violators of the prohibition on performing plural marriages, and about his intentions for the future. They gave him advice on ways to handle delicate situations when approached about the subject. "We want you hereafter to join with us in putting this thing down," President Ivins said. "If anybody comes to you for information or encouragement, tell them it can't be done, that it is wrong to desire and that no attentions whatever should be bestowed upon the sisters with this in view." Musser replied: "President Lyman, I cannot do that, but I suggest if you have any instructions to give me, it should be done through my Stake President, with whom I am in harmony and I will endeavor to remain so."[20] Musser was sufficiently confident of his stake president's position on the subject to decline to side with the apostles of the Church.

The situation was further complicated by the presence of apostles who Musser knew had sanctioned plural marriages after 1890, including Rudger Clawson and John Henry Smith, who had approved his earlier post-Manifesto marriage. He was pressured to "get in harmony," to which he answered in a way similar to others who had been questioned that day, and which prompted Lyman to question whether or not the answers were rehearsed. Soon, Musser would move even further from the center. On 14 December 1909 the Church of Jesus Christ of Latter-day Saints disfellowshipped Musser for his continued belief in a plurality of wives.[21]

Despite the investigation (which Musser called an inquisition) and his disfellowshipment, Lyman called Musser to preside over the India Mission. Clearly, there was ambiguity and division among the twelve over the seriousness of the offense. During this transitional period, many leaders of the Church were themselves polygamists or were relatives or friends of Mormons continuing in the practice, a fact which greatly confused the efforts at discipline.

This new calling was an assignment that Musser could perform through the mail. In a letter dated 6 January 1910 Lyman wrote Musser saying, "Keep your hand in the good work and the Lord will bless you abundantly and so will your father and the good, good saints of India. I bless you and will continue to do so and appreciate your work as if done to me; for they seem like my own." The letter was signed, "Affectionately your brother, Francis M. Lyman."[22]

Musser recorded in his journal that in 1915 an apostle (whom he did not name) conferred upon him the "sealing power of Elijah, with instructions to see that plural marriage shall not die out. He wrote:

"President Snow had said that I must not only enter the law, but must help keep it alive. This then, was the next step in enabling me to help keep it alive. I have tried to be faithful to my trust."[23]

During the second decade of the twentieth century Musser could feel himself growing in the "work of the Lord" although his brother Donald pulled away and announced that he would forsake the Principle. At the same time, Musser became increasingly conscious of the lines drawn between those who continued to practice plural marriage and those who did not. His most significant associations were with those whose ideas matched his own, particularly those who seemed to have answers to the question of priesthood authority. Perhaps partly because of this and his stubborn refusal to defer to the authority of the Church president, and because of his continued belief in the doctrine of plural marriage, Joseph White Musser was excommunicated from the Church by the Granite Stake High Council on 23 March 1921.[24] Thus, Musser passed from being a leader of the faithful to becoming one not only outside of but actively challenging the legitimacy of the Church. As an excommunicated Mormon, Musser could no longer participate in Church services, enter the temples, partake of the sacrament, or hold Church callings. Yet Joseph W. Musser, former high councilman, bishop, and missionary, in many ways continued to perceive the world from the Mormon point of view, as an insider might. Mormonism continued to define much of his behavior and beliefs.

Joseph continued to see himself as a champion of Mormonism unjustly cast out from "its functions and benefits."[25] He claimed that he and his wives continued to pay a full ten percent tithing plus fast offerings to the Church through the late 1920s despite the fact that Church regulations barred them from temple attendance.[26] In June 1929 these restrictions barred Musser and his third wife from witnessing the marriage of their daughter Ellis in the temple, even though his wife was what Musser described as a "tithe payer and in good standing in her ward."[27] Musser would record counsel he had given to a small group of fundamentalist Saints concerning temple work: "Don't worry about not being able to do temple work. Get your genealogies ready and the day will soon come when the temples, which are literally the houses of the Lord, will be 'set in order,' and then the work will count. Much of the work now being done will have to be done over."[28] Joseph Musser and his wives continued to wear temple garments and respect the ordinances that were performed in the temples.[29]

It was during this time of confusion and ambiguity that Musser and six other polygamist leaders met in Salt Lake City in 1929 to form a priesthood council. This seven-member council would become the center of ecclesiastical power and authority for many fundamentalists. Besides Lorin C. Woolley and Joseph W. Musser, members of the first council included J. Leslie Broadbent, John Y. Barlow, LeGrand Woolley, Louis Kelsch, and Charles F. Zitting. Musser described the idea of the council: "It was this body of men who Moses brought before the face of the Lord. This body, when properly organized, is presided over by seven Presidents of the Great High Priest Order, the worthy Senior member being the presiding officer and the mouthpiece for the seven."[30] According to Musser, this body was the only proper conduit for the word of the Lord. "When the voice of the Lord penetrates to the Church, it will be relayed through this Presidency, the Church being a subordinate organization. This order is difficult for the Church to see now, but it will have to come to it. This organization is a Theocracy, receiving its direction and authority direct from God, while the Church is a quasi-Democracy, all things in it being done by common consent."[31]

Lorin C. Woolley ordained Joseph W. Musser a "High Priest Apostle and Patriarch to all the world" at that time and exhorted him to see "that never a year passed that children were not born in the covenant of plural marriage."[32] Musser wrote, "I was instructed to give patriarchal blessings to those applying for same and [who] were denied access to real patriarchs in the Church."[33]

Lorin Woolley was the natural leader of the fundamentalist movement, as other fundamentalists felt that he had been set apart for the work by Church President John Taylor. The Mormon Church excommunicated Woolley in 1924 for "pernicious falsehood," a decade after his father John Woolley was dropped from the records of the Church.[34]

In 1928, the year of his father's death, Lorin Woolley made a convert who later would occupy a central place in the history of Short Creek polygamy—Leroy Johnson. Johnson would lead the colony for almost forty years between 1949 and 1987. Of their meeting, Johnson reported, "I shook hands with him and heard his story of the 1886 revelation, and I believed it."[35] Johnson already believed in a plurality of wives but had "not taken any action about it any further than to express feelings."[36]

When Lorin C. Woolley died on 19 September 1934, Barlow succeeded him as senior member of the council. Before Barlow died in 1949, he had called Leroy S. Johnson and J. Marion Hammon and set them apart as "Apostles of the Lord Jesus Christ"; and he also had called Guy H. Musser and Rulon Jeffs, Richard Jessop, Carl Holm, and Alma Timpson to positions of authority.[37] The history of plural marriage in the next half-century would become, in large measure, the history of these men and their posterity, a group who by their union selected for themselves a peculiar destiny.

The fundamentalists never intended to form a new church separate from Mormonism, and they continued to identify themselves as members of the Church of Jesus Christ of Latter-day Saints.[38] In the 1930s the fundamentalists began to refer to the "corporate church" or the church as separate from the "priesthood." The Church was, Johnson said, "a vehicle of the Priesthood, instead of the Priesthood being a vehicle of the Church."[39]

Johnson welcomed the name "fundamentalist." He wrote: "I was grateful when I heard that Mark E. Peterson [sic] branded us as 'FUNDAMENTALISTS.'"[40] He pointed out that more than the one issue of plural marriage was important to the fundamentalists:

> Some people think because we speak of the everlasting Gospel and the law of Plural Marriage, that we have pulled away and left the Church of Jesus Christ of Latter-day Saints, and that we have hung on to one principle of the Gospel, namely, plural marriage, and discarded everything else. This is not true. For we believe that no man can receive the Celestial Law without first coming in at the door of Baptism for the remission of sins and keeping himself clean and pure from the sins of the generation in which we live.[41]

However, the fundamentalists also were quick to point to the wall that divided them from the main body of the Church. In a manner perhaps somewhat reminiscent of the way that John Winthrop and the Puritans set themselves up as a "City upon a hill" as an example to the Church of England, Johnson and the fundamentalists believed that theirs was a more pure and direct way to God. As Johnson observed in 1952, "We have separated ourselves from the Church of Jesus Christ of Latter-day Saints as it now stands."[42]

Johnson would frequently return to this theme in his sermons to the polygamists during his thirty-seven years as senior member of the priesthood council:

> There is only one thing in which we differ from those who profess to be Latter-day Saints today, and this is in living the higher principles of the Gospel as they were revealed to the Prophet Joseph and given to him. Because they conflict with the laws of the land seemingly, they have been abandoned and laid on the shelf. And because we contend that they are as true today as they were the day they were given to Joseph Smith, we are condemned; and they say we are trying to establish something new and advance new ideas in the earth.[43]

The polygamous lifestyle was nothing new for Leroy Johnson. His father Warren Johnson had two wives and seventeen children at the time of the 1890 Manifesto. Leroy was born on 12 June 1888, two years before the Manifesto prohibiting polygamy. Like most Mormon boys, he was baptized and indoctrinated in the gospel of Jesus Christ according to the Mormon Church. Leroy and the other Johnson children grew up in southern Utah, a place where upwards of two out of five men married into polygamous unions during the 1880s, and where most women and children were part of plural families.[44] Leroy attended school in Kanab until age eleven, when he reached the sixth grade. He was sufficiently motivated to become educated that he returned to school at age twenty-two to complete the eighth grade.[45]

Many years of Johnson's childhood were spent in Big Horn County, Wyoming. Frequent visitors to his family's ranch there included Apostle Abraham Owen Woodruff, who testified that "except the people woke up [*sic*] and accepted the fullness of the gospel and lived it and applied it to their lives, they would not be able to obtain the blessings that the Lord had in store for them in the country."[46] Abraham Woodruff, who in 1897 at the age of twenty-four was ordained as an apostle by his father Wilford Woodruff, advocated plural marriage long after the Manifesto was issued. However, Abraham died before his thirtieth birthday in 1904, a decade before the Church began to discipline others like him who continued to teach the Principle. The fundamentalists considered Abraham Woodruff a special witness of the Principle. Johnson recalled:

> I was only a boy about thirteen years old when Abraham O. Woodruff passed away. I heard him talking to my father. He [Woodruff]

said "I hope the Lord will take me home before I do anything that
will deprive me of my salvation." This was in Wyoming. He went
back to Salt Lake, was asked to go down and preside over the Mexican mission. He went down and established himself there. His wife
took small pox and died. A week later, he died with small pox. So,
the Lord takes us at our word.[47]

Leroy Johnson's attitude about the Manifesto matched that of
Abraham O. Woodruff. Both men believed that it was a political ex-
pediency. "We all know that Wilford Woodruff signed a manifesto in
order to make the Church of Jesus Christ of Latter-day Saints a part
of the world, or in other words, in order to save our dignity with the
world, he made a covenant with them that we could do away with
the Celestial Law."[48] Johnson maintained that the Manifesto left
room for the choice to continue in plural marriage:

> After Wilford Woodruff signed the manifesto, the Lord told him
> that it was now pleasing in His sight that men should use their own
> judgement·regarding these principles. He also says in this book, the
> Doctrine and Covenants, that except a man obeys the laws that per-
> tain to the blessings of Celestial Glory, he cannot obtain it. So, we
> are only trying to keep alive the principles of life and salvation.[49]

On another occasion Johnson more forcefully condemned the
Manifesto for the destruction it wrought upon the Church:

> In 1890 the Manifesto was signed by the President of the Church of
> Jesus Christ of Latter-day Saints; and not only did they sign away
> their privileges to the New and Everlasting Covenant, or the law of
> Plural Marriage, but they broke every other commandment that
> God has given. Why? Because God says: Break one of these com-
> mandments and you are guilty of the whole.[50]

During 1935, Leroy Johnson's stake president Claude Hirschi,
the Church leader who had ordained him to the office of high priest
the year before in 1934, confronted him on several occasions and unsuccessfully attempted to schedule meetings to force the issue of
Johnson's attraction to the principle of plural marriage. Johnson,
who was forty-one years old at the time of his private conversion to
the Principle, was deliberating a decision that would commit him to a
life of sacrifice and persecution, yet simultaneously bring him great
joy.

"I had been laboring for some time to get the Spirit of the Gospel," Johnson related in a later sermon. He stated that when he

learned that President Heber J. Grant would be speaking at a stake conference in Kanab, Utah, "I went to the Lord and told him I was going to that meeting and for Him to cause that Brother Grant would give me the key as to whether plural marriage could be lived this day or not." Grant expounded that day on the dangers of associating with the polygamists. His condemnation of plural marriage, though he called it the "celestial law," was particularly harsh. Yet his remarks seemed to be what Johnson had been waiting for, and he heard the voice of revelation at last: "Every once in a while he dropped a word to let me know that the true principles of the gospel were always discarded by the majority of the people."[51] The idea of being one of the elect minority inspired Johnson, and he decided to enter plural marriage.

Leroy's brother Price also became a fundamentalist. By 1935, Price William Johnson was fifty years old and the husband of five wives and the father of eleven children. His first two wives were sisters. Ester Heaton, the first, willingly moved from Idaho to Arizona with him, hoping "to find prosperity and peace."[52] Her sister had been widowed by the death of her husband in World War I before she married Johnson. His third and fourth wives had been raised on ranches in the Rainbow Bridge country of southern Utah. Helen Hull was a college-educated Mormon who came from Salt Lake City where she had been impoverished by the Depression to live in Short Creek with the fundamentalists. Price Johnson, like his full brother Leroy, was raised by polygamous parents at St. George, Lee's Ferry and Byron, Wyoming in the pioneer tradition. It was at home that he said he received a testimony of the sacredness of the principle of plural marriage.

John Y. Barlow also was raised in the Church.[53] His grandfather Israel Barlow had been a bodyguard of Joseph Smith, Jr. and had traveled west to the Great Basin with Brigham Young. Barlow, like Johnson, had grown up in the tradition of polygamy and had never ceased to believe in its importance in the Mormon plan of salvation. Barlow served in the Northwestern States Mission under Apostle Melvin J. Ballard. As was customary, the First Presidency—Joseph F. Smith, Anthon H. Lund, and Charles W. Penrose—had signed his minister's certificate on 9 April 1918 certifying:

Elder John Y. Barlow, who is in Full Faith and Fellowship with the Church of Jesus Christ of Latter-day Saints, has been ordained a minister of said Church, with authority to preach the Gospel and administer in all the ordinances thereof pertaining to his office and calling. And we invite All Men to give heed to his teachings as a servant of God, and to assist him in his travels and labors, in whatsoever things he may need.[54]

Ballard soon discovered that Barlow was teaching polygamy among his missionaries. Ballard confronted the young missionary: "I asked him about it and he defended the doctrine so vigorously that I said to him, 'If you do so any longer you will be sent home.'"[55] Barlow persisted and was sent home early and later excommunicated for his continuing belief in plural marriage.

Others traveled an even more painful road to dissent. After the publication in 1933 of his father's defense of polygamy, *A Leaf in Review*, Rulon C. Allred initiated correspondence with Apostle Anthony Ivins during the summer of 1933. Allred was adamantly opposed to polygamy and begged Ivins to begin action to discipline his father for his condemnation of Church leadership and continuation in a polygamous lifestyle. Ivins assured Allred that he had sent a pamphlet to all local ecclesiastical leaders setting forth more clearly than ever the Church's position on plural marriage and the consequences for disobedience of this direction. Ivins was familiar with Byron Allred's book and its contents which directly contradicted the Church president's instructions on polygamy. Allred described the Manifesto as an accommodation to the government rather than a revelation from the Lord. *A Leaf in Review* was a call to the fundamentalists proclaiming the importance of keeping the Principle alive. Ivins wrote to Rulon: "It is a great surprise to me, knowing him as I do, that he should assume the attitude that is set forth in this book. However, it is his right to do so and he must be responsible for the issue which he has raised."[56]

For Allred, who had prayed long and hard on the matter, words of sympathy and compassion were not enough. He lay the blame for his father's heresy at the feet of others (including former Apostle Matthias Cowley) who were continuing to "further the work of Lucifer among many groups of the Saints in Idaho and Utah.... They have so fervently and extensively persisted in this propaganda that my Father and many of his family and also many other noble and good Saints have been deceived."[57] Particularly painful to Allred were the plural marriages of his sisters Rhea and Olive to Morris Kunz.

His father's involvement in polygamy became such an obsession with Allred that he made it a matter of almost constant prayer. He wrote to Ivins:

> I feel certain that, as in days of old, even now God will hear our constant prayers and that if we are diligent will, through His infinite wisdom and might, prevail upon them to repent before it is too late or before they are allowed to lead others of the Church astray. What can be done? What may I do?[58]

Thus, Allred looked to Ivins. "Maybe only immediate excommunication can be followed. Perhaps your influence will bring about repentance, I cannot say."[59] In October 1933 Rulon C. Allred was so convinced of the wickedness of a choice in such obvious defiance of the Church president's word that he urged Ivins to excommunicate his own father.

Allred's wife Katherine kept a journal that details the next few months while documenting her increasing apprehension. "Rulon is neglecting his practice terribly. He spends all available time in reading up on polygamy, in order to dissuade his father, he says.... He won't stop reading up on polygamy, regardless of my pleas and tears. I am afraid."[60] His studies continued, and according to Katherine his obsession became worse. Eventually his views changed. "Rulon won't even listen to my pleading any more. Everything he says is in favor of polygamy. He [*sic*] is like some demon possesses him. When I try to tell him what he's doing to me, he says I'm doing it to myself in not being willing to accept the word of the Lord. When I really get frantic, he leaves and says he is going out into the hills to pray. Several times he hasn't come back until morning. My heart is breaking."[61]

Before too much longer she wrote: "Rulon is now beginning to teach polygamy to everyone he sees. He is obsessed with the idea."[62] The following January Katherine Allred wrote Anthony Ivins. In a letter dated 20 January, she referred to Allred's series of letters of the few months before. Alarmed and distressed, she described Rulon as a changed man who had joined his father in his beliefs. "I was about to take my babies and leave him this morning," she wrote, "but decided to write to you first before making this drastic decision, as I love my husband with all my heart, and don't want to feel at some future time that I hadn't done all I possibly could."[63] According to Katherine, Rulon based his changed viewpoint on three things:

1. My husband says, according to the prophecy of 1882, page 9, that President Grant and others were not eligible to be apostles unless they lived polygamy.

2. He says that his sisters' polygamous marriage outside the Temple were necessary because of the wickedness of men and will be binding in eternity.

3. He says the Manifesto was drawn up by outsiders and had nothing to do with revelation. He says the church intended it to continue but had to put a different face on it, complying with the U.S. laws.[64]

During the same time period, Katherine also wrote to President Heber J. Grant, similarly asking him for advice. President Grant encouraged Katherine to stay with the Church but to leave her husband. She wrote to Ivins, "that the women Rulon will take will be no better than women of the streets. Today I am taking my sweet babies and leaving the husband I love."[65] Within two years Katherine divorced Rulon Allred and began a new life.

The poignancy of Katherine's narrative underscores the theme of sacrifice that the fundamentalists required of themselves. Men and women left families and friends to follow what they considered a straighter line to God. Some like Katherine Allred rejected polygamy and chose to live apart from the ones they loved rather than challenge the authority of the president of the Church. Increasingly, the fundamentalists grouped together in isolated communities throughout the region.

Short Creek, Arizona was one such community, and was considered by many fundamentalists to be a place with a special purpose. Leroy Johnson would later teach that it was the only place "upon the earth that you can hear the fullness of the everlasting gospel preached."[66] Short Creek provided a safe place for the flowering of the Principle. According to Johnson, "The evil powers tried to destroy that which God had set up, but before He allowed this condition to transpire, He provided an escape for this revelation to be continued."[67]

Johnson viewed the Manifesto as the single most important test to come to the Latter-day Saints, one that the main body of the Church had failed. The Church "tried to make peace with the enemy by signing away their rights to Holy Priesthood," he wrote. However, God's plan was not frustrated because the Lord "caused a division to come upon the Latter-day Saints."[68] In the future, the Saints would divide into what Musser called the "visible" and the "invisible" church, a distinction which largely reflected those who believed that the Church prophet continued to receive revelations from God and those who continued in the "original" doctrines of the Church. In a 1976 sermon Johnson articulated the distinction:

> "But," says the enemy of righteousness, "we live in a different age. What was good for the people in the days of the Prophet Joseph is not necessary in the lives of the people in the day in which we live." This is not so, my brothers and sisters, for God says: "My word is one eternal round, and what I say to one I say to all. My purposes never fail. And all who will not listen and put into their lives the Gospel of Jesus Christ will fall by the wayside."[69]

As they were excommunicated from the Church of Jesus Christ of Latter-day Saints and ostracized from the community of Saints, the fundamentalists gathered during the early 1930s in small groups—in living rooms or in summer beneath the boughs of a tree—to listen to the testimony of Woolley, Musser, Barlow and others who made claims to continued priesthood authority.

During this same time, Musser was increasingly frustrated in his efforts to find work as the official Church effort to stamp out polygamy intensified. Blacklisted, painfully and acutely aware of the increasing boundaries between them, he mourned the loss of his friends and the support of his loved ones: "I am out of employment and many of my erst-while friends and loved ones now shun me. To them I seem something unclean."[70]

His former friends who publicly separated themselves from him but privately supported his independent stance complicated his situation. At the funeral of Musser's wife Mary in November 1930, Church general authority J. Golden Kimball spoke of a lifetime association and friendship he had shared with the Mussers. He continued by acknowledging how unfairly the Church had treated the couple, causing Mary to suffer in her final years: "Oh, I know we are supposed to say nothing about this thing—we are afraid to tell the truth; it isn't always wise to tell the whole truth, but I want to say that Brother Musser has been unjustly dealt with; he has been persecuted. The principle of polygamy is true. . . . I was of that origin and I am proud of it."[71]

Theological Roots of Fundamentalist Dissent

The controversy between the Mormon Church and the fundamentalists was deeper than the argument about plural marriage. It
centered on the idea of changes in doctrine. The fundamentalists
claimed that if an "eternal principle" was valid at one time it was
valid for all times. This principle of original doctrine would become
the unifying concept of their theology. Besides the change in the practice of plural marriage, the fundamentalists also pointed to the dissolution of united orders throughout the Church, a new missionary
system policy,[72] the changed nature of the office and calling of the
Seventy, and what they claimed were the radical new conceptions of
the gathering of Israel, of the idea of Zion, and of the political Kingdom of God.

As Joseph W. Musser departed from the center, from the visible
church, he began a rough, often uncertain path in search of what
might be called the "invisible church"—what he distinguished as the
"Priesthood," separate and distinct from the "Church." He wrote in
1940, "It should be observed here, that while the Church Authorities
have changed many of the ordinances, the Priesthood, as a separate
organization, has not thus gone astray; and one day it will rise up
and save the Church from final rejection."[73]

In Musser's understanding, the "Church is subservient to the
Priesthood, any action taken by it against those entering the law [plu-
ral marriage] is null and void. A man or woman cannot properly be
cut off from the Church for keeping a law of God, for the Church be-
longs to God and God cannot act a lie and remain God."[74] According
to Musser, the President of the Church might or might not have been
the President of the Priesthood.

> By reason of their seniority in the higher Priesthood calling, Brig-
> ham Young, John Taylor and Wilford Woodruff, each in his turn,
> became President of the Church, but always their Church calling
> was subordinate to their Priesthood positions. The greater orga-
> nizes the lesser—the lesser cannot organize the greater. By authority
> of his Priesthood Joseph Smith organized the Church and ever after
> the Church was subject to his direction, because he was President of
> the Priesthood; a calling above that of the Church.[75]

Therefore, Musser reasoned he was subject only to direction from his
immediate priesthood leader on the issue of plural marriage. For

Musser this was Granite Stake President Frank Y. Taylor. Musser was aware of the fact that Taylor and his counselor John M. Cannon had performed plural marriages during the first decade of the twentieth century. This created an ambiguous environment for those, like Musser, who were questioning the Manifesto.

By 1935 Musser was increasingly critical of the Church that had cast him out. That year he wrote:

> Peace is taken from the earth. Men's hearts and thoughts are evil continually. Greed reigns supreme. Even the Temple of God is polluted. The Gospel, as changed, has lost much of its power and the Saints are being rapidly drawn away from the truths as revealed to Joseph Smith. Wickedness is established in the Church, and those who are sincerely trying to live the Gospel are being excommunicated and cast out.[76]

Musser's relationship with Church President Heber J. Grant was particularly complicated. "I love the Gospel," he said; however, "I do not endorse all that President Grant does, and many things about him I cannot admire; and yet I love and respect him as the leader of the Church, and I have it in my heart to help him in his arduous labors."[77] This respect would deteriorate during the next decade as the distance between the two increased. In 1939 he described Grant as being prejudiced against him, and spreading that prejudice through the council.

Musser reacted to the flood of anti-polygamy literature and persecution by the official Church with a new publication—*Truth* magazine. It had from its inception in 1935 a single-minded dedication to the perpetuation of the principle of plural marriage among the Mormons. And it was through this medium that Musser exerted his most profound influence on the loosely organized fundamentalist community. Here, through editorial comment, Musser portrayed the polygamist lifestyle as he saw it, offering advice on marriage, child-rearing, spirituality, and community life. As editor he quoted extensively from nineteenth-century polygamous leaders, using the voices of Joseph Smith, Brigham Young, and George Q. Cannon to justify the modern practice while always emphasizing its eternal and revelatory nature. The rhetoric of fundamentalism was, in the pages of *Truth* magazine, the language of Mormonism, an insider's point of view written on the outside. The magazine also provided a forum for discussion, and a means of reconciliation among the different factions of fundamentalist Mormons. Bound together by their belief in the Principle, they were increasingly split asunder by competing claims to priesthood authority, the issue that also divided them from the mainstream Church. *Truth* magazine would become the primary focus of Musser's life as he grew increasingly wary of the relationship between the Church and those excommunicated for their practice of polygamy.

In a journal entry of 8 March 1939 Musser reflected: "I have regretted more than I can tell the necessity of opposing my brethren of the Authorities, but the doctrines they are putting out are so rank with error I cannot refrain from publishing the truth. My desire is to establish the truth—to strike straight and fair; let the blow rest where it will." He also spoke to the issue of his position outside the faith: "But we are said to be apostate, and yet our apostasy rests wholly on our adherence to the fullness of the Gospel as Joseph Smith established it. It seems so strange to me—and not strange in the light of scripture—that I should be singled out and lied about, shunned and in many ways forsaken, because I believe in the Gospel in its fullness and insist on my right to live it."[78]

The assumption that God required great sacrifices of the faithful provided meaning to Musser's hardships. However, Musser never deviated in his testimony of the truthfulness of the Church. His words are a poignant reminder of both the ties that bound him to the Church and the walls that separated him.

> The Church of Jesus Christ of Latter-day Saints is the very and only Church of Jesus Christ on earth today; its members who are living the fullness being members of the Church of the First Born.... While in many respects the Church is out of order, a condition in which the Church has always fallen through the weaknesses of men, it has not been rejected—it is still the Church of Jesus Christ, and will always remain so.... Meantime those attempting in perfect good faith, though weak, to live the higher law—the law of Consecration and of Celestial Marriage in its fullness, the latter of which the Church rejected in the Manifesto of Wilford Woodruff, must continue on; they must endure the stigma hurled against them—of apostasy and excommunication, persecution, imprisonment, with other abuses, until the Lord sees fit to take a hand. And my faith is that when the Lord rights the wrongs of His leaders the faithful Saints will be crowned with glory and eternal lives, a consummation worth suffering for, as many are now doing.[79]

Musser's piety is a key to understanding his separation from the Church. For Musser, as for many other fundamentalist Mormons, a private conviction of the correctness of one's position was more valid than a pronouncement from a supposed religious authority. Yet also, Joseph White Musser emerged as a dissenter from the Mormon faith due to his position in time—to the anxiety and tension of a time when the Church effort at accommodation, at Americanization, in attempting to compromise with mainstream America produced a confusion for those inside the faith as well as those outside. Pride in the reckless, independent Mormonism of the nineteenth-century Church attracted him as the Church changed, and this provided Musser with a powerful rationale for restructuring ecclesiastical institutions.

The discrepancy between his belief as an insider and his life as a Mormon fundamentalist outside the Church became more complicated with each year. On his fifty-eighth birthday Musser recorded in his journal:

> The Church withdrew fellowship from me because of my active adherence to the principle of plural marriage, but I have a definite testimony of the truth and am seeking to live in accordance with the Gospel as the former Apostles and as the Spirit of God interprets it to me. I teach my children to pray for and sustain the Authorities. I attend my meetings and am honestly trying to "Love my neighbor as myself."[80]

Musser considered his children to be useful members of the Church and community despite the stigma attached to them by the Church and society: "Yet they are my crime. How can this be? Will a corrupt fountain bring forth pure water, or a wicked tree bring forth good fruit?"[81] he questioned.

As the early twentieth-century Mormon Church strained to become accepted by mainstream American society, as it became a missionary church marketing not only a message but an image, it seemed to many to become more like other "protestant" religions. To maintain the pure and unadulterated church, the "invisible church," the church of the original teachings of Joseph Smith, the fundamentalists chose a road often running parallel to the visible Mormon Church, but more often moving into increasing isolation, separation, and what they considered a more true path to God.

Short Creek:
First Settlements, 1860–1935

The turbulent history of Short Creek, Arizona, the center of Mormon fundamentalism, begins with Mormon Church President Brigham Young, whose vision of an expanded ecclesiastical and agricultural empire extended south from Utah into northeastern Arizona. According to a tradition taught in Short Creek, in the 1850s Brigham Young traveled through the area with George Q. Cannon, then his first counselor. Passing between St. George and Kanab, Young ordered his driver to halt so he could admire the magnificent landscape, saying, "This will someday be the head and not the tail of the Church. These [fields] will be the granaries of the saints. This land will produce an abundance [of] sufficient wheat to feed the people."[1] Church leaders were familiar with the reports of explorer John C. Fremont which paved the way for settlement of what came to be called the Little Colorado region.

A few years later, in 1862, at Brigham Young's request, seasoned Indian scout Jacob Hamblin first explored the rich red Arizona Strip country of the Grand Canyon plateau. Hamblin met with some success: he found a feasible Colorado River crossing (soon known as Pierce's Ferry), helped to build a Mormon outpost at Lee's Ferry in 1870, and opened up a new Mormon road into Arizona. His work helped begin the corridor of Mormon settlements that soon stretched far into Mexico, providing yet another escape route from federal harassment.[2]

Hamblin was not the only one who confronted the challenges of the Arizona Strip country. Two hardened frontiersmen had matched their strength against the desert land of Short Creek itself in the 1860s. Both had failed. William B. Maxwell and his family first settled Short Creek in 1860 but did not last even a full growing season before admitting defeat.[3] A few years later, Nathan Tenney, owner of a sawmill on Mount Trumbull, tested his fortitude against the desert conditions and frequent raids from the neighboring Navajo Indians and found it wanting.[4] After a single growing season, Tenney moved his family to Toquerville, Utah.[5]

Unlike Tenney's and Maxwell's aborted attempts at settlement, Hamblin's exploration had a more enduring impact on the region. Particularly important in the saga of Mormon settlement of the region was Lee's Ferry. Named for Mormon John D. Lee, Lee's Ferry was established with a working ferryboat in 1873 and was located just above Marble Canyon where the Paria River meets the Colorado. Lee ran the oupost until his arrest in 1874 for his involvement in the Mountain Meadows Massacre. One of his plural wives, Emma, along with family friend Warren Johnson, assumed management of the ferry in Lee's absence. Two years after her husband's execution in 1877, Emma and her family crossed the river to settle further south in Arizona. Representing the Church, Warren Johnson bought the ferry from Emma with one hundred cows contributed by Mormons from the surrounding area. Johnson's family continued to run Lee's Ferry until 1929 when the Marble Canyon bridge was completed.[6]

Warren Johnson carefully considered the ambigious language of the 1890 Manifesto officially ending plural marriage among the Mormons. Concerned about his future and that of his two wives and seventeen children, including son Leroy, he wrote Apostle Joseph F. Smith on 15 December 1891 for advice about how best to meet his responsibilities. Smith responded that the Lord did not want the Saints to put aside their plural families, because these marriages had created commitments that endured beyond the Manifesto. "What the Lord requires is that we shall not bring upon ourselves the destruction intended by our enemies, by persisting in a course in opposition to the law."[7] Leroy Johnson would later say that his father Warren was "a man that had lived the law, but he refused to give up his plural families after the Manifesto."[8]

In 1893 Warren Johnson broke his back in an accident on a road between Kanab and Fredonia while working in the unrelenting heat.

He and one of his wives traveled the long journey from Kanab to Salt Lake City in a wagon for a blessing from President Wilford Woodruff. "When he came back," Leroy Johnson would later recall, "he had a wheelchair—given to him by President Wilford Woodruff. He taught us children to honor and obey the leaders of the Priesthood. That was his great charge to his children, especially his sons—to honor and obey those who presided over them in [the] Priesthood."[9]

Partially paralyzed, Warren worked the ferry from the confines of his wheelchair. But eventually it proved to be too much for him, and in 1900 he and his wives moved from the Little Colorado region to the Big Horn country of Wyoming. Johnson spent the entire journey in his wheelchair in the back of a wagon staring at the vast expanse of sky and land they were leaving. He loved the country of southern Utah but needed land for his twenty children to start their own lives. Later that year, seven years after he broke his back, Warren died and his family buried him in Byron, Wyoming. Members of that family would figure prominently in the story of fundamentalism in Short Creek, Arizona.

Three years after the establishment of Lee's Ferry in 1873, the first group assigned by Church authorities to settle the Little Colorado region went into Arizona but soon returned to Utah, discouraged by the harsh environment. That same year, in 1876, Lot Smith, hero of the 1857–58 guerilla raids that had delayed Johnston's Army in the Utah War, led a better-supplied group into the area. He established four Mormon villages and a base for missionary work among the Indians. The Mormon Church was the driving force behind these settlements and was the hub of their social, religious, and recreational activities. As was the Mormon colonization pattern, cooperative efforts of the citizens built these towns—colonists dug dams and ditches for irrigation, built houses and barns and cleared fields.[10]

Sparse settlement coupled with geographic isolation from other towns in both Utah and Arizona defined the Strip country. Though nearly the size of New Jersey, it contained only a sprinkling of settlements that lasted long enough to appear on a map. Repeatedly, however, in 1865, 1902, and 1909, the Utah legislature unsuccessfully petitioned Congress for the Strip because it provided Utahns access to the Colorado River. Utah argued that most of the Strip's inhabitants were Mormons with close ties to Utah, that the area was primarily grazing land used by Utah residents, and that "it was a no man's land as far as justice was concerned because Utah had no jurisdiction there and Arizona peace officers were mainly on the other side of the Grand Canyon." However, the government awarded the Strip to Arizona when it fixed the state boundaries.[11]

The Arizona Strip was a stern taskmaster that demanded stiff payment for even the meager rewards of subsistence farming. The growing season was short, and water, when it could be found and controlled, was often too salty for crops. Much of the area could only be used for grazing cattle or sheep, and it proved vulnerable to overgrazing. Short Creek was fully part of its desert environment.

However, in the 1870s Church leaders considered such rugged, inaccessible land a blessing. "If there be deserts in Arizona," exclaimed George Q. Cannon, "thank God for the deserts. . . . The worst places in the land we can probably get, and we must develop them. If we were to find a good country how long would it be before the wicked would want it and seek to strip us of our possessions?"[12]

The first permanent settlement at Short Creek came in the second decade of the twentieth century, more than forty years later. In 1911, long after the Navajos had become pacified, monogamous Mormon Jacob Marinus Lauritzen left Richfield, Utah for the Arizona Strip. He left behind his wife, Annie Eliza Gardner, and nine of their ten children.[13]

Lauritzen first saw Short Creek from the top of a mountain ledge high above Canaan Ranch. "It was a breathtaking panorama that spread out before us. Two lakes sparkled in the evening sun. They were the Canaan Lake and the Short Creek Lake both full of water."[14] Lauritzen gazed out on this spectacular sight as if in a trance:

> How this virgin paradise lay vast and silent spread out before our view like a gib [sic] new page from the book of nature. It is therefore not surprising that I should gaze upon it all as in a dream. I seemed to see this vast expanse dotted with cities and towns, fields and forests. It was only a day dream and yet I am sure it was prophetic of the day when the great Colorado shall contribute of water to the development of this great empire.[15]

Jacob and his son who accompanied him raised their tent home at the base of the high vermillion cliffs that cast an evening shadow over the creek winding down from the canyon. Within a few weeks Jacob petitioned the Arizona legislature for culinary and irrigation water rights, estimating that he would need to dig at least three miles of ditches to fully tap the canyon water and bring it into the valley. The rough terrain would make this a costly and difficult task. After he had secured the water rights, he set to work on what would become known as the Lauritzen Irrigation Ditch.

He also received a visit from a representative of Utah cattlemen who had worked out a rough but effective system of grazing and water rights. Lauritzen's farming plans directly threatened the status quo and, as he recalled in 1968, "I was duly warned that if I persisted in my activities, I would probably turn up missing some morning. . . . [A]n emissary of the cattlemen, who was said to be expert at horse whipping prospective settlers, came out here and warned me and made a lot of threats but did no one bodily harm, although he came duly prepared with his horsewhip or black whip, he constantly fondeled [*sic*] and prominently displayed."[16] When their threats didn't work, the cattlemen backed down.

For several months Lauritzen worked under the blazing blue skies clearing the land, planting crops, and tending his animals in the fields. His family remained behind in Richfield until Lauritzen had prepared a tent home for them. He partitioned a large tent that had housed a box-ball alley in St. George into three rooms. This provided all the privacy and shelter the Lauritzens would have for two years until they could build a permanent house.[17] The generally mild weather made a tent home perfectly satisfactory, however. Their chickens needed to be shooed out of the shady tent during the hot part of the day, and roosted at night at the base of a nearby cedar tree, guarded from predators by the sounds of a ticking clock Lauritzen had placed in the lowest branches.[18]

Leaving behind two married daughters, Julia and Annie Joy, and sending a son, Jacob McLloyd, on a mission to England, Lauritzen brought his family to Short Creek in the spring of 1912. He also invited his "impoverished" brother-in-law, William Rust, to join him, and together the two men camped in the canyon, moving downstream as they finished each section of ditch.[19] Eventually, only 1,000 feet of ten-inch pipe were needed to carry water to the Lauritzen farm. Twice the family ran out of provisions altogether. Once Lauritzen walked the fifty miles to St. George in thirteen hours, with only two soda biscuits and a handful of raisins to sustain him.[20] The first water that flowed through the ditch that year marked the real beginning of the community of Short Creek. Their nearest neighbors were Andrew Silver, who lived five miles to the west at Canaan Ranch, and Jonathan Heaton, twenty-five miles to the east at Moccasin, Arizona.

Jacob later expressed pride in his accomplishments. "As soon as we had the water out and began growing crops it looked like a permanent settlement.... It began to look like law and order had at last made its appearance on the Strip. Homeseekers took courage and soon we had neighbors."[21]

During the next four years other families settled in Short Creek. Lorin Covington, Orlin Frank Colvin, Frank Johnson, Isaac W. Carling and a few other Mormons brought their families and tents from southern Utah, extending the irrigation ditches and plowing straight furrows to mark the land as their own. Orlin Frank Colvin and Isaac W. Carling came to Short Creek from Pipe Springs in 1913 and immediately began clearing land and building fences for a homestead. They began digging their own ditch, later known as the Short Creek Irrigation Ditch, and built a dugout home.[22] After Lizzie Colvin joined Frank in 1914, he started building her a wood house, hauling the lumber in from a sawmill in the Kaibab Forest. Lizzie's brother, Frank Johnson, joined them later that year.

Lauritzen's own six school-age children and the two children of his brother-in-law and sister, William and Sara Rust, satisfied the Arizona minimum of eight children required for a school appropriation. Public education had arrived at Short Creek, Arizona. Short Creek's first school started in September 1912 in a nine-by-twelve-foot tent located near the Arizona state line. Classes were taught by Charles Hafen of Santa Clara, a Mormon settlement a few miles from St. George. Hafen boarded with the Lauritzens and taught grades one through eight. His students included the six Lauritzen children: Tennyson, Marion, Miriam, Reed, Dean, and Dawn, as well as their two cousins, Maida and Ray Rust. The next year, the townspeople received a fifty-dollar grant from Arizona's Kingman County school superintendent. They used the money to buy lumber, and with cooperative labor built their first "real" schoolhouse under the cottonwoods near the wash. The school's new teacher was Robert P. Woodbury from Hurricane, Utah. The students worked on wooden tables and benches built of rough timber by Jacob Lauritzen himself. The Colvin and Johnson children swelled the ranks of the one-room school by eight.[23]

In 1916 Lydia Covington, the wife of Lorin Covington, became the town's first postmistress and thereby its first representative of the

U.S. government. Lydia first moved to Short Creek in the summer of 1913 and lived in a dugout at the center of town. The government granted the petition to establish the post office on the condition that the inhabitants of Short Creek carry the mail themselves, at their own expense, for six months. Jacob Lauritzen traveled the distance between Hurricane and Short Creek on horseback once a week to pick up the mail. In 1916 the townspeople also petitioned the county to organize a justice precinct. That same year, the town's residents unanimously elected Jacob Lauritzen as justice of the peace and Isaac Carling as constable.

James Edwin Black and his wife Sarah Lavina Foot moved their family to Short Creek from Ferron, Utah in April 1918. Their five children increased the total number of students at the school to twenty-two.[24] Short Creek continued to steadily grow over the next few years.

Life on the Arizona Strip was not without its challenges. Frequent droughts and unpredictable shifts in the weather made agriculture a difficult way to make a living. When crops failed in 1924, Isaac Carling traveled to Salt Lake City to find a job to support his family. He found employment working at the Baldwin Radio plant, and through Nathaniel Baldwin he became acquainted with excommunicated Mormons continuing in the doctrine of plural marriage. He also heard the testimonies of the inner circle of priesthood leaders, who were convinced that they had continuing authority to perform plural marriages.[25]

Some were more successful than others in Short Creek. Through the early 1920s, Lauritzen's ranch was in good condition. By dry farming as well as with irrigation it produced enough food for his family's needs and provided a surplus to sell to his neighbors as well as in St. George. Sheep and cattle grazed in his fields. He wrote, "We owned about one hundred head of young cattle, mostly cows and heifers, and they were all grazed in the canyon so that very little riding was necessary to look after them. The boys and I had all worked hard and faithfully to achieve this result."[26]

In 1919, on a visit to his daughter Tana in Provo, Utah, Jacob came across a pamphlet that drew his eye away from his dream of a paradise at the base of the vermillion cliffs. It described a settlement project at Atascadero in central California. The pamphlet, which highlighted the cooperative and socialistic aspects of life in this attractive, modern California town, beckoned him: "In contrast there would appear before me mental pictures of the dry and dusty desert and the almost impassable road between here and Hurricane and then would come the longing for the scenes pictured before me. It is true that I had traveled considerable and had seen large and diversified portions of the earth but they were all in the colder climates and I longed to sit under the palms in a tropical or sub-tropical atmosphere."[27] Jacob, who was fifty-six years old in 1924, dreamed of the cool breezes blowing through the orange groves of central California.

Jacob decided to move to California. He left the care of his ranch to his sons. It included one hundred head of cattle and forty new calves. Two years later, because of overexpansion and poor planning, Jacob's sons (Mack, Marion, Pratt, Jon Reed, Joseph, and Richard) had run the ranch into the ground. Before Lauritzen returned to the Strip eight years later, all of the family members had joined him in California. In April 1932 Jacob and Annie returned to Short Creek, their determination undaunted. He bought a cow with a lug of pine nuts that he had gathered on the way into town and started anew. A lone goat grazing near the house was the only remaining livestock. With hard work, however, his ranch was soon in working order again.

Independence, imagination, self-sufficiency, and a gritty willingness to work at backbreaking toil day after day characterized Jacob and Annie Lauritzen, and these traits were replicated in the first generation of settlers who stayed in Short Creek for more than a single season. Isolated from surrounding communities—the closest, Hurricane, was twenty-eight miles, while the nearest city, St. George, was fifty miles away across the Utah border—these colonists understandably became something of a law unto themselves. And, by 1935, one law—the divine law of plural marriage or polygamy, referred to simply as "the Principle"—had come to identify the community and make it a center of fundamentalist Mormonism.

—4—

The Search for Refuge and the First Raid, 1935

Warren Johnson and his family were the ones who first proposed Short Creek as a potential refuge from the intense and heated confrontation between the fundamentalists, the Church, and the government. The polygamists first came to Short Creek in 1928. Polygamists Leroy S. Johnson, Edner Allred, and Carling Spencer, as well as monogamist Price Johnson, left their homes in nearby Lee's Ferry to lead their families to Short Creek "as a starting point for the gathering of the Saints."[1]

Lauritzen found the newcomers a "friendly and sociable" lot but doubted that they would prosper because he and his sons controlled much of the water rights to the most promising areas.[2] But the fundamentalists believed that the problem would be resolved because of a prophetic promise. In 1935, the presiding elder from Salt Lake City, John Y. Barlow, taught the little colony of less than one hundred members that the dry creek beds and sagebrush-covered fields of Short Creek were the "Land of Bountiful" spoken of in the *Book of Mormon* where Christ had blessed the little children on his visit to the Nephites and promised that the land would be rich and yield abundant crops.[3] "Thus while this section was unattractive and unproductive," recalled Lauritzen later with some amazement, "it acquired a hallowed and secret aspect for these people by reason of these teachings."[4] Johnson remembered that the fundamentalists offered the site "as a starting place for the gathering of the Saints,... choice above all other spots of ground in the surrounding country."

48

In fact, the statement was made that the time would come when one acre of this ground would "produce more than ten acres of the best soil in the Salt Lake Valley."[5] The fruits of this richness would only materialize, Johnson reminded the fundamentalists, "when you are united."[6]

The quiet movement of the polygamists into this isolated corner of the Grand Canyon country did not go unnoticed. Within a matter of months, commented Lauritzen, Short Creek became a "mecca for news reporters and curiosity seekers."[7]

The story of the LDS Church's involvement with the Short Creek fundamentalists began in 1929. The Church of Jesus Christ of Latter-day Saints established a branch of the Rockville Ward in Short Creek when the Zion Park Stake was organized that year. Isaac Carling presided over the branch for the first four years of its existence. The fundamentalists were active members of the branch: they held leadership positions in the Sunday School organization and spoke in sacrament meetings. Some were advanced by stake leaders in priesthood offices.[8]

It was at one unspecified occasion during this time that Leroy Johnson, Price Johnson, Isaac Carling, and their wives drove from Short Creek to Salt Lake City for October general conference. While the women sat under the dome of the Tabernacle for three days of instruction from the Church's general authorities, the men gathered beneath the boughs of a spreading cottonwood tree in Cottonwood, a suburb of Salt Lake City, with other fundamentalists to discuss their beliefs, the price they might have to pay for the practice of their beliefs, and the possibility of uniting together. Here, the Johnson brothers first met Joseph W. Musser and John Y. Barlow, prominent excommunicated Mormons and polygamists.

When the Mormon Church excommunicated Musser, Barlow, and Johnson they set them adrift—separated from the official Church and the fellowship of Saints. Those ostracized from their mother church grouped together to form a new order. They discussed how best they might restructure their lives. Not surprisingly, out of this period of anomie when these men and their families were unbound by traditional religious laws and regulations they proposed a way of living that looked backwards and resembled more than anything else the nineteenth-century Mormon Church.

During the next few weeks in Short Creek, Leroy and Price Johnson talked long and fervently about the Principle, with the older brother Price being the more ardent. Gradually, Leroy began to feel less severe toward those who had chosen to leave the Church to pursue a different path. He had been particularly influenced by Barlow, whom he believed had been genuinely ordained by Lorin C. Woolley with authority given him by John Taylor, and who therefore held the all-important authoritative keys of the priesthood.[9] Therefore, the trauma was cushioned when their own excommunications came.

In the fall of 1934 Barlow and Musser traveled to Short Creek, thereby solidifying the bond between the clusters of polygamists who were scattered across the state. In 1940 Barlow moved some of his families to Short Creek. He had a close relationship with Leroy Johnson and in 1941 ordained him as a member of the Priesthood Council and appointed him as successor to the leadership of the community. Barlow died eight years later in Salt Lake City in 1949 at the age of seventy-four, a few years after serving seven months in the Utah State Prison after the Boyden raids.

In April 1935 Joseph W. Musser, John Y. Barlow, Ianthus W. Barlow, and Richard S. Jessop, leaders of the fundamentalists, traveled to Short Creek to examine the community and discuss the possibility of organizing under the umbrella of a formal trust "and controlling the same in the interest of the work of the Lord." Musser remembered: "We met with the Priesthood there; held several meetings, and decided to go ahead with the proposition."[10] Yet it would be almost a decade before they formally would organize a religious charitable trust—the United Effort Plan.

By the end of the summer of 1935, there were clearly two settlements—one on the Utah side of the creek and one in Arizona. Many of Short Creek's twenty-odd houses predated the flood of polygamists to the community. A small combination store and gas station, a post office, a lumber mill, and the one-room schoolhouse were the only public buildings. Only one structure in town had electricity, no one had refrigeration or other modern conveniences. Two wells and a nearly completed irrigation canal provided the town with water. Over two hundred head of cattle grazed in nearby fields. Already the group was trying to cooperatively buy and sell their produce. "The benefits of their efforts are divide, share and share alike."[11]

The Civilian Conservation Corps came to Short Creek in the early 1930s to lay three miles of two-inch pipeline from Jan's Canyon into town. The CCC camp included several barrack buildings and a gas generator which supplied electricity. The fundamentalists avoided the corps men and considered them a bad influence on their children. After the CCC moved out, the town used the barracks for community functions.

During this same time Isaac Carling and John T. Spencer started a store in Carling's living room, calling it "The Spencer and Carling Mercantile Company." With $103 of capital stock between them they purchased and hauled in supplies from Cedar City in Carling's truck (the only truck in town). They bought staples such as flour, lard, sugar, salt, soap, and lye in bulk; customers would bring their own containers to purchase as much as they needed.

Local education did not extend beyond a junior high school level, and few felt sufficiently motivated to continue. Cars bumped down the rutted road only when someone from "the outside" brought in gasoline. If gas and an automobile were available, the town's young people (properly supervised) drove into the red and rugged hills or the thirty-four miles to evening dances at Fredonia. A battery-operated ham radio connected this quiet town with the world outside, bringing news of the Depression, of Franklin D. Roosevelt, of war clouds gathering in Europe, of problems so widespread and pervasive that they seemed to lend proof of the rightness of their efforts to remove themselves from the world.

The monogamous Mormons of Short Creek adapted to their new neighbors—some finding much to admire in their cooperative lifestyle. Annie Lauritzen went so far as to say she didn't "know of finer folks anywhere. My grandfather was a polygamist. He had ten wives and they all loved him dearly. They loved each other, too. Those wives would divide up the housework, help him with his missionary duties and watch and care for him. A carnal-minded world is always thinking in terms of sex, often acuse [sic] believers in polygamy of wanting more wives in order to satiate their lusts. This is a deliberate lie, the worst kind of trash." She continued on the issue of the polygamous men. "Every man I have known in the polygamist faith has lived morally honest. Most of them have been gentle and considerate of their wives and followed strict and wise rules in regard to sex. Many people, especially women, don't understand how several wives can live and work in harmony and at the same time share the affections of one man. The trouble is they don't understand the religion of the polygamists."[12]

According to Lauritzen, fundamentalists in Short Creek were for the most part happy, felt vindicated by their faithfulness, and were thankful to find refuge.[13] They lived a cooperative lifestyle, working and playing together. Old-timers remembered that everyone joined in with enthusiasm on work projects or recreation. Typically, polygamists built homes as large as they could afford and usually filled them with two or three wives and as many children as possible.[14]

However, the line between the fundamentalists and the Mormon Church had already been drawn—Isaac Carling and his fellow polygamists had challenged the authority of Church President Heber J. Grant. On 30 August 1934 Isaac Carling was excommunicated from the Church by the Zion Park Stake High Council.

The polygamists felt that theirs was a righteous cause and thus they took excommunication in stride. Increasingly, fundamentalists moved into the isolated region of the Arizona Strip so that their families could be raised in an environment where the traditions they held sacred were respected. John Y. Barlow moved two of his wives and their thirteen children to Short Creek in 1935. His brothers Edmund and Ianthus as well as Ianthus's son Albert came the same year.

From the 1930s Short Creek was essentially a community of fundamentalist Mormons separated from the Mormon Church but attempting to live lives in accordance with their beliefs. They met together in church meetings but also found other ways of coming together for community activities. The fundamentalists' tradition of holding community-wide socials continues to the present. Their "social" was a true "mixer." Flushed elderly matrons twisted and turned, dipped and sashayed with adolescent sons, who, when the music stopped, formally bowed to thank their partners for a quadrille, waltz, or polka—the only dances allowed in town. It was customary for mothers who had young children to stay away from the dances to attend to their little ones, so extremes of age groups were prominent.

The children of Short Creek, unconcerned by the illegality of their parents' lifestyle, played the way children have always played, including roller-skating up and down the dusty road in front of the white schoolhouse.

Both Arizona and Utah had constitutional mandates prohibiting plural marriage, but Short Creek was no longer within Utah's reach. However, the growing community on the Grand Canyon's north rim was a source of particular irritation to Arizona's Mohave County Attorney E. Elmo Bollinger. He listened with vexation to complaints from local cattlemen, local Mormon Church officials, and other neighbors in the area who felt threatened by the growing strength of the fundamentalists.

Bollinger was best known in Mohave County for his "American-ism" campaigns during the 1930s. Patriotism was for him a religion, the lawbreaker a sinner. One unnamed journalist described E. Elmo Bollinger as "peppery," yet he underestimated the spirit of this man who threw himself into his work with such energy that he often of-fended many.[15] Ironically, Short Creek residents had voted unani-mously for Bollinger in the 1934 elections.

The distance from Mohave County's seat at Kingman to Short Creek—a single-lane twisting nightmare of an unpaved road—was a continual impediment to Bollinger's repeated law enforcement ef-forts. Although "Short Creek is only 90 miles by crow's flight, he has to bump over 425 miles of road through California, Nevada, and Arizona to reach the hamlet," wrote one journalist. "His complaint was it gives the ladies of the harem time to skin out."[16]

Bollinger may well have felt pressure from the Mormon Church to make the necessary effort. He certainly had its encouragement. Ac-cording to an article in *Truth*, in early August, Church Presiding Bishop David A. Smith in Salt Lake City told the press: "We feel that it would be a good thing for the Government agents to take strong action against the offenders and make an example of them. Persons using the Church as a cloak for such practices are bringing ill repute to us, and we are cooperating, whenever possible, in obtaining en-forcement of the law."[17] Earlier, at the April general conference of 1931, Heber J. Grant had pledged the resources of the Church to support the prosecution and imprisonment of the fundamentalists.[18]

In 1935 Grant was given cause to rejoice. According to the *Mohave County Miner*, government investigators researching wel-fare claims obtained information supporting the charges of plural marriage. It included the information that "there was a social organi-zation in that particular section of Mohave County where, if polyg-amy did not exist in its usual meaning, there did exist open cohabita-tion, it being alleged that some of the women admitted they were 'plural wives.'"[19] The *Miner* described the families as members of the "Brethren of the United Order"—polygamists. The information gathered for the relief board also included one case where three chil-dren were born the same month with the same father but different mothers.

On 16 August 1935 Bollinger succeeded in surprising the fundamentalists with warrants and arrested six of their most solid citizens: John Y. Barlow and Mary Roe Barlow, Price W. Johnson and Helen Hull Johnson, I. Carling Spencer and Spencer's plural wife Sylvia Allred Spencer, then four months pregnant with her fifth child. John Y. Barlow filed a demurrer and succeeded in having his and Mary's cases dismissed, although he was the most notoriously polygamous of the group.[20] Helen Hull Johnson's case was dismissed because of insufficient evidence to convict her. Price Johnson, Carling Spencer, and Sylvia Spencer appeared before Justice of the Peace Jacob Lauritzen, Short Creek Sheriff Ernest Graham, and Bollinger to schedule a preliminary hearing for 6 September. Local papers immediately announced the proceedings, which promised first-class entertainment.[21]

Bollinger's picture appeared in the *Los Angeles Examiner* on Thursday 29 August 1935 together with a statement about the so-called "polygamy" cases. Bollinger was in Los Angeles consulting about the case with Fred W. Maryon, an attorney and former resident of Kingman.[22]

Musser represented the polygamists as their legal advisor when the county attorney served the complaints in Justice Lauritzen's office.[23] Jack Childers was cited as the complaining witness in the cases of Johnson and Spencer. Lauritzen recalled the scene:

> I well remember the day when the County Attorney prepared these complaints in my office. Jack Childers was present and when the allegations in the complaints were read to him he frankly stated that he had no personal knowledge of those matters and therefore could not swear to them. Mr. Bollinger seemed baffled for a moment and then said: "Well, you have heard a lot, have you not." Yes, I have responded Mr. Childers. The County Attorney then said he would fix the complaints so that Mr. Childers could swear to them. He then inserted a clause in each complaint stating that the same was sworn to upon information and belief.[24]

The defendants promptly filed a demurrer to these complaints, contending they were not sworn to according to law.

Bollinger clearly intended to signal what would happen to all polygamists who did not abandon their pernicious practice. The warrants charged the defendants with cohabitation, which implied not only coresidence but also sexual intercourse, because the court had succeeded in locating the birth certificates of four children who had been born to the three defendants outside the parameters of a legally binding marriage. All three defendants were released on bail.

The *Miner* noted the extraordinary media attention the polygamy cases inspired:

> The columns of publicity that have gone the rounds of the press from the Atlantic to the Pacific coasts and north and south from Canada to the Mexican border about the alleged polygamous modes of living in Mohave county's northern strip is unique in that it has brought to the attention of the people of the nation a section of the country that heretofore has been practically unknown to the public because of its isolated situation. Some of the comments have been in particularly good syndicate form and appeal to the morbid and the curious.[25]

The hearing on the demurrer convened at the schoolhouse on the morning of 6 September and quickly turned into a comedy of errors. One account somewhat wryly described the central players in this drama:

> J.M. Lauritzen, smug astute justice of the peace, presiding; County Attorney Bollinger, representing statutory law in a land of religious tolerance; J.W. Musser, Salt Lake City, lay advisor to the defendants and court, author of numerous works on the sanctity of the "Everlasting Covenant of Marriage," and its full embracement of the doctrine of plurality of wives. The alleged polygamist defendants present were J.Y. Barlow, Price Johnson, I.C. Spencer, and Silvia Allred.[26]

Although his own case had been dismissed, Barlow, as the group's leader, continued to attend the hearings. The reporter went on to say that Bollinger raged and boiled, adding passion to the proceedings.

Lauritzen, unimpressed, pointed out that the complaint against the three had been sworn on "information and belief" ("information" being the legal equivalent of rumor), and declared it null and void.[27] The court further denied Bollinger's plea that the three be held while new complaints were drawn and warrants issued. Musser at this point delivered an impassioned denunciation of the proceedings. He said that although the defendants were polygamists, they were at the present living with only one wife. He maintained that the government was showing incredible intolerance toward the fundamentalists and was persecuting them for their religious beliefs by "attempting to carry the men off to jail and leaving the women and children on relief, when the big business men of every city were doing the same thing under the guise of wife and mistress, without molestation, and contrary to their religions."[28]

Just ten minutes later, Bollinger brought new complaints before Lauritzen; they were sworn, issued, and placed in the hands of Deputy Sheriff Millard Black for service. However, during that same ten minutes, the defendants had filtered through the crowd of bystanders gathered in the yard of the little white schoolhouse and had disappeared.[29] Black searched for ninety minutes. There were few cars in Short Creek, and the dust cloud that billowed behind his truck provided ample warning to the three, who darted through houses, behind outbuildings, and across the state line into Utah. Black returned frustrated and dejected.

Jacob Lauritzen, according to the *Mohave County Miner*, turned from Bollinger and Black saying that as far as he was concerned he had nothing upon which to hold the trio until after new charges were filed. He expressed his chagrin that such a thing could happen in his community.[30] On Wednesday, 20 September 1935, Kingman Rotarians watched films taken by their local news crews of the notorious escape of the defendants.[31]

The air crackled with excitement in Short Creek on 11 October 1935, the day of the rescheduled preliminary hearing. This time professional counsel—Los Angeles attorney Victor C. Hayek—represented the polygamists. The schoolhouse filled to overflowing with visitors from all across the state. Reporters representing half a dozen newspapers noted every moment of this legal confrontation with the polygamists.

The *Paramount News* set up a movie camera in the schoolhouse and filmed the entire proceedings. Flashbulbs exploded across the makeshift courtroom as Justice Lauritzen, County Attorney Bollinger and the three defendants entered the room. Lauritzen later wrote: "It was so strange for a small place like Short Creek. You would have thought it was the Supreme Court of the state in session and that some sensational case was about to be tried. Those in charge of affairs were certainly putting on a big show."[32] After Bollinger admitted the birth certificates as evidence against the defendants, counsel on both sides moved to discontinue the proceedings in this court and move to Kingman so that the case could be heard before the Superior Court.[33]

The day after the first attempt at a preliminary hearing, Zion

Park Stake President Claude Hirschi presented to the members of the Short Creek Branch a "loyalty" oath designed to test their allegiance to President Heber J. Grant and their conformity with the Church's anti-polygamy stand. As reproduced in *Truth* magazine it stated:

> Short Creek, Arizona, September 7, 1935
> To the Stake President and High Councils of Zion Park Stake and to Whom it May Concern: I, the undersigned member of Short Creek Branch of the Rockville Ward of the Church of Jesus Christ of Latter-day Saints, declare and affirm that I WITHOUT ANY MENTAL RESERVATION WHATSOEVER SUPPORT THE PRESIDENCY OF THE CHURCH and that I repudiate any intimation that any of the Presidency or Apostles of the Church are living a double life, and that I repudiate those who are falsely accusing them and that I denounce the practice and advocacy of plural marriage as being out of harmony with the declared principle of the Church at the time.[34]

Fundamentalists in the group, many of whom had entered into the Principle, unanimously refused to sign the document. Then they waited. But not for long; partly because of their connections with the Barlow group, that same day, 7 September 1935, the Zion Park Stake presidency and high council moved to excommunicate twenty-one adult members of Short Creek Branch without a formal Church court, close the branch altogether, and remove the Mormon Church from Short Creek, Arizona. They dispensed with the traditional methods of Church adjudication which would have allowed the defendants to present evidence and question the witnesses. According to *Truth*, Claude Hirschi was the liason between the Church and Elmo Bollinger. Pledging his support to the county prosecution Hirschi "expressed [the] willingness of the High Council and the Stake Presidency to assist in any way possible to bring the accused parties to trial."[35]

Many fundamentalists, including Leroy Johnson, marked their lives from this moment and remembered passionately this critical juncture in their lives. "The high council came out to Short Creek in 1935 and called us on the carpet and told us our die was cast and that we were only to accept or reject their edict, there would be no argument. I held up my hand and they gave me a chance to speak," Johnson reported. He then asked, "President Hershey [Hirschi], do you mean to say by this, that whatever takes place here today, you and your counselors will be responsible for?" Hirschi answered, "Yes, sir." Johnson concluded, "That will be all." He then sat down.[36]

After the council had announced their decision and described what they intended to do, the ward clerk passed around the "loyalty oath" to be signed. Leroy Johnson examined it and passed it to his wife. She asked, "Are you going to sign it?" He answered, "I have signed all I am going to." Leroy estimated that perhaps four or five people signed the paper. President Hirschi stood at the close of the meeting and said, "We will send you our decision in a few days."[37] Stake President Hirschi notified Johnson and the others who refused to sign the document of their excommunication.[38]

The reactions of those excommunicated varied. Johnson felt it was a "great load . . . lifted off my shoulders." His wife, however, felt "like the earth had fallen out from under her."[39] Nevertheless, she supported her husband. Johnson would later acknowledge having been "handled" by the Church, but denied the validity of the excommunication. "They may have gone through the motions of excommunicating me, but how can they excommunicate a man for believing what Joseph Smith taught?"[40]

Fundamentalists elsewhere reacted with indignation. Musser responded to the excommunications in *Truth* magazine:

> We class ourselves with the youth of Zion, and as such feel that we have been betrayed: that the present authorities of the Church are trying to compel us to accept false doctrines, not only by robbing us of our rights in the Church, [but also because they] have pledged the resources of the Church to persecute, in the civil court, our parents, ourselves and all other Latter-day Saints who dare believe and uphold the word of God in relation to this matter.[41]

After the trial, Hirschi sent a returned missionary to reclaim the lost Saints. An Elder Crawford of Rockville, Utah, traveled to Short Creek to preach repentance to the excommunicated fundamentalists. In a later sermon, Leroy S. Johnson described him as "an ambitious young man full of faith, as far as the Church was concerned. He was very definite of his explanation of what he was sent out to Short Creek for." His fervor matched that of the polygamists themselves. "He went on at great length to let us know that we had committed one of the greatest sins a people could commit in breaking away from the Church and claiming plural marriage to be a great saving principle";[42] but he reclaimed no lost sheep.

Years later, in a 1973 sermon given to the fundamentalists, Leroy

Johnson spoke about the connection he felt with the Mormon Church. "I did everything that was asked of me by the Church authorities. That is where I got my training. But I did have the presence of mind enough to say 'no' when I knew people were trying to get me to do things that were not right."[43]

Although their excommunications would be what most fundamentalists would remember about the fall of 1935, for the defendants the court case was also an immediate issue. Finally, on 11 October 1935 at the Kingman, Mohave County Courthouse, Johnson, Spencer, and Allred appeared before Judge M. T. Phelps of Maricopa County, who was brought in for the case because he was not known to have any sympathies with the polygamists.[44]

Joseph Musser assisted attorney Victor Hayek in the defense. The *Mohave County Miner* reported the event. The first witness called was Howard Rourke, a case investigator in the public welfare service. He testifed that two of the defendants—I. Carling Spencer and Sylvia Allred Spencer—were cohabitating, living in the same house, and had children.[45]

The second witness, John J. Cunningham, head of the welfare board, also attested to the rumor that the defendants were living plural marriage. Buck Lowry, deputy sheriff and hotel manager at Marble Canyon, gave his testimony concerning "the reputation of the defendants during the few years they lived at Lee's Ferry."[46] Charles Heaton, president of the LDS Church Moccasin Stake, and his sister Ester Heaton Johnson, the wife of Price Johnson, confirmed the presented testimony and added the information that the polygamists were excommunicted members of the Church of Jesus Christ of Latter-day Saints. Mr. Hayek objected occasionally both to the questions asked and the method of answering, but he was for the most part overruled.[47]

Carling Spencer defended his beliefs saying: "In living my life I have sinned against neither God or man, and if I am to be condemned for living the normal married life with a woman whose virtue and high ideals are beyond question, even though I may have another wife in another State, I am prepared to rot in jail before surrendering my faith."[48] The primary evidence against the trio included birth certificates and the testimony of Charles Heaton, who had reported that the Mormon Church had excommunicated the defendants earlier based on the same evidence. Trial was set for 13 December 1935.

The reporter from the *Miner* interviewed Lauritzen after the

hearing, asking how he felt about polygamy. Lauritzen replied that
he considered the problem of polygamy "a social one rather than a
criminal one." He added: "The question of arresting and convicting
a few individuals is of small moment when compared to the problem
of finding a permanent solution."[49]

Several years later Lauritzen would write: "The polygamists are
law breakers and they are advocating an unpopular practice but that
is no reason why they should be rail roaded thru [sic] the courts with
utter disregard for their legal rights.... The only reason I can be accused of favoring the polygamists is that I have firmly declined to be
a party to unscrupulous practices. I would have violated my oath of
office and lost my self respect if I had."[50]

Lauritzen's wife Annie, ironically, disagreed with her husband's
views on polygamy. She often told her believing but inactive Mormon husband that he was not "worthy" to live the life of the
polygamist.[51]

Elmo Bollinger felt differently than both Jacob and Annie Lauritzen. The presence of the polygamists was a source of continuous irritation to him, a problem that mocked both his authority and responsibility as county attorney to uphold the Constitution. *Truth*
reported that he had said: "Section 21 of the Constitution of the
State of Arizona guarantees religious liberty, allowing all men to
worship God as they choose, but forever prohibiting polygamy. Conditions here at Short Creek are an outrage; and so far as my jurisdiction goes I am going to clean up the foul situation. However, conditions have got so bad it is time that the Federal Government steps in
and takes a hand."[52]

Polygamists from all over Utah united in their criticism of the
court's actions. *Truth* published articles, letters to the editor, and
even poetry that decried the actions of the government and called for
fairness and justice. "Why come up 400 miles to that desert Arizona
strip to pounce upon a peaceful, hard-working, struggling, Christian
community, suspected only of having more married women than
men?" asked Musser in one editorial.

> Surely the great state of Arizona—great in its western atmosphere
> and broad tolerance—is not so free from moral delinquencies as to
> justify its officials leaving the more populous sections of the state to
> train their legal artillery on this little community. It seems small
> business in this age of open immorality to invade an outpost of civi-

lization, such as Short Creek, break up homes and fasten unreasonable hardships upon men and women—with their children—whose only offense is to make sexual virtue a crowning point in their lives.[53]

At the same time, the press queried Church officials about the existence of the "polygamy problem" in southern Utah. Apostle Melvin J. Ballard was a key figure in the public dialogue, often giving a standard Church response to media inquiries. The *Kansas City Times* quoted Ballard as giving this typical statement: "The Church does not countenance this pernicious practice and just as fast as violations are brought to our attention the guilty parties are handled for their standing in the Church."[54]

The *Kansas City Times* interview also quoted Elder Ballard as admitting the Church's partial responsibility for the prosecution of Spencer, Allred, and Johnson when it shared information with the government that had been gathered for Church trials. Ballard added that John Barlow, a former missionary, was "following his occupation as farmer [in Short Creek] last spring [1935] when the authorities [of the Church] urged Arizona officials to act against him and his followers."[55]

Outsiders took the case less seriously. Alexander J. Wedderburn, Jr., covering the trial for the *Washington Post*, headlined his article as follows: "Polygamy again causes half-amused, half-bitter Arizona-Utah furor. President of Mormons involved in quarrel. Court ruling incites religious controversy. Charges and counter-charges fly between sects over plurality of wives in colony at Short Creek. Judge freed defendants on plea that 'Big Business Men' are polygamists under clandestine system."[56]

On 13 December 1935, Elmo Bollinger argued his interpretation of the Constitution's freedom of religion amendment against that of Victor J. Hayek, counsel for the defense, before Judge Jesse W. Faulkner of Mohave County Superior Court and a jury of twelve men. Hayek made a motion for a mistrial but it was denied. Bollinger's arguments were apparently more persuasive, for Price Johnson and Carling Spencer were found guilty of "open and notorious cohabitation" and were sentenced from eighteen to twenty-four months in the Florence, Arizona, penitentiary. Bail was set at $1,500 each. Although Johnson's wife, Helen Hull, was questioned during the proceedings, no formal charges were leveled against her. After receiving the judgment of the court, Johnson maintained that if he had in fact "violated the laws of this state it was because he had obeyed the laws of God and eternity. That in the choice of the temporal laws of man and the laws of God, he would obey God, for His word was eternal and the opinions of man extend no further than this earth."[57] In response to the decision, John Y. Barlow, head of the group, said that he had "been on the fighting line for 20 years in just such cases as this and we will never rest until the highest tribunals have made their rulings."[58]

Sylvia Allred Spencer's case was delayed until her baby was born in February 1936; she then received a suspended sentence from Judge Faulkner. She continued to defend plural marriage throughout the proceedings:

> I have already given birth to four boys. They are the crowning glory of my life. I am praying that I may have more children so that my happiness through eternity may be greater.
>
> We who believe in polygamy are joyed at the role that the Lord has given us. Unlike so many mothers of today, we do not fear childbirth. We don't worry because of the extra expense that another mouth will bring. We know that the Lord will provide and care for us.
>
> Bringing children into the world is the main function of womankind. Everything else is subordinate.[59]

In January, one month after the convictions, Johnson's wife, Helen Hull, petitioned for his release. The parole board was willing to grant the request if Johnson would sign a statement agreeing to "straighten out his family affairs." Johnson voiced his own attitude with the typical ardor of the polygamist: "I am not only willing to go to jail for my family and my religion but I would be willing to give up my life as did Joseph Smith and his brother Hyrum. When this case is taken before the supreme court our cause will be vindicated and we will be permitted to obey the dictates of conscience unmolested."[60]

The parole board returned Johnson to the penitentiary where he and Carling were model prisoners. Prison officials appointed the two fundamentalists to be trustees of their wings of the prison after their first three days. They spent the next eleven months gardening, working in the tannery and dairy, and supervising the work of their fellow inmates. They were released early because of good behavior, and the two returned to their families in Short Creek on 8 November 1936.

Like the more than 1,300 Mormon men and women during the 1880s who had been "prisoners for conscience's sake," the three were heralded as folk heroes. This first of the three "raids" on the fundamentalists had, from the Church's and government's points of view, backfired. It had aroused public interest and sympathy while generating greater growth and hardening the determination of polygamy's adherents.

When a *Literary Digest* reporter questioned a Mormon Church official after the December 1935 trial, the official enthusiastically supported future legal action.[61] However, Arizona government officials were more cautious: "The matter is being treated warily; under the law the colony as a unit may not be punished, altho individuals may be enjoined from violating the law. The trials of Spencer and Johnson proved costly, and there is distinct agitation against bringing others to trials."[62] Arizona Governor B. B. Moreur declined to comment at all.

In less than a decade, however, this view would be reversed. The story of the mechanisms that locked the fundamentalists, the Mormon Church, and the governments of Utah and Arizona in irreversible conflict is not just an aberration in the fabric of Utah's cultural history but part of the larger pattern of American values during the 1930s and 1940s.

The Boyden Raid
and Prosecutions, 1944–1950

Beginning in the late 1920s, in part as a reaction to the growing influence of men like Joseph Musser whose charismatic leadership drew the fundamentalists together, the hunt for polygamists stepped up. To counteract the growing numbers of fundamentalists, in 1938 the First Presidency of the Church authorized a number of loyal Mormons to conduct surveillance of persons attending meetings in private homes in Salt Lake City and Midvale, Utah.[1] According to *Truth*, one of them, Casper Fetzer, would later testify in a court that David O. McKay had given him a "calling" to find offenders and bring them to justice.[2] On 5 June 1939, Paul C. Child, president of the Salt Lake City Pioneer Stake, reportedly instructed bishops that fundamentalists were "in very humble circumstances, being practically destitute, and if we help them we are helping to support plural families."[3]

A Church bulletin which went to all stake presidencies and bishoprics told leaders to deny baptism to the children of polygamous parents until they were old enough to "repudiate the principle that gave them birth." J. Reuben Clark, Jr. also used his ecclesiastical power to promote change in the secular environment by urging the Salt Lake City postmaster to prohibit the mailing of fundamentalist tracts; and throughout the 1930s and 1940s he encouraged the immediate prosecution of the "new polygs."[4]

During the late 1930s the Church through Clark conducted extensive surveillance of the polygamists. Local bishops would privately solicit the assistance of ward members to watch the homes of suspected polygamists and note license plate numbers of visitors to the home. The Hawthorne Ward bishopric described one of their surveillance efforts in a letter to Clark. "As per your request we will continue to investigate this case, and will give you another list of cars owners at the end of two weeks so they can be attached to the list given above. At the meeting last Tuesday Evening at 7:30 P.M. there were over forty people in attendance.... We have also found out that Mr. Joseph Musser and Charles Zitting also attend these meetings."[5]

In a series of excommunication proceedings, Church leaders questioned members who had attended meetings at the homes of polygamists. When asked to characterize the gatherings, a woman identified only as R. Gordon answered, "They opened the meeting with prayer. The women were in one room, the men were in another. After opening the meeting with prayer, they began a discussion of plural marriage and denounced President Grant. That's about all they talked about."[6]

Bishop Fred Curtis questioned Gordon's husband about the way they had been invited to attend the discussion at the Jeffs' home. Gordon related that he had been a teacher in the Hawthorne Ward with Rulon Jeffs, who was himself the "Gospel Doctrine" teacher. Jeffs told Gordon that there were some things that one must do because of extraordinary circumstances. "The first meeting I attended," Gordon said, "was a testimonial meeting." He continued:

> That was a meeting where the men and the women were gathered together in one room. It was a very interesting meeting and I learned quite a lot.... I noticed after a while that there was a certain amount of backbiting and no harmony among the men that were supposed to be conducting these meetings. Their teachings, while somewhat similar to ours, had a marked personal opinion and fostered that opinion at the expense of the doctrine of our Church.[7]

Gordon was particularly disturbed by the polygamists' attitude toward Church President Heber J. Grant. It was Gordon's understanding that they funded these meetings with the proceeds from the publication of *Truth*. In the case of Rulon Jeffs, the members of the

Church court concluded that he was "out of harmony with the Church and its policies."[8] Jeffs was subsequently disfellowshiped from the Church.

The meetings described in the Church court included religious services, informal social gatherings, and lectures on the principle of a plurality of wives and other subjects. A series of free lectures on "Ancient Mormonism" given by fundamentalist Francis M. Darter was held in 1940 at the Moose Club in Salt Lake City, located at 161 South and 2nd East. There fundamentalists could hear the doctrinal defense of the Principle and purchase the latest literature published on the subject, including *A Leaf in Review* by Byron Harvey Allred, a book depicted in one leaflet advertising Darter's next lecture as a "faith building, authentic, timely message, [that] portrays [the] present condition of the Church—second to none."[9] *A Leaf in Review* has been called the single most influential piece of literature of early fundamentalism. Church leaders carefully watched Darter's free lectures and recorded the license plate numbers of those in attendance.[10]

Although the governments of Arizona and Utah refrained from "raiding" the community of Short Creek for the time being, they continued to prosecute individual polygamists. In 1938 Utah brought a number of polygamists before the court; they included three Short Creek fundamentalists, Richard Jessop, Fred Jessop and Grover Cleveland LeBaron. In Washington County the next year, the trial of one of them, Richard Jessop, charged with cohabitation, received considerable attention and raised issues that would dominate the debate over plural marriage for the next three decades.

A major concern of the defense in *State of Utah* v. *Jessop* (100 p.2d 969, 27 March 1940) was whether a polygamist could receive a fair trial in Utah, where Mormons not only held most court positions but also constituted a majority in the makeup of most juries. Defense attorney Claude Barnes, who would continue to defend the fundamentalists through their many complicated trials and appeals, told the court that he felt there were not eight men in the entire state who could judge the polygamists fairly. Joseph W. Musser and other fundamentalist leaders were alarmed at what they perceived to be an LDS-dominated legal system. Musser wrote in his journal on 21 September 1939:

> The trial of these boys was a farce. It was a Church fight, the Co. Atty [Orval Hoit] being a counselor in the Stake Presidency there.

The Dist. Atty. is a Mormon; the Sheriff who served the papers and furnished the chief testimony, AB [sic] Price, and the Judge, Will L. Haft, were Mormons. The Jury of course, was comprised of Mormons. It was an effort to stamp polygamy out . . . thereby bringing rejoicing to the heart of pres. Grant. Today the word "JUSTICE": both in the Ecclesiastical and Civil or Criminal Courts, in Mormon communities, is no. [sic][11]

These court cases with their elaborate judicial and enforcement machinery not only disrupted the lives of the families directly involved but also forced an increasing number of other fundamentalist families into hiding or into deliberately transient and secretive lives. Rather than live life on the run, during the 1930s some families had chosen to join Johnson, Barlow, Carling, and others in the relative isolation and safety of Short Creek. A 1936 snapshot of the Short Creek Sabbath School (the LDS Church dismantled its branch there that same year) showed 125 smiling Mormon fundamentalists. "One may never expect to meet up with a finer, cleaner or more intelligent group of Saints than here pictured," its caption in *Truth* read. "They are fundamentally sound in their religious and social ideals."[12]

In 1938 the fundamentalists organized cooperatively under the United Trust. Steeped in the tradition and doctrine of the early Mormon law of consecration and stewardship, cooperation was nothing new to these people, whose roots ran deep into nineteenth-century Mormonism. Because of their religious convictions, they believed that community economic life should be organized according to, and subject to, ecclesiastical directives under the direction of the priesthood. Like their nineteenth-century predecessors, religious belief rather than hope for material gain motivated their communal economic organization in the United Trust. From the late 1930s on, the belief in and practice of economic organization in the spirit of the law of consecration and stewardship as taught by Joseph Smith was as much a part of fundamentalism as was plural marriage.

However, although the Arizona community and Utah fundamentalists shared a common way of life and similar convictions, they were drifting apart over the issue of authorized leadership. During the 1940s, Barlow continued to consolidate his influence in Short Creek while Joseph Musser and Rulon Allred came to dominate fundamentalists in the Salt Lake Valley.

The Boyden Raid

The next police assault on Short Creek was part of what the press dubbed the "Boyden Raid," named after one of its architects, U.S. Attorney John S. Boyden. He collaborated with Utah State Attorney General Brigham E. Roberts, grandson of B.H. Roberts, one of the early Church leaders and a polygamist. The pair visualized ending the polygamy problem once and for all with a massive roundup of offenders. Under their direction the executive branch of the Utah State government, along with FBI agents, U.S. federal marshals, deputy sheriffs, Salt Lake City police, support units from Washington County, Utah and Maricopa County, Arizona, as well as deputy sheriffs from Pocatello, Idaho, served warrants for the arrest of those accused of "unlawful cohabitation" in polygamous enclaves throughout the region.[13] Boyden told the press: "These arrests take into custody the leaders of the group which called themselves 'fundamentalists.' They are the most active and we feel we've got them all."[14]

At six o'clock on Tuesday morning, 7 March 1944, a cold drizzly day, a heavy knock on the main door of the Rulon Allred home in Midvale wakened the entire family. A group of policemen pushed past the family patriarch, clutching warrants for the arrest of Rulon C. Allred and his plural wives, twin sisters Mabel and Melba Finlayson.[15] His other wives were not served warrants at this time. The children screamed and ran for their mothers, while several of the women burst into terrified tears. Their fear cooled the officers' zeal and led them to pursue a more restrained approach as the policemen searched for their "evidence," confiscating issues of *Truth* and additional documents. They had, however, neglected to obtain search warrants and thus confiscated the material illegally.[16]

Simultaneously, a similar scene was repeated in other fundamentalist homes in Salt Lake City, Short Creek, and at several other locations in Arizona, Utah, and Idaho.[17] In Short Creek, Mattie Jessop Barlow, plural wife of John Barlow and mother of twelve children, was arrested and taken from her sickbed where she lay terminally stricken with cancer. Seven months later, on 22 October 1944, she died while free on bail. Sixteen-year-old Gwen Balmforth, the future plural wife of Leroy Johnson, lived in a tent at Short Creek when law officers burst through the front flap demanding information about the whereabouts of alleged polygamists. Leonard and Vera Black saw officers in the town and so they took their small children and ran for the foothills, taking what food they could snatch on their way out of the house. Federal officers arrested Leroy Johnson and L.R. Stubbs in Short Creek and booked them into the county jail.[18]

That same morning of 7 March in Salt Lake City two heavily armed FBI men and two Salt Lake City police officers entered the home of Joseph W. Musser at 6:00 A.M. "I was in my bathrobe working on the *Truth* magazine, (My habit was to rise at 5 a.m. and work a couple of hours before dressing for the day).... They followed me into the bathroom and into my bedroom where I dressed,"[19] Musser related. After placing Musser under arrest, and despite his numerous protestations to stop, the intruders searched his office for records even though they presented no search warrant. "This search continued until about 11:00 A.M. when the officers took me to the county jail. Arriving there, I found a large congregation of my brothers."[20] Musser was charged with federal conspiracy, state conspiracy, and cohabitation.

The men and women taken from their homes that March morning were immediately eulogized by their fellows as enthusiastic martyrs for the cause. They had long anticipated just such a confrontation. Earlier, John Y. Barlow told a *Deseret News* reporter that "his followers would go to jail or lay down their lives in defense of their beliefs, including plural marriage."[21] What *Truth* called the "Honor Roll of 1945" included Oswald Brainich, Joseph W. Musser, Louis A. Kelsch, Dr. Rulon C. Allred, Albert E. Barlow, Ianthus W. Barlow, John Y. Barlow, Edmund F. Barlow, David B. Darger, Charles F. Zitting, J. Lyman Jessop, Heber K. Cleveland, Arnold Boss, Alma A. Timpson, Morris Q. Kunz, and Follis Gardner Petty.[22] The prosecution also gathered enough evidence to arrest twelve women. As in the judicial crusades of the 1880s and 1890s, the charges against the polygamists included more accusations than just that of polygamous living itself.

Tuesday afternoon, the officers handcuffed the defendants and led them through the streets to the Federal Court where large bonds were set for them. The judge also set dates to hear their pleas, to hear motions, and for the beginning of their trials. Friends of the prisoners tried to raise over $50,000 for bonds for the men of $2,500 each. The bail was subsequently raised to $4,500 for two of the men, Heber Kimball Cleveland and Follis Gardner Petty, who had been carrying firearms at the time of their arrests.[23]

The Mormon Church immediately endorsed the police action

with a statement signed by the First Presidency—Heber J. Grant, J. Reuben Clark, Jr., and David O. McKay:

> Since the manifesto by President Wilford Woodruff was adopted by the church the first presidency and other general authorities have repeatedly issued warnings against an apostate group that persisted in the practice of polygamous marriage, illegal both as to the church and the state. Members of the church who have let this warning go unheeded and have violated the rule and doctrines of the church by entering into these illicit relationships have been formally dealt with and excommunicated as rapidly as they could be found out. This is the extreme punishment which the church can inflict. . . . Notwithstanding excommunication some of these persons have persisted in propagating false ideas regarding the doctrine of plural marriage. Their attitude is one of rebellion against the church.
>
>   We commend and uphold the federal government in its efforts through the office of the United States district attorney and assisting agencies to bring before the bar of justice those who have violated the law.[24]

Officials established a makeshift dormitory on the basketball court of the Salt Lake County Jail for the prisoners from the Salt Lake area. After releasing four women—Ruth Barlow, Mary Mills Johnson, Juanita Barlow and Zola Chatwin Cleveland—to return to their children, they walled off part of the room for the eight remaining female prisoners, Leona Allred, Jean Barlow Darger, Myrtle L. Allred, Rhea Allred Kunz, Mabel and Melba Finlayson Allred, Marie Barlow Cleveland, and Nita Barlow Smith. To make the space livable Chief Deputy George Beckstead also set up cots, tables, benches, and a large cookstove where the prisoners cooked their own meals of food furnished by friends. "'We're in a stew, but we're not stewing,' one of the forty-six men and women arrested Tuesday on polygamy charges facetiously remarked today as he was served stew cooked by the prisoners themselves at the Salt Lake county jail,"[25] wrote a *Deseret News* reporter.

The sixteen men and eight women struggled to accept their arrests calmly. Rhea Kunz led the women in Mormon hymns to keep their spirits elevated.[26] Soon the words of "Come, Come, Ye Saints," "A Mighty Fortress," "A Poor Wayfaring Man of Grief," and "The Spirit of God Like a Fire Is Burning" resounded through the gymnasium. The music added a sense of a harmonic connection with the early Mormons. One visitor noted that "the men are cheerful and in no way reticent to discuss their imprisonment and the charges against them. They spend their time exchanging experiences, taking turns over the cookstove, walking about and reading."[27] During one reporter's visit to Rhea A. Kunz and Marie Beth Barlow Cleveland, he wrote that "Mrs. Kunz was engaged in washing the walls of the bathroom."[28] Rhea, a thirty-seven-year-old mother of eight children, defended her beliefs: "Of course we believe in what we are doing. . . . This thing is far bigger than the individual, for it will inevitably encompass much more than the man-made laws by which the world lives and will become a fundamental component in the lives of all right-living people."[29]

While their mother was in jail, Rhea Kunz's older children were staying home from junior high school to care for their younger siblings. A sister wife cared for the children of her cellmate, Marie Beth Barlow Cleveland. After bail of $1,000 each was paid, seven of the women were released from the Salt Lake County Jail on Wednesday night, 8 March.[30]

After he had been released on bail, Joseph Musser confronted reporters for the first of what would be several times over the next few years. The *Salt Lake Tribune* tried unsuccessfully to interview Musser but instead carefully described him and the scene for their readers.

> A tall, erect man, 71-year-old Joseph W. Musser, husband of four wives and father of 20 children, walked coatless out of his cell in the Salt Lake county jail, head held high. He was clad in a black suit and a heavy gold watch chain hung from his vest. A day's growth of beard showed on his face, but his white moustache was carefully trimmed. "What do you wish?" he asked in a clear steady voice. Asked whether or not he would like to tell his side of the story, he declined. "No," he said, "We will present the case of the Fundamentalists in court. If you want any more, I refer you to our magazine, *Truth*."[31]

Wednesday, March 8, in Salt Lake City, preliminaries to the trials opened. Forty-six total arrested fundamentalists accused by the state and federal governments of a variety of charges began the long judicial process. Thirteen of the twenty individuals charged with federal offenses appeared with attorney J.H. McKnight before Federal Judge Tillman Johnson. McKnight petitioned the court to continue

the arraignments until Friday afternoon to give him more time to prepare. The trial was set for March 20. On Wednesday afternoon the
fundamentalists facing state unlawful cohabitation charges appeared
before Salt Lake City Judge E.G. Foxley at the City and County
Building.[32] The families of the fundamentalists filled the courtroom to
overflowing. Salt Lake County Attorney Harold E. Wallace, Deputy
County Attorney W. Stanford Wagstaff, and Earl M. Lowry, investigator for the county attorney's office, represented the state. After the
hearing concluded, defendants and their families tearfully embraced
each other, not knowing what was to become of them.[33]

Also on 8 March the *Deseret News* published a photograph of
the judge and assistant prosecuting attorney conferring on the case.
The caption unabashedly read: "He prepared for one of the most difficult and extensive criminal trials of his long career. Eighty-seven
year old Federal Judge Tillman D. Johnson confers with Assistant
U.S. District Attorney John S. Boyden on matters of the polygamy
case before him."[34] Defense attorney Claude Barnes promptly filed an
affidavit and motion for disqualification, which Tillman Johnson accepted, disqualifying himself as trial judge and providing a delay that
gave the defendants more time to prepare a defense.[35]

Mormon attorney Claude R. Barnes eventually would argue
twenty-seven separate matters for the fundamentalists before the
United States Supreme Court. Barnes was a man of many talents. A
published author of volumes of poetry and a scientific treatise on the
mountain lion, Barnes was consumed by a passion for science. He
was a charter member of the American Society of Mammologists and
of the Society for the Study of Evolution, and he was the first president of the Utah Audubon Society. Barnes celebrated his sixtieth
birthday anniversary in 1944 and was just five years away from re-
tirement; but he proved to have the strength of a wildcat and was a
fearless, unrelenting supporter of the fundamentalists, their single
most loyal friend on the outside.

The Boyden Prosecutions, 1944–1950

The State of Utah and the United States government accused the
fundamentalists of five separate categories of offenses. The state leveled charges of unlawful cohabitation and criminal conspiracy
against the largest number of the polygamists. In perhaps the most
serious matter, the federal government charged some members of the

group with mailing obscene literature, Lindbergh Act (kidnapping), and Mann Act (White Slave Trade Act) violations.

United States v. John Y. Barlow, et al.,
(56 F. S., 795)

The first case to be heard before the federal court dealt with the accusation of conspiracy/mailing obscene literature. Newly appointed Judge J. Foster Symes of Denver heard the case, replacing Judge Tillman D. Johnson who had disqualified himself on the basis of personal prejudice on the case. Twelve men were charged with conspiring to commit an offense against the United States: mailing obscene matter. The law read:

> Every obscene, lewd, or lascivious, and every filthy book, pamphlet, picture, paper, letter, writing, print, or other publication of an indecent character,...is hereby declared to be nonmailable matter.... Whoever shall knowingly deposit, or cause to be deposited, for mailing or delivery, anything declared by this section to be nonmailable...shall be fined.[36]

The defendants filed a motion to quash the indictment, alleging that it did not state a specific federal offense. This lack of specificity seemed to be the weak link in the prosecution's case. Claude Barnes produced sample editorials from *Truth* for the perusal of Judge Symes. *Truth* was largely the work of its editor Joseph W. Musser and therefore expressed a rather consistent viewpoint on the subject of a plurality of wives.

The prosecution countered by calling witnesses who figured prominently in the LDS Church, including Samuel O. Bennion and Richard L. Evans. The fundamentalists felt it was significant that Boyden, the prosecuting attorney, was himself an active Mormon.

Judge Symes failed to see the evidence of lewdness in the documents he surveyed, concluding,

> It might be said that the natural reaction to reading a publication setting forth that polygamy is essential to salvation is one of repugnance and does not tend to increase sexual desire or impure thoughts. We also bear in mind that one cannot pick up a national magazine, or go to the theatre or movie without being confronted with illustrations and advertisements that tend more to incite sexual desire than do any of the publications in this magazine that have been called to our attention.[37]

Symes therein supported the defendants' motion to quash the indictment and dismissed the hearing, freeing the defendants from that charge. His decision was dated 18 March 1944, just eleven days after the raid.

Syme's decision seemed to the fundamentalists to vindicate three principles: 1) that a man may have a belief; 2) that he may express that belief; and, 3) that he may advocate changes and amendments in the laws to conform to that belief.[38]

This was an important victory for the fundamentalists. It fueled them with the belief that success would be met with in each separate indictment. "Our magazine is now free as the air," exclaimed Joseph W. Musser upon hearing of the decision. "We will continue publication, and with the same editorial policy."[39] Although this decision encouraged the fundamentalists immensely, it did not affect the other cases continued in the courts.

United States v. *William Chatwin, Charles F. Zitting,*
Edna Christensen; and *Chatwin* v. *United States,*
326 US 455, 66 S. Ct. 233, 90 L. Ed. 198 (1946)

Another charge accused William Chatwin, Charles F. Zitting, and Edna Christensen of the seizure and abduction of a fifteen-year-old who was not only a minor but had married without the permission of her parents. The Federal Court assigned Judge T. Blake Kennedy of Cheyenne to come to Utah to hear the case. The court brief attested that in August 1940 farmer William Chatwin of Goshen, Utah, employed fifteen-year-old Dorothy Wyler as a housekeeper. A previous IQ test had placed her mental age at seven years and two months.

Dorothy's parents not only approved of her working in the Chatwin home but had visited her upon occasion. Lula Cook, who also lived with Chatwin as a plural wife, made friends with Dorothy, introduced the subject of plural marriage, and suggested the idea of Dorothy's marriage to Chatwin—a man sixty-three years her senior.

Dorothy apparently understood that the arrangement would not only give her a husband and a secure home, but also a lifelong friend in Lula. Dorothy and William married in a common law ceremony on 19 December 1940 without the knowledge or consent of her parents; within weeks, she was pregnant. Dorothy's parents alerted Washington County juvenile authorities about the polygamous nature of this peculiar family (*United States* v. *William Chatwin*). In early August 1941, after Social Services finally located her, the seven-months-pregnant Dorothy was taken into the protective custody of juvenile authorities.

On 10 August 1941 Dorothy went to the movies with her probation officer. During intermission she went into the foyer of the theater for some candy, met one of Chatwin's daughters, perhaps by design, and drove away with her. She rejoined the Chatwin family then living in Juarez, Mexico (a nineteenth-century Mormon polygamy enclave). This scenario had the ingredients of a romantic thriller, despite the unlikely combination of a mentally deficient teenager and a skinny but spry seventy-eight-year-old patriarch. Two years later, Washington County juvenile authorities discovered Dorothy, then the mother of two children, in Short Creek during the Boyden raid. Chatwin, along with Charles Zitting and Edna Christensen, had allegedly told Dorothy to live "God's law not man's."[40]

The three were accused of kidnapping Dorothy for immoral purposes and charged with violations of both the Lindbergh Act and the Mann Act. Dorothy Wyler's mental deficiencies made the charges even more serious. Judge T. Blake Kennedy, who had earlier waived a jury for the trial, tried the three defendants as a group. He found all the defendants guilty and sentenced each of them to a term in a federal prison. Judge Kennedy imposed a lighter sentence on Edna Christensen, mother of seven children, because Boyden had proved to him that "Zitting ruled his wives with a domineering hand and . . . occasionally spanked them when they disobeyed him, and that Edna Christensen might have been compelled to make the trip."[41] Edna did testify that she accompanied her husband on the trip to Arizona to be with the younger mother, and that if given a choice she would have preferred to stay at home with her own family.[42]

The decision was appealed, but the Tenth Circuit Court of Appeals at Wichita, Kansas, sustained the decision of the lower court. The case eventually went to the United States Supreme Court, which reversed both lower courts in the kidnapping cases and discharged the three defendants. The appeal of *Chatwin* v. *United States* was grouped for judgment by the Supreme Court of Utah with *Cleveland* v. *United States* (1946). In a unanimous vote, the Supreme Court handed down a judgment written by Justice J. Murphy stating: "The purpose of the act was to outlaw the interstate kidnapings rather than general transgressions of morality involving the crossing of state lines, and the broad language of the statute must be interpreted and applied with that plain fact in mind."[43]

The Court further argued that the language of the Lindbergh Act was sufficiently vague as to leave room for interpretation and "conceivably could lead to the punishment of anyone who induced another to leave his surroundings and do some innocent or illegal act" across state lines. "The absurdity of such a result, with its attendant likelihood of unfair punishment and blackmail is sufficient by itself to foreclose that construction." Dorothy Wyler was not held for ransom, which is implicit in a definition of kidnapping under the federal kidnapping act.[44] Finally, the Court ordered reargument of cases involving the conviction of six other fundamentalists on Mann Act charges.

United States v. Cleveland and Five Others
(56 F. Supp. 890 h [D Utah 1944])

The defendants in the Mann Act accusations were Heber Kimball Cleveland, David Brigham Darger, Vergel Y. Jessop, Theral Roy Dockstader,[45] Lawrence R. Stubbs, and Follis Gardner Petty. The federal government charged these six fundamentalist men, who had each moved a plural wife from one state to another, with Mann Act violations—taking females across state lines for immoral purposes. The Federal Court at Salt Lake City assigned this case to Judge Kennedy of Cheyenne. Invoking the Mann Act in a polygamy case was an example of legal ingenuity on the part of the prosecution to avoid a direct attack on polygamy. The Mann Act, sometimes called the "White Slave Traffic Act," was originally created to halt the interstate transportation of prostitutes.

On 20 March 1944, just weeks after the men's arrests, the prosecution obtained twelve federal court convictions after a non-jury trial that was based upon stipulated facts, not live testimony.[46] On 7 June 1944 *United States* v. *Cleveland and Five Others* affirmed the convictions of Heber Kimball Cleveland and the other five for violations of the Mann Act. Judge T. Blake Kennedy, who had presided at Teapot Dome scandal cases twenty years earlier, sentenced the six men as well as the two men and one woman from the Chatwin case in United States District Court for Mann Act and Lindbergh Kidnapping Act violations. Sentences ranged from one to four years. "The courts have frequently paid their respects to the practice of polygamy,"

Kennedy wrote in his fifteen-page opinion, "and in each instance so far as I have been able to discover, it has been condemned." He continued: "When such beliefs lead to practices which contravene to violate the laws of the land, then such beliefs must yield and be subordinated to such laws for otherwise government by law would amount to chaos."[47]

Claude Barnes started immediately to work on an appeal to the decisions while the defendants were released on bail bonds. By October 1944 he had filed a brief with the United States Circuit Court of Appeals, Tenth Circuit. The charges were upheld by the Tenth United States Circuit Court of Appeals.[48]

By May 1945 the Supreme Court of the United States had accepted an appeal to review both the Mann Act and the Lindbergh Act charges. This appellant brief presented by Barnes to the Supreme Court stressed the sacred nature of the polygamous marriage relationship and the difference in biblical interpretation between the concubine or paid mistress and the polygamous wife.

Cleveland v. *United States* was argued on 10 October 1945, reargued on 17 October 1946, and decided on 18 November 1946. Assistant Solicitor General Judson argued the case for the United States justifying the use of the Mann Act against the polygamists.[49] Despite the appeals, the Supreme Court upheld the convictions of the six men who had been found guilty in lower courts of taking females across state lines for immoral purposes, which violated the Mann Act. Justice William O. Douglas read the Court's six-to-three decision. A majority of the Court concluded:

> It is a violation of the Mann Act, 36 Stat. 825, 18 U.S.C. 398, for a man to transport a woman across state lines for the purpose of making her his plural wife or cohabiting with her as such—notwithstanding the fact that the practice is founded on his religious belief.
>
> It expressly applies to transportation for purposes of debauchery, which may be motivated solely by lust.
>
> Polygamous practices are not excluded from the Act, have long been branded as immoral, and are of the same genus as the other immoral practices covered by the Act.[50]

In a dissenting opinion delivered on 18 November 1946, Justice J. Murphy identified the central legal question as whether taking plural wives across state lines constituted "transportation for immoral purposes." The answer, he argued, hinged on whether plural marriage was of the same genus as prostitution. He concluded that it was not—that polygamy was instead a form of marriage "built upon a set of social and moral principles. It must be recognized and treated as such."[51] Murphy maintained that polygamy and prostitution are very different practices and should not be confused.

Central to the convictions was the principle established in *Reynolds* v. *United States* that polygamy was a "notorious example of promiscuity" and that such unions had long been branded as immoral under the law. Justices C.J. Wade Larson and J.J. Turner concurred: "Whether an act is immoral within the meaning of the statute is not to be determined by the accused's concepts of morality. *Congress has provided the standard.*" (*United States* v. *Cleveland*, 329 U.S. 1). Although this decision had brought despair to the Mormons in the 1880s, it must have been exactly the decision J. Reuben Clark, Jr., had longed for. As long as the judgment stood against plural marriage, this argument could be raised against the polygamist.

State v. *Barlow et al.*
(153 p. 2d 647)

In *State* v. *Barlow* fifteen fundamentalists were charged by the State of Utah with unlawful cohabitation. Those charged included Albert Edmund Barlow, Morris Quincy Kunz, David Brigham Darger, Ianthus Winford Barlow, Dr. Rulon Clark Allred, Oswald Brainich, Edmund F. Barlow, Arnold Boss, Heber Kimball Cleveland, Louis Alma Kelsch, John Yates Barlow, Joseph White Musser, Joseph Lyman Jessop, Alma Adelbert Timpson,[52] and Charles Frederick Zitting. As was the case in the nineteenth century, unlawful cohabitation was more easily proven than was plural marriage, for the only evidence required for conviction was an indication of the *appearance* of marriage—not sexual intercourse or actual marriage.

The defendants appeared before Judge Ray Van Cott, Jr., on 12 May 1944, and were committed to the custody of the sheriff. The attorneys for the defendants immediately served notice of petition for a writ of habeas corpus. The defendants were detained in the county jail pending hearing of the petition in the court of Judge J. Allan Crockett. However, Crockett had already heard the arguments on 14 and 15 April and denied the petition. The defendants, no longer having any recourse other than appeal, were admitted to the state penitentiary for an indeterminate period not to exceed five years.

One defendant, Albert Edmund Barlow, a fundamentalist from Salt Lake City, was accused of cohabiting between 14 October 1941 and 30 March 1944 with Amanda Kate Kilgrow, Violet Frazer, and Marine Owen. Their association was based upon the belief in the doctrine of plural marriage. The prosecution provided no testimony concerning sexual intercourse between Barlow and any of the three women.

On 20 May 1944 the fifteen fundamentalists were convicted of unlawful cohabitation with fifty-five separate wives. They each faced a maximum sentence of five years in prison. E.G. Valens described the case in a United Press story as "one of the strangest cases in Western legal history—in which one man, District Judge Ray Van Cott, Jr. acted as both jury and judge—the 'paper trial' was based on written stipulations and involved no witnesses."[53]

These individual cases involved the same legal questions and were again grouped together for appeal. Each of the defendants was charged with violation of Section 103–51–2, Utah Code Annotated, which reads:

If any person cohabits with more than one person of the opposite sex, such person is guilty of a felony. Any person, except the defendant, may be compelled to testify in a prosecution for unlawful cohabitation; *provided, however,* that the evidence given in such prosecution shall not be used against him in any proceeding, civil or criminal, except for perjury in giving such testimony. A person so testifying shall not thereafter be liable to indictment, prosecution, or punishment for the offense concerning which such testimony was given.[54]

Knox Patterson, second counsel for the defense, began his arguments with reference to cases in which statutory laws had been cast aside in the interests of the resolution of the matter at hand.

The religious beliefs held by these defendants, is out of the realm of prosecution. We feel that there has been no violation of the law, not because there isn't a law against it, but because there is a higher law which overrules that of the state.

The court has never passed on a more important case. It will affect the lives of many persons. There are hundreds of others doing the same thing and there are hundreds and hundreds of children which will be affected by the court's decision. Would you condemn innocent little children by finding them born out of wedlock?[55]

Although the defense continued with a complicated attack on the cohabitation law on several points, the constitutional question remained central to the defense. The fundamentalists maintained that cohabitation was backed by religious belief and therefore should be provided with constitutional immunity under the First and Fourth Amendments. However, *Reynolds* v. *United States* had already disposed of this argument; and the U.S. Supreme Court had already upheld cohabitation's nonprotected status in 1944 and would again in 1946.

In his final arguments before the jury in *State* v. *Barlow*, Brigham E. Roberts, prosecutor for the state, argued that when the law of God and the law of the land conflict, citizens must obey the law of the land, according to a *Deseret News* report:

> Despite the fact that the defense might argue that such associations are based on a religious doctrine, violations of the statutes are defined as criminal intent. The fact that the defendants did cohabit with more than one woman, he argued, is criminal intent and a violation of the cohabitation statute of Utah.[56]

When these cases came to the Utah State Supreme Court on appeal in December 1944 the court broadened the definition of unlawful cohabitation and permissible evidence to include the following standards: if the woman used the defendant's surname; community recognition of membership in a family; if the woman occupied a bedroom next to or near the man's; if the children used the defendant's surname and called him "father." Therefore, birth certificates, school records, anniversary cards, and so forth were admissible proofs of cohabitation.

The cohabitation laws had themselves undergone alterations in the fifty years since statehood. In 1944, the defendant was considered a felon, and all persons except the defendant himself were required to testify in the prosecution. One argument of *State* v. *Barlow et al.* centered on the "irrevocable clause" of the Utah State Constitution dating from 1896 that provided that polygamy was forever prohibited in the state of Utah. Counsel for the defense argued that these provisions had been inflicted upon the state under duress and were therefore invalid. In its concluding judgment, the state supreme court said that the issue of duress could have been argued in 1896 but had since solidified into law through legal precedent.

Defense attorney Claude Barnes also attempted to invoke the

1848 Treaty of Guadalupe Hidalgo, stretching its guarantee of religious freedom to Mexican citizens in what had been Mexican territory. However, this piece of legal ingenuity was scuttled by its bad history: Mormons in the Mexican colonies had never claimed Mexican citizenship and the rights provided by Mexico to its citizens. It also was clear that the treaty dealt with a specific and limited time period—before the territory was ceded to the United States. The court found each of these arguments to be not only absurd but indefensible and rejected the appeal. All fifteen men were declared guilty of unlawful cohabitation. The Utah State Supreme Court denied the petition for a rehearing in the cases involving the unlawful cohabitation charges. In 1945 the United States Supreme Court upheld all fifteen convictions by refusing to review the cases.[57]

Judge Will L. Hoyt of the Fifth District Court in St. George dismissed the cases of Fred M. Jessop and Edson P. Jessop, two of five fundamentalists from Short Creek who were arrested and accused of cohabitation. On 7 February 1945 the motion for dismissal of the charges was made by the prosecution after a request for additional time to prepare evidence against the two men was objected to by defense attorney J. H. McKnight.

State v. *Musser et al.*
(175 Pacific Reporter, 2d Series, 724)

State officials hoped that the case of *State* v. *Musser et al.* would be the coup de grace in its fight against polygamy. Here the law against conspiracy was stretched to its limits in the effort to prosecute polygamists.

The state conspiracy cases were set for hearing before Judge Ray Van Cott, Jr. of the Utah Third District Court and they involved the largest group of polygamists: thirty-three persons who were accused of criminal conspiracy to "commit acts injurious to public morals." The charges against them further claimed that they did "advocate, promote, encourage, urge, teach, counsel, advise, and practice polygamous or plural marriages."[58]

As evidence, the prosecution pointed to the publication of *Truth* magazine, the purchase of a house at 2157 Lincoln Street in Salt Lake City for a group center, and an attempt to convince a Salt Lake woman named Helen Smith and her husband to enter polygamy.[59]

Claude Barnes's legal brief cast the alleged conspiracy in these terms: "Does the advocacy of a practice that is considered a felony within the State of Utah constitute *acts* injurious to public morals?"[60] Since the courts had established that cohabitation was a felony, countered the prosecution, then it must follow that to teach, advise, or counsel the practice was also a crime.

The state bore the burden of proof as to whether there had actually been a conspiracy—meaning that the defendants not only were united in agreeing on plural marriage and in promoting it but also tried to affect the opinions of others. Witnesses testified that meetings favoring polygamy had occurred, and they described direction from leaders like Joseph W. Musser and John Y. Barlow that was designed to influence those in attendance. One witness testified that Musser had said that if plural marriage was a divine law then it *must* be lived, that legislation prohibiting the practice violated the spirit of the Constitution, and that the state law made no difference.[61]

The state also charged that the fundamentalists were abusing the state welfare system; and a witness for the defense declared, "Public relief was instituted of the Lord for the polygamist people."[62]

Helen Smith testified that Musser had at one meeting described the process for courting underage girls. In fact, two of the girls, Juanita Barlow and Jean Barlow Darger, who were originally indicted in the conspiracy case, were under eighteen years of age at the time of their alleged offense and were transferred to the juvenile court.

This case also featured extensive cooperation from the LDS Church on behalf of the prosecution. Musser reported in *Truth* rumors that the Church had excommunicated members who had acted as bondsmen for the defendants. Others supporting the defendants were allegedly reprimanded or threatened with excommunication. One Mormon woman told Joseph Musser that her bishop had threatened, "If you will covenant not to repeat the act [meaning support for the defendant], I will renew your recommend to the temple, otherwise you will be handled."[63]

One of the more dramatic moments in this trial occurred 25 May 1944 during the sentencing before Van Cott. During the imposition of the sentence, Betsy Lee, an outraged plural wife of Joseph Musser, stood in the courtroom, pointed her finger at the judge, and exclaimed: "Judge Van Cott, if you sentence this man I will call the vengeance of Almighty God upon you."[64]

Momentarily taken aback by the disturbance, Judge Van Cott stared at the woman. After a deep inhalation, he said: "Just a minute. Bailiff, take that woman into custody." She was subsequently charged with contempt of court for causing a "commotion willfully contemptuous," and delivered without bail to the city jail. "This is the first time I've been in jail," said the fifty-seven-year-old Betsy Lee, who explained to the reporters that she had been reborn about ten years earlier when she had joined the fundamentalists and had "ever since devoted most of her time to her religion."[65]

After the preliminary hearing, the defendants petitioned for a new justice. The *Deseret News*, not learning from experience, published a photograph on 16 August of Van Cott with state prosecutor Roberts, which delayed the trial until the October term of the court when District Court Judge M. J. Bronson was assigned to be trial judge. Van Cott disqualified himself from the case after pressure from the defense. Their argument was based on three grounds: 1) he had already ruled on evidence in a similar case and convicted fifteen fundamentalists on charges of unlawful cohabitation; 2) he was a member of the county attorney's office that did the preliminary investigations that led to the raid; and, 3) he was a member of the Church of Jesus Christ of Latter-day Saints.[66]

The complicated process of jury selection began on 19 September 1944.[67] After calling the first 100 prospective jurors, Judge Bronson ordered another 100 called. He explained that many of the prospective jurors were elderly persons "engaged in war work or were farmers, upon whom jury duty would work a hardship."[68]

Although agreeing with Judge Bronson that no one should be disqualified because of membership in any particular church, defense attorney Knox Patterson raised the issue of having members of the Mormon Church, a church that had openingly excommunicated the fundamentalists, sit as jurors. He maintained that the ideal jurors would be members of the Sons and Daughters of the Utah Pioneers, who, in his opinion, "have a better understanding of the religious background of the case than do 'gentiles,' who always have been against polygamy."[69] Bronson asked potential jurors whether or not they believed in the doctrine of plural marriage; if they believed others should be allowed to have a plurality of wives without interruption; and whether or not they were more or less inclined to convict the defendants on charges of polygamy than other violations of the law.[70] Two hundred potential jurors were examined before eight were found who were sufficiently neutral on the issue to serve. Among those eight were, according to Barnes, members and officers of the Mormon Church.[71]

A major concern for defense attorney Claude Barnes, himself a Mormon, was again the possibility of a fair trial in Utah where Mormons filled most court offices and juries.[72] Barnes told the court that he felt that once again there were not eight men in the entire state who could fairly judge the matter: "Some of these jurors had formed opinions which would require evidence to change, and this under the constitutional provision that in the United States all men are presumed to be innocent."[73] On 3 October 1944, the jury selection was finished and twenty-two men and eleven women were tried in Utah State Court for criminal conspiracy to commit polygamy and unlawful cohabitation.

The trial lasted thirteen days and resulted in the conviction of all the defendants.[74] The prosecution called a series of disgruntled former wives of polygamous men as witnesses. Cathryn Cosgrove, at one time a wife of Heber Kimball Cleveland, testified about the process of recruiting new wives. "I was told it was up to me to encourage other girls to become plural wives."

She went on to tell the court about delivering babies in the Cleveland home because of her training in nursing. According to Cosgrove, when she had her own baby she was told by Cleveland that it would be given to another wife, Zola, "who was unable to have children of her own and that she [Cosgrove] could have other babies."[75]

Cathryn detailed her courtship when she was a student nurse and Cleveland had first suggested she marry him and enter into plural marriage during August 1941. "Mr. Cleveland had picked her up at the hospital, given her a wedding ring and driven her to the home of Joseph W. Musser, 1153 3rd Avenue, for the ceremony which took place in an upstairs bedroom, with the only witness a small boy lying in a basket." Mr. Musser told her this fact was unimportant for they were "in the presence of God and the angels."[76] These marriages were difficult for the court to track because "no record of marriages was kept for 'obvious reasons.'"[77]

The case then went to the United States Supreme Court which remanded the case to the Utah court for further interpretation of the cohabitation section of the law. This rehearing ended in a final dismissal of the case by concurring votes of Utah State Supreme Court Justices Eugene E. Pratt, James H. Wolfe, and Roger I. McDonough on 21 October 1950. They ruled that the statute was so vague and indefinite that it failed to adequately define the offense or give reasonable standards for determining guilt.[78] In appeal, the Utah Supreme

Court eliminated all the remaining men and women from conviction.

This date would be noted in *Truth* as the "Last Chapter of the 1944 Church Crusade."[79] The cases had cost the federal and state governments more than $500,000 to prosecute. The wives and children of the fifteen fundamentalists serving sentences in the state penitentiary awaited their fathers' return.

The Aftermath
of the 1944 Raid

The Role of the Mormon Church

There is no evidence that the general authorities of the Mormon Church attempted to impose their opinions or directives upon members of the court in the cases that resulted from the raid of 1944. However, Church cooperation seems to have included a careful sharing of lists of names and observations as well as other information gathered for Church courts. LDS Church leaders naturally scrutinized the proceedings and cooperated with the prosecution. In a statement published by United Press International and printed in part by the *Tribune* and the *Deseret News*, Apostle Mark E. Petersen in November 1944 responded formally to curiosity about the Church's involvement in the cases:

1. All the cultists are not former members of the Church. Some have been recruited from various protestant faiths.
2. All cultists who have held membership in the LDS Church have been excommunicated by the Church, some of them, as Joseph Musser, the ringleader, having been excommunicated many years ago.
3. The Church was actively assisting federal and state authorities in obtaining evidence against the cultists, and helping to prosecute them under the law.
4. Among witnesses for the prosecution are men who have been appointed by the Church to search out the cultists, turning over

such information as they gather to the prosecution for their use; these men have also been appointed by the Church to do all they can to fight the spread of polygamy.

5. The cultists use the name fundamentalists which is regarded by the Church as a misnomer. They are not fundamentalists in the sense of holding to the fundamental doctrines of the Church, for the fundamental doctrine of the Church is now opposed to polygamy. Use of this name has caused confusion in the public mind and has tended to give the impression (which is what the cultists sought) that they are old line Mormons, which they are not.[1]

Basically, Petersen reiterated the Church's position of excommunicating violators of the prohibition against polygamy, referred to a sharing of information gathered for Church courts by members called to conduct surveillance of suspected fundamentalists, and emphasized the theological differences between the two groups.

Defense attorney Claude Barnes sought to have the Mormon jurors impeached for alleged religious prejudice. This motion was filed 13 September 1944 by Claude Barnes.[2] The motion was denied 21 September 1944. By way of compromise, Judge Bronson then allowed Barnes to question jurors about their membership in the Church, knowledge of the case, etc.[3] In an attempt to disqualify the Mormons, Barnes asked prospective jurors questions that guaranteed all would be privy to damaging information and conclusions about the defendants. Judge Bronson allowed Barnes to ask the jurors three questions about their previous knowledge of the case; Barnes prefaced each with the words, "Did you know . . ."

1. That some of the defendants had been excommunicated from said Church for advocating or practicing polygamy;
2. That no one is ever excommunicated without a trial at which evidence is produced, and the member charged with misconduct; and
3. The judgement of excommunication is based on a finding that the communicant has been guilty of "teaching" preaching or practicing polygamy.[4]

In other words, the defense apparently assumed (or wanted the prospective jurors to assume) that the polygamists were in fact proven felons and excommunicated Mormons.

After the early convictions in the state cohabitation case, Barnes publicly announced that the trial had been decided before it began because of the climate of opinion in Utah surrounding the issue of polygamy. According to Barnes, this was due to the makeup of the jury (half of whom were Mormons), to what he called the court's favorable attitude toward the prosecution, and to the Mormon Church's publicity campaign against the group.

Imprisonment

The first fundamentalists to enter the state prison did so on 15 May 1945. The *Salt Lake Tribune* reported: "Defeated in yet another court battle, fifteen convicted polygamists entered the Utah state prison after a year of hard-fought courtroom battles late Tuesday afternoon to begin serving indeterminate terms not to exceed five years."[5]

The lengthy appellate process lasted from October 1944 to October 1950. The fifteen defendants were imprisoned during part of the appellate period but attempted to provide for their families by running family businesses from their prison cells. While incarcerated, members of the group were, for the most part, model prisoners, and prison officials treated them well. Although technically convicted felons, the fundamentalists were atypical criminals and were given special privileges. While in the state penitentiary the fifteen fundamentalists met together for religious services, worked on the prison farm, and wrote voluminous letters to their numerous loved ones. The rules of the prison stipulated that each prisoner was allowed to write two one-page letters weekly. For a man like Rulon Allred, with six wives and forty-eight children, the rule was manifestly unjust; John E. Harris, warden of the Utah State Penitentiary, granted special permission for Allred to write one letter a week to each wife.

During the appellate stage, wives of the prisoners were not allowed to visit their husbands because of the publicity it would generate. The letters exchanged, however, reflect the lofty convictions of men convinced they were being persecuted for a noble cause but who were also homesick and lonely. They expressed concern for their families, pled with them to stay together, urged them to remain faithful, and warned them to avoid temptation.

Joseph W. Musser was seventy-two years old at the time of the raid. While in prison he was frequently ill and suffered an attack that perhaps precipitated the massive stroke he later suffered in March

1949. He wrote: "The food did not agree with me, neither did the treatment nor the iron cell in which I was encased; though I would have died there rather than renounce my faith."[6]

During these months, the fundamentalists made repeated unsuccessful appeals for release to the board of pardons.[7] Finally, in November 1945, after wrestling at length with the issue of compromising their principles, nine men of the group signed the "prison manifesto" and secured a release on parole: John Y. Barlow, Joseph W. Musser, Alma A. Timpson, Edmund F. Barlow, Oswald Brainich, Ianthus W. Barlow, Rulon Clark Allred, Joseph Lyman Jessop, and David B. Darger. They pledged: "... to refrain hereafter from advocating, teaching, or countenancing the practice of plural marriage or polygamy in violation of the laws of the State of Utah and of the United States. The undersigned officers of the religious group above referred to further pledge ourselves to refrain from solemnizing plural marriages from and after this date contrary to the laws of the land."[8]

These nine men were paroled on 1 December 1945 after serving six and a half months in the state prison. Musser's parole from prison allowed him to continue to publish *Truth* magazine.

> We were told by the Parole Board we would have to live with our legal wives. We might visit the others and support our children, but we must not live with them. As Rose was my legal wife, but had not lived with me for nearly 20 years, and as my office, records, library etc., were with Lucy, the mother of my two youngest children, Rose divorced me, thus permitting me to marry Lucy legally and maintain my residence with her. This arrangement was also endorsed by my wife Ellis. Rose made it clear she did not want a temple or a priesthood divorce; she wants our relationship to continue in eternity; and, of course, I am supporting her the best I can, as I have always done.[9]

State attorney Brigham E. Roberts later questioned the parole board's decision of granting parole to the fundamentalists, and testified before the board that recent articles in *Truth* had "eulogized the prisoners as martyrs and commended the inmates for 'upholding the practice of plural marriage' while the 'cultists' still advocated polygamy in their meetings. I questioned the good faith of their pledges." He continued, "These people have practiced polygamy for years knowing it was against the law." He accused them of signing the prison manifesto "for their own convenience and advantage" and pointed out, quite accurately, that "no security is given that the promise will be kept."[10]

Four other prisoners—Zitting, Boss, Kelsch, and Kunz—did not sign the manifesto and remained in prison. On 22 June 1946 Warden John E. Harris told them that he had been authorized by the Utah State Board of Pardons to make them an offer. As Kelsch recalled, Harris said that "it would not be necessary for us to remain at the Utah State Prison another day if we would promise to obey the laws of Utah."[11] They had already served two years and one month. They refused. It would be another six months before the final decision.

In a letter to Governor Herbert B. Maw and the Utah State Board of Pardons reprinted in *Truth* more than one year later Charles F. Zitting explained his position:

> Now, entirely aside from my religious views regarding Plural Marriage, I cannot agree to compromise my conscience and obey all laws, just or unjust, without question. If I did, I would be letting my sons down, who offered their lives by fighting for nearly three years in the South Pacific for the four freedoms, and I would be helping to sow the seeds of Totalitarianism in the structure of our Government. I think too much of true democracy and true democratic laws to agree to do that, and I cannot agree to do something I don't intend to live up to.[12]

With the convictions and sentencing, only time would tell whether or not the raid would successfully eradicate polygamy. It did not. Breaking their pledges, the defendants returned to their fundamentalist lifestyle upon their return to their homes and families. On 13 May 1945 Church President Heber J. Grant died. His legacy endured, however, as the Church and the fundamentalists locked into a cold war that would crystalize into an enmity both broad and deep. Leroy Johnson would later remember Grant's role in the prosecutions:

> Sometime along the line, President Grant made remarks that he would like to live to see all these polygamists behind bars. And he did. When the 1944 Raid came along, they arrested Brother Musser and Brother Barlow and put them in jail along with Brother Zitting, Brother Kelsch and others. And do you know what happened? After the prison gates closed behind these men, President Grant passed away. So, he lived long enough to see them behind bars.[13]

Life at Short Creek

The six years between the launching of the Boyden raid in March 1944 and the final decision of the U.S. Supreme Court in April 1950 were ones of stress for the fundamentalists at Short Creek and elsewhere in Utah. Although their consciousness of being persecuted for their religious beliefs offered the solace historically available to martyrs, the fundamentalists who were imprisoned also experienced periods of discouragement and weariness. Predictably, after the raid and the six years of trials there was confusion and rivalry over who was the leader of the priesthood council. Musser, who at the time of the raid was seventy-two, had a debilitating stroke in 1949 and was under the medical care of Dr. Rulon Allred. John Y. Barlow died that same year, three years after signing the pledge allowing him to be paroled from the Utah State Penitentiary.

Musser appointed Allred to be his successor to the senior spot in the council, passing over Barlow's choices of Leroy Johnson, Louis Kelsch, and others who Barlow felt had a superior claim to seniority. The council was divided into those who followed Allred and those who recognized the leadership of Leroy Johnson.

Earlier, in 1940, Barlow had dissolved the original trust—the United Trust—because of the disaffection of some of the participants. That trust was always quite loosely organized, and the lands which had been conveyed to the trust by disaffected members were returned to them. Some, however, including Leroy S. Johnson, refused to accept a reconveyance of the property they had contributed because they believed it would be wrong to accept the return of lands donated as consecrations based on religious belief.

Soon after the United Trust was dissolved, Barlow, along with Musser, Johnson, Hammon and Rulon Jeffs, proposed to establish a new United Order. Musser studied law books on how best to structure a cooperative venture, drew up a proposal, and brought it to attorney Claude Barnes for his advice. Barlow's primary concern was to create an indissoluble trust, or irrevocable trust, that neither lawyers nor apostates could break apart.[14] Short Creek polygamists, under a plan called the "United Effort Plan," organized according to Utah law on 9 November 1942. The land that remained unreturned from the United Trust became the original holding of the United Effort Plan Trust. Copies of the Declaration of Trust, the charter document, were filed with county recorders in the following counties: Salt

Lake, Washington, Garfield, Kane, and Iron counties in Utah, and Mohave County in Arizona. The fundamentalists' second effort to formally apply United Order principles to their community's economic life was again, as was the case with the United Trust, not a corporation. The organization of the trust did not require any specific statutory authority under Arizona law.

These trust organizers were convinced that when the law of consecration and stewardship was reestablished among the fundamentalist people they would be brought closer to God. Musser said: "It has also been said that the blessings of the Celestial Kingdom shall be realized when the people become united. So, in order to bring about a condition whereby Zion might be redeemed, we must promote a spirit of unity among our people. That unity must be centered upon one object, and that object is the principles of the Celestial Kingdom, or to bring ourselves into a condition where we can assimilate ourselves into the likeness of our Father in Heaven."[15]

The United Effort Plan helped provide for the families whose lives had been disrupted by the court proceedings and imprisonments. A complicated plan for the regulation and cooperation of its members, it embodied many essential elements of the Mormon United Order, a cooperative effort lived first and briefly in Missouri a century earlier, and, again, more seriously but still with limited success, in the 1870s in Utah until the system fell apart under the strains of anti-polygamy prosecution that disrupted Utah life in the 1880s.

The charter of the United Effort Plan is almost entirely concerned with the legal organization and governing procedures of the organization. It identifies the original settlers and the original corpus of the trust (the real property contributed by the original members; specifies offices of the trust and the various duties and responsibilities associated with those offices; and outlines rights of the members. It does not contain provisions that regulate the day-to-day lives of the members or non-members who live in the community, nor does it require a specific code of conduct. Regardless of the fact that the fundamentalists who designed the trust believed it would help them to live righteous lives, the document itself makes no assumption whatsoever concerning plural marriage.

The twentieth-century United Effort Plan was from the first a religious charitable trust. Perhaps the most basic belief that bound members together was the belief that communalism created an environment where plural marriage could flourish. According to the fundamentalists, the purpose of the United Effort Plan was "charitable and philanthropic." Ideally, it would be "governed in a true spirit of brotherhood."[16] An attorney could have pointed out that this fluid definition opened the door to any legitimate business venture or project undertaken in the name of the group's good. It was, nevertheless, in the truest sense a religious charitable trust as defined by English common law and the laws of Utah: "A charitable trust is a fiduciary relationship with respect to property arising as a result of a manifestation of an intention to create it, and subjecting the person by whom the property is held to equitable duties to deal with the property for a charitable purpose."[17] Most fundamentalist members of the community either contributed donations or consecrations in the form of property, income, and labor to the United Effort Plan.

The language of the document creating the trust itself described this entity as one devoted to the accomplishment of good for the community:

> It is understood and agreed that we and such other members as may hereafter come into said association are associated together merely and solely for the purpose of being *cestui que trustents* of the trust hereby created, thus being entitled to the equitable and beneficial interest of all profits and property, both personal, real and mixed, of the trust estate hereby created, *in accordance with their respective just wants and needs as determined from time to time by the board of trustees and as the trust estate may be able to respond thereto.*[18]

Members received assistance from the trust based on their "just wants and needs" rather than on the basis of their material contributions to the trust.

In spirit, the United Effort Plan reflected the nineteenth-century Mormon doctrine of consecration and stewardship. Mormons were taught that they were "people of the covenant," bound together by spiritual as well as economic temporal bonds. *Doctrine and Covenants* 82:15–17 served as a reminder and an exhortation to consecrate their all for the good of the group.

> Therefore, I give unto you this commandment, bind yourselves by this covenant and it shall be done according to the laws of the Lord. Behold, here is wisdom also in me for your good. And you are to be equal, or in other words, you are to have equal claims on the properties, for the benefit of managing the concerns of your

stewardship, *every man according to his wants and his needs, inasmuch as his wants are just* [italics added].

This Mormon scripture had potent meaning in the lives of the fundamentalists, for they believed it was the word of God through his prophet Joseph Smith. For them, the United Effort Plan was one way to help the faithful obey the Lord.

The UEP's primary function was to hold real property. Under the provisions of the plan, members consecrated private ownership of all their property, both personal and real, to the bishop. When Warren E. Johnson and Viola Johnson transferred their Short Creek property to the UEP, they received one dollar in return.[19]

All earnings also went into the bishop's storehouse. Ideally, women and children who were old enough to work and contribute were included "into the service of the group, and during fruit picking, canning, and such work they were transported by truck to and from their work in the nearby towns," recalled Jacob Lauritzen.[20] As an outsider, Lauritzen observed the way the fundamentalists rallied together for their work projects. But he failed to make the important distinction between ownership of land under the United Effort Plan and donated labor. The fundamentalists functioned according to a cooperative model. They donated their labor to projects on land owned by the UEP just as they donated time and energy to work projects on city property. The cooperative labor itself was not organized under the United Effort Plan. The UEP was primarily a land-holding entity for faithful members of the fundamentalist community. Efforts to push it beyond these finite limits were confined to the period between 1945 and 1949 when many of the principal economic leaders, the heads of families, were incarcerated.

Although it was not called for under the UEP, during that period all produce from individual gardens went into a central warehouse—Bishop Jessop's storehouse—where the people kept everything from wheat and milk to finished clothing. A rickety dumptruck made daily rounds to the homes of members and nonmembers in the community to distribute milk, food, clothing, fuel, or whatever else the families required. Again, this was not an expression of the UEP trust, but was instead the simple efforts of the fundamentalists to group together in a community struggle for survival. The bishop's storehouse, like its nineteenth-century Mormon antecedents, was owned and operated by the fundamentalists on land provided by the UEP.[21]

The single barn in the community became a dairy for members who supplied the necessary labor. When they created the United Effort Plan the fundamentalists brought all their cows to this barn, built earlier by Frank Colvin and Isaac Carling. Under the direction of Fred Jessop, "Container boxes were built, mail-box style, in the east wall of the barn which had little doors that opened to the outside where people could come and get their milk. Each family received their portion according to size."[22] Joseph Jessop often drove the milk wagon through town on deliveries.[23]

In 1943, Fred Jessop purchased 3,500 baby chicks for the UEP to start a poultry business. With native rock and lumber left by the CCC construction crews he constructed a chick brooder at the base of the hill. Jessop liked the spot so much that he built a home nearby for his family.

Monogamous Mormons were also welcomed to donate to and benefit from the charitable trust. Nevertheless, the unity and conviction of the fundamentalists, who had been involved in United Order efforts since their arrival in the early 1930s proved too much for Jacob and Annie Lauritzen, who finally sold their property and moved to neighboring Hurricane in 1949. The success of the United Effort Plan further strained the tenuous brotherhood with Mormon fundamentalists outside of Short Creek.

Women in the group also benefitted from the provisions of the trust although they did not serve on the board of trustees. The structure of power was clear: it was patriarchal and priesthood oriented.

Lauritzen saw modern polygamy as being substantively different from its nineteenth-century Mormon antecedent. In this later version a man could marry as he desired. Inasmuch as faithfulness was the basis of future glory, the man who had the most wives and the greatest number of children would receive the greatest glory and exaltation in the next world if he remained faithful. Thus, the begetting of children became of the greatest importance. They were waiting spirits who must be given bodies.[24]

In true pioneering tradition, the fundamentalists sacrificed enormously during the formative stages of their community-building activity and adapted to scarce services and goods. Obviously, although the ideal was very generous and sweeping in its intent, the trust, in actual practice, had difficulty satisfying all the needs of its members in its early years. It would be four decades before the standard of living created under the provisions of the United Effort Plan matched that of comparable rural communities in the region. They were years complicated by the continued harassment of the community by the governments of Utah and Arizona. During these decades Short Creek was essentially a frontier town organized along the cooperative lines of the United Effort Plan—not all that different from a nineteenth-century rural Utah Mormon town. No one really prospered or dominated the economic life of the community under the Plan, but most did survive.

Ultimately, the United Effort Plan would more adequately provide for its members. One fundamentalist commented in 1988 that she believed that the trust took care of people's needs adequately—better than if they had to do it themselves.

The Women
of Fundamentalism

A girl growing up in the shadow of Short Creek's red butte knew the boundaries of her world. Geographically and socially isolated, she and the other women of Short Creek lived in a carefully gender-marked patriarchal world. The powerful male world of fundamentalist Mormonism did not exist without the supportive and obedient female world, however. Bearing children to a righteous husband as one of his several wives is, in these women's views, not only the husband's will, but it is also God's will. One fundamentalist woman expressed this idea by saying that women had to have the strength of character to stand up for their beliefs, have the strength of character to know where their obedience should be placed, and then place it there only. One of the government's motives in the 1953 raid was to "free" these women from a form of sexual slavery and to "protect" the young women of Short Creek from an untenable situation of limited choice—their sexuality during early adolescence became the property of a husband who was usually much older.

How did these women function as individuals? How much did they have to say about how they lived their lives? Possibly the most crucial question surrounding polygamy was that of arranged marriages, perhaps the single custom, after plural marriage itself, which ran most deeply counter to American culture. In 1955, two years after the third raid, the Senate Subcommittee on Juvenile Delinquency heard testimony about social conditions in Short Creek. One senator asked whether young girls had been free to choose their own husbands, and Robert S. Tuller, a judge of the Pima County Superior Court, emotionally testified that they had been denied that right, then added:

> To force a young girl not yet competent to think or speak for herself into a plural marriage with a man not of her choosing, is to force her into bondage. To say that a fifteen-year-old girl who marries a thirty-, forty-, or fifty-year-old man, selected for her by a committee of other men, does so voluntarily without force or duress is merely to quibble with words. Our law wisely decrees a child of such age is incompetent to make any voluntary decision in that.[1]

Mrs. Alfonzo Nyborg, a monogamous resident of Short Creek who had been raised in a polygamous home and was the wife of the town's deputy sheriff, testified before the same committee. Polygamous society, she said, allowed teenage girls and boys very little autonomy in comparison with the larger society: "The children, they don't have a mind of their own. They [the male leaders] just live their lives for them. The same way with the young boys. They go out and work and do what they tell them to do, and they hand the money over, and they [the male leaders] give them back what they want." Mrs. Nyborg expressed pessimism about young fundamentalists' ability to break out of the system: "It seems that once they get them it is awfully hard to get loose." She also reported upon once commenting to a girl, who was a daughter of polygamists and also the wife of a polygamist, "They must hold something over you so that you do like that." The girl answered, "They do, but I can't explain it."[2]

The doctrine of individual free agency, one of the foundational beliefs of Mormonism, occurs repeatedly in fundamentalist literature. However, the context and examples usually assumed that the reader, like the speaker, was male, and the issue of choice was most frequently invoked in the context of being free from the constraints of society to live a polygamous lifestyle. Women in Short Creek had few choices to make as adults. Here the culture of fundamentalism coincided with the limited opportunities offered in an isolated, rural, frontier community.

One young woman interviewed by the author, Sharil Jessop Blackmore, the daughter of Edson and Alyne Jessop, grew up in Short Creek and married there into polygamy, but later moved from the town. She described her adolescent awakening to her situation, claiming that when she was sixteen she first realized that she would probably never see the world, that Short Creek and the few miles of fields around it might be all she would know. She summarized what she had seen as her choices: finishing high school and then getting married—as a teenager. If she left the town, it would bring disgrace to her family and shame to herself.

She also realized that she was ill equipped to fend for herself. She was not trained for a job, and knew no one outside of Short Creek; the thought of a world full of strangers terrified her. Therefore, leaving was simply not an option. Neither was discussing her concerns with her father or her mother. They would have considered such questioning a form of treason, or a sin to be repented of. Thus, the youth of Short Creek had to wrestle privately with their problems about polygamy.[3]

Short Creek itself reinforced the authoritarian nature of fundamentalism, allowing its young people little room for independence. In 1953, Short Creek was still essentially a frontier community. Homes had no electricity or central heating, and often had no plumbing. The sheer physical labor required of women to care for their children and houses under these conditions should not be underestimated. Furthermore, the typically large fundamentalist families meant that pregnancy, childbirth, and nursing intensified the physical demands on a woman every two or three years from the time she was married until she was past childbearing, typically in her mid-forties. Daughters worked with their mothers in the domestic environment from childhood until the time of their own marriages, learning there what it meant to be a woman of fundamentalism.

In 1953, no local public high school or avenues to trade or higher education existed in the community, although the school did sponsor a correspondence program through Phoenix Union High School. The Short Creek Academy (the local school) offered only limited classwork. Partially as a consequence, the marriage pattern of the school-age children differed markedly from general United States norms. The average age at first marriage for fundamentalist women in Short Creek was sixteen years old, although fourteen and fifteen were not uncommon ages at which girls married.

Eight of the sixty-four women involved in the 1953 raid were minors. Four teenage wives testified at the Senate hearing investigating the raid and agreed with Mrs. Nyborg that women in Short Creek typically married in their teens and had frequent pregnancies. In preparing for the raid, the Arizona Attorney General's office (with cooperation from the Utah Attorney General) compiled profiles of each family unit based on census records, birth certificates, and school census records.[4] Their study listed thirty-one men and eighty-eight women, and the children of two elderly wives who had died before 1953 were also included. Therefore, there were ninety separate family units.[5]

The average number of children per female was 3.27. The number of actual children per fertile female would be higher because fourteen women in the study had not had any children before 1953. Males in this sampling had an average of 9.1 children, a total that included the offspring of all of their plural wives. In 1953, fifteen married fundamentalist women (seventeen percent of the total women) were under the age of eighteen. Excluding the fifteen women who were under eighteen years of age, thirty-two of the other women had been under the age of eighteen at the time of their first childbirth. The average age at first birth for this group was seventeen. Approximately two-thirds of this group were married by the time they were sixteen.

At the time of the raid, at least a dozen girls between fourteen and seventeen years of age were either pregnant or were the mothers of up to three children.[6] Those in school would leave class to nurse their babies. The juvenile justice system particularly concerned itself with all girls between the ages of eleven and eighteen—perhaps fifty in number—for they were potential plural wives and mothers.[7] The 1944 raid seemingly had done nothing to dissuade these young girls from marrying polygamous husbands.

Evidence indicates that the girls in Short Creek tended to marry so early because of their limited opportunities. As the local public school system improved over the next two decades, the women's average age at first marriage increased dramatically until, by 1988, it had leveled off at age nineteen, an age that more closely approximated the state average of twenty-one years.

The community considered marriage decisions to be religious and private, made with the advice of the presiding patriarchs. Sect leaders John Barlow and Leroy Johnson exerted tremendous influence on their followers' choices of future mates. When approached, they advised men when and who to marry, as well as how to live in plural households. Even when one middle-aged polygamist married his wife, he deferred to the judgment of his patriarchal leader, Leroy

Johnson. Because he believed that Johnson was the mouthpiece of the Lord, he was predisposed to accept his advice.

Such a system is not necessarily coercive or exploitive. When fewer than five hundred individuals lived in Short Creek, the patriarch knew everyone and probably had reasonably accurate ideas about how well two people might be suited to each other. But more importantly, the fundamentalists believed that the patriarch spoke the word of the Lord.

In some cases, parents arranged marriages. Also, a young man usually married a girl near his own age for his first wife, although later marriages tended to reflect increasing gaps in the ages of the bride and groom—a pattern that had also been true for nineteenth-century Mormon plural marriages. In these early marriages, and even in later plural marriages, romantic involvement was a frequent element of the courtship. Polygamists esteemed the value of love in marriage, no matter what the age of the partners.

The fundamentalists preferred to use the term "plural marriage" in reference to their polygamous lifestyle, believing it to be the Lord's term.[8] Johnson often reminded the group of the seriousness of their peculiar form of family life:

> The Prophet Brigham Young said that the law of plurality would damn more than it would save. And this is true. Why? Because we treat lightly that ordinance. We do not know how to train ourselves when we get them. We labor under a great delusion. Many of us think that when we have wives sealed to us that we have our calling and election made sure, and we need not go further, but this is not so.[9]

The primary aim of marriage, however, was not love, but a celestial social order. Plural marriage was part of a deferential and hierarchical society strictly ordered along patriarchal lines. The child was subordinate to the mother; the mother bowed to her husband's authority; he, in turn, looked to the prophet for direction; while the prophet was answerable to and spoke for Jesus Christ. As God was at the head of the world, the husband was the earthly head of the family. The appropriate behavior directed toward one's superior consisted of deference and obedience. The appropriate behavior directed toward one's subordinates consisted of instruction, benevolence, and the meting out of either rewards or punishments.

The official fundamentalist requirements for women are summarized in one of Musser's editorials in *Truth* in 1948: "Thy desire shall be to thy husband, and he shall rule over thee. In placing man at the head, he bearing the Priesthood, a law, an eternal law, was announced." Rigidly prescribed roles existed for men and women: "Man, with divine endowments, was born to lead, and woman to follow, though often times the female is endowed with rare talents of leadership. But women, by right, look to the male members for leadership and protection." Women were taught to "respect and revere themselves, as holy vessels, destined to sustain and magnify the eternal and sacred relationship of wife and mother." A woman was the "ornament and glory of man; to share with him a never fading crown, and an eternally increasing dominion."[10]

Musser also spelled out these male-female roles in more secular matters: The man "shall fight the physical battles in protection of his loved ones, and bring into the home the necessaries of life." The wife "adorns the home, conserves the larder and renders the habitation an earthly heaven where love, peace, affection, gratitude, and oneness shall abound, she the queen and he the king."[11]

Men were encouraged to look for women with a "kind and amiable disposition; love, unaffected modesty, for industrious habits, [and] for sterling virtues." The ideal wife had "cleanliness in person, in apparel, in cooking, and every kind of domestic labor." She was cheerful and had "genuine religion to control and govern every thought and deed."[12]

If a wife was found wanting in any of these areas, it was the husband's responsibility to instruct her and help remedy her deficiencies: "Let him realize the weighty responsibility now placed upon him as the head of the family, and also let him study diligently the disposition of his wives, that he may know how to instruct them in wisdom for their good." Because men were superiors to women, who were "weaker vessels," and because they were working toward the same goal, it was the husband's responsibility "to nourish, cherish, and protect; to be their head, their patriarch, and their savior."[13]

Alongside the advice given in Musser's series of essays, Leroy S. Johnson and John Y. Barlow instructed their followers from the pulpit. For instance, Johnson asked this question in 1974: "Are you training those wives so they will be in harmony with you and take you into the highest degree of the Celestial Glory and give eternal increase?"[14]

A dress code reinforced traditional gender assignments. It spelled out modesty for the women, but not for the men. The women were discouraged from wearing pants, scanty attire, and makeup. "The female cannot wear men's attire and display to the world those finer and more sensitive qualities that crown her with beauty and grace known only to herself," Musser editorialized in 1947. "When a corpulent woman forsakes her protective skirts for overalls she displays a figure that is anything but attractive. Her feminine charms have forsaken her."[15] Polygamist Edson Jessop of Short Creek explained in a national news story: "We believe in covering our bodies and we frown upon make[-]up; silence itself is reproof enough if one's wives come out with short sleeves or painted faces."[16]

Johnson made the observation in 1973 that keeping women modestly dressed remained a difficult task. "We have been trying for the last thirty-five years that I know of, since I have been acquainted with this work, to get our women folks to notice their dresses, bring them down where they ought to be, cover up their nakedness, and let us not be found wanting when the day of grace is over."[17] Johnson also bemoaned the fact that "the daughters of Zion would walk the streets of our great and glorious city of Salt Lake as harlots; and you will not be able to tell the face of a Saint from a Gentile."[18] He taught parents to not allow their children to run naked, but to clothe them, and to teach them modesty "and the sacredness of their bodies."[19]

Interestingly enough, these prescriptions—right down to the prohibition against pants—could have appeared in any nineteenth-century Mormon publication without sounding even faintly strange; what is more, they also could have appeared in any twentieth-century Mormon publication up to approximately the mid-1970s and still have sounded completely familiar to orthodox Mormon women and men. Even today, it is the intensity of the decree, rather than the concept itself, that sounds extreme to orthodox Mormon women.[20]

Perhaps the only substantive difference in how Mormon and fundamentalist women viewed their position in society was the literalness with which the latter took this advice, and the pervasive belief in fundamentalist society that women were a separate class from men. Women willingly took their place in this carefully defined society and—conditioned by tradition, history, and spiritual experiences which reinforced such roles—considered it to be God's will for them as well as a source of great personal happiness. One young plural wife in a Salt Lake City fundamentalist family said in a recent interview that she and her sister wives gladly looked to their husband's leadership as a priesthood holder. "We are lucky to have one of the elect of God in our home," she emphasized. Her sister wife added, "When you only get a small part of your man, you glory in what you have."[21] Even more than that attitude was a sense that fundamentalist men and women were united in a common goal for the hereafter, which seemed to vindicate their efforts in this temporal existence.

Clear gender roles can have a useful social function of providing social and cultural stability. Against the turmoil, materialism, and juvenile delinquency which they claimed characterized post-war America, the psychological security and emotional reassurance of a profoundly religious, home-centered life must have been deeply consoling for many fundamentalist women. As the "outside world" came to be characterized as a threatening place of persecution, legal action, and imprisonment, the ideal of home as a haven acquired additional power.

The polygamist also married in order to follow God's biblical injunction to Adam and Eve: "Multiply and replenish the earth." Accordingly, sex was for procreation and was governed by strict guidelines based on theological considerations. The fundamentalist patriarch spoke of sexual activity in puritanical terms, again an echo of nineteenth-century Mormonism, and saw in plural marriage the cure-all for the world's problems of prostitution, homosexuality, infidelity, and sexual debauchery. Monogamy, claimed Musser in *Truth* in 1949, was a lesser sexual law which had put "many women . . . in their graves [as] the victims of the sexual over-indulgence of their husbands." Polygamy "will at least modify this trouble and subdue the natural animal in man."[22]

Rulon Allred described first approaching patriarch Joseph Musser in the early 1930s with the idea of marrying a plural wife.[23] Musser, one of the original fundamentalists, put him through a grueling interview regarding his private life, sexual experience, past history, and attitude toward religion and women. Musser seemed to look straight into Allred's heart with his piercing dark eyes. "If you are ready to enter the Principle," he said, "this is the law." Musser then declared the purpose of plural marriage to be producing children; he forbade sexual intercourse between the time of conception and the child's weaning, and warned, "A man who looks upon his wife with lust is damned. A man who can live this law is worthy of his exaltation, but don't enter the Principle unless you can meet the requirements."[24]

Musser's declaration of "the law" of abstinence during a woman's pregnancy and lactation seems to have been a generally accepted rule.[25] Leaders counseled polygamous husbands to exercise "self-control and moderation; then, the sexual relation, properly employed, rather than reflecting mortal weaknesses and being immodest, lewd, coarse, vulgar or indelicate, and something to blush over, would be elevated to a higher plane and become a divine principle dedicated by the Gods for the perpetuation of life and birth of earths."[26]

The rhetoric of fundamentalism does not celebrate sexuality, but instead treats it with respectful caution as a necessary evil—at best a force which men must learn to control and from which pregnant women must be protected. Still, sexual consummation sealed the marriage with a powerful bond. Musser went so far as to say "a real man could not live sexually with a woman without loving her."[27]

Although the polygamists fundamentally opposed contraception, sharing a husband with five other women could serve as a sort of birth control. Nor is there any reason to believe that all husbands expected to provide or were capable of providing sexual intercourse every night, since "tempering the lust of the husband" was also one of the "residual effects of righteous living."[28] Perhaps the most effective contraceptive device was the commandment to observe gestational abstinence, thus insuring that children would be spaced at least eighteen to twenty-four months apart, "thereby conserving [the mother's] health and enabling her to bring forth healthy and beautiful children."[29] It was the bearing of these children that, for the fundamentalist woman, was the ultimate blessing and her unique role in the plan of salvation. Fundamentalism viewed barrenness as a reproach—God's curse on a woman and her husband.[30]

Musser and other fundamentalist leaders derived their philosophy of gestational abstinence, or the "sexual law," from extensive readings in pseudo-medical journals (as, for example, some of the articles written by Dr. Walter Siegmeister, editor of the magazine *The Regeneration*) about the relative virtues of abstinence during pregnancy. They then picked from those readings a combination of ideas that made sense in their minds. It is virtually impossible to document how extensively this doctrine was practiced, but the ideal existed by

the 1940s. For the fundamentalist, gestational abstinence emphasized the theologically sacred nature of birth. During gestation and
lactation, the woman was separated from earthly passion and joined
with God in the act of creation.[31]

Other practical arguments in fundamentalist literature concen-
trated on the benefits of gestational abstinence for both mother and
unborn child. According to one mother writing in 1944, such abstinence "results in superior brain development, while the reverse leads
to idiocy. Intercourse during pregnancy drains the nerve-vitality of
the mother and child . . . when the nervous system of the mother is so
sensitive and may be so easily upset."[32]

Another polygamous woman expressed this same concept in
highly colored language: "The embryo and fetus destroying practice
[sexual intercourse during pregnancy] is hideous. It is little short of
involuntary baby slaughter. An ugly unholy picture it makes."[33] She
continued with a poignant observation that told much about the
complicated nature of these marriage relationships: "Yet the loving,
faithful wife submits, usually without protest, because she wants to
please her man and keep him loving her alone."[34] Fundamentalist
women were often reluctant to speak about sex outside of the context of reproduction. This woman, at least, acknowledged its role in
the husband-wife relationship.

Short Creek was the "lambing ground" where the women of plural marriages from all over the region came to give birth in a home
setting with the assistance of an experienced midwife. For example,
in the east wing of her lovely plantation-style home in Short Creek,
nurse midwife Lydia Johnson Jessop, the first wife of Fred Jessop, delivered hundreds of babies. She brought to her work a sense of pro-
fessionalism and care that county health officials acknowledged.

During the three Short Creek raids, officials dealt more leniently
with the women of Short Creek as *mothers*. They indicted several
women on charges similar to those of their husbands, but, except
for a week in the county jail, none of the women were imprisoned.
Rather, the women stayed with their children under the protective
custody of the state. However, the state also recognized that it was as
mothers that these women exerted power and influence. Although
the state "protected" them, it also punished them by separating them
from their husbands, for they were recognized as crucial in perpetu-
ating both the doctrine and practice of plural marriage.

In fact, the role of fundamentalist women was involved in a distinct shift in the evolution of polygamy's defense. Nineteenth-century Mormon polygamists defended their constitutional right to freely practice their religion; twentieth-century fundamentalism defended a woman's "inalienable right to motherhood."[35] In the 1950s, fundamentalist Mormon polygamy was sometimes seen as a "cult of motherhood." Musser called polygamy a "woman's rights program." What mattered most was not marriage, he said, but "quality" motherhood; "and to try and withhold the right thereof from any fit woman of our breed and nation is an infamy as well as national insanity."[36]

Idealized motherhood thus counterpoised patriarchal power in fundamentalist society, and it was as a mother that a woman in Short Creek exercised what influence she had. "Motherhood was the grand capstone of the life of the woman," lauded Musser in 1948: "Greatness, glory, usefulness await her otherwise, but here alone all her powers, all her being can find full play."[37]

In 1944 a plural wife and mother claimed, "We don't worry because of the extra expense that another mouth will bring. We know that the Lord will provide and care for us."[38] "We cooperate together, caring for each others' children and for each other in times of illness and need," Rhea Kunz would write. "We are proud of our beautiful, intelligent children and our loving, faithful husband. . . . We are proud of our associate sisters in this Gospel." For Kunz, the law of celestial marriage included more than just a plurality of wives but stimulated "the saving virtues of every religion—humbleness, gentleness, kindness, love, charity, self-sacrifice, devotion to God."[39]

According to Musser, polygamy offered to all women the possibility of marrying a man of her choice and becoming a mother. From his perspective, "every normal woman yearns for wifehood and motherhood. She yearns to wear the crown of glory. The most precious and yearned for jewels are children to call her mother."[40] Polygamy also served the practical social function of integrating the "thousands of American women who are [otherwise] a permanent surplus on our marriage market and doomed to spinsterhood and childlessness."[41]

How did this practice of plural marriage work? Behind the theory and the theology of fundamentalist "celestial marriage," how did polygamous families live out their united lives? First, fundamentalists viewed their unions as both sacred and eternal, thus increasing the significance of all relationships in the home. Much official counsel warned against anger and criticism while encouraging harmony:

> Speak not the faults of your wives and others; for in so doing you speak against yourself.
>
> Never seek to prejudice the mind of your husband against any of his other wives, for the purpose of exalting yourself in his estimation, lest the evil which you unjustly try to bring upon them, fall with double weight upon your own head.
>
> Let each mother teach her children to honor and love their father, and to respect his teachings and counsels.
>
> Suffer not children of different mothers to be haughty and abusive to each other; for they are our brothers and sisters the same as the children of the patriarch Jacob.... Always speak well of each of your husband's wives in the presence of your children.... If you consider that some of the mothers are too lenient with their children and too negligent in correcting them, do not be offended, but strive, by the wise and prudent management of your own, to set a worthy example before them.[42]

In Short Creek, a polygamous woman typically spent much of her married life in the same household with her sister wives and their children. She was also expected to generously love each of them. Making a plural marriage work thus required enormous sacrifice, self-control, and commitment to the Principle.

One plural wife, in an anonymous interview, acknowledged the difficult times: "Sure we became angry and jealous. We are, after all, human beings. But when I felt most hateful I went into my room and closed the door." There she inhaled slowly, and "prayed for the strength to endure—or at least to be pleasant."[43]

Husbands endeavored to minimize jealousy in various ways. Rulon Allred carefully expressed his affection only privately to his wives. Allred believed that to flaunt his romantic involvement with six separate women would have resulted in discord. They all knew such involvement existed, but it was easier not to witness it.

A second patriarch, Edson Jessop, attempted to encourage thinking first of the group as a whole and considering the plural family as "above all a unit. My wives trust me. A man of our faith never walks the chalk line as does the man with only one wife." Jessop tried to "spend my time where I'm most needed, perhaps where there is sickness or trouble," and claimed that his wives "trust me to do whatever is best for the family as a whole."[44]

Jessop saw his role as being that of a "diplomat" and explained, "Even when my families lived separately, I rotated my evenings; once a week we met together at one Home Evening." In this setting it was possible to "pray and sing together, air your problems and your grudges, play games and visit and afterward sample Marie's special angel-food cake or Alice's cream puffs. You not only have fun—you forge bonds that will endure a century."[45]

In one family, the five wives felt most content by alternating weeks spent doing household chores in the kitchen, garden, and laundry.[46] Another family "specialized": one woman cared for all of the children; her elder sister wife, who was more proficient in household skills, sewed, laundered, and ironed; while the third wife baked bread and prepared meals.

Edson Jessop's six wives were nearly all the same age and were good friends. "They cooperate efficiently, one handling the sewing for the family, another the cooking and so forth," he commented. "What counts is not the number of wives, but the number of united wives. In fact, there are times when I wish mine would at least get mad at me separately instead of all together."[47]

In answer to the oft-voiced question about the nonexclusive nature of plural marriage, polygamists simply turned away from metaphors and images of romantic love. Instead, they explained it with analogies to a mother's love for her several unique and individual children.[48] Jessop also used the image of friendship: "Naturally a man values his wives for different qualities, just as he values his friends. Perhaps one wife has pretty hair, and another is wonderful with the children, perhaps one is witty and keeps him cheerful, and another brings him closer to God."[49]

After childbirth or during illness, sister wives assumed the incapacitated woman's roles. "It is a joy to have a companion with whom to share sorrow and happiness, sickness and health," commented one woman; "[to have] in times of distress someone to lean upon and turn to for assistance; when sick, to know that your children are receiving a mother's loving care."[50]

This type of close companionship seems more analogous to the friendship in a husband-wife relationship in a close monogamous marriage than it does to the more usual women's friendships of today. Perhaps, in the frequent absence of their husbands, these women learned to meet most of their social and emotional needs with each other. In one family, when two plural wives were offered the option of living in separate homes, they chose instead to share a home as "best friends." One first wife, preparing to meet a potential third wife, remarked candidly to her husband, "After all, it's more important that she get along with us than with you. A plural wife doesn't see much of her husband, but she is entering into the family of her sister wives."[51]

The shared feelings of persecution brought about by the three raids, through which the women saw themselves and their children as martyrs for a holy cause, also increased their shared commitment. Furthermore, the raids dramatically reinforced an ongoing saga that encouraged the women to see themselves as part of a larger family, the community of believers. Polygamy served as a boundary separating those inside the community from all outsiders, including blood kin who did not accept the principle of plural marriage. It functioned as a powerful adhesive that enhanced the resolve and unity of the group.

Unlike Mormon polygamy of the nineteenth century, which had its roots in the marital tradition of monogamy, this highly enmeshed society looked for guidelines in its own one-hundred-year Mormon history of the practice. In the 1950s, mothers of the new generation of young polygamous women taught their daughters what it was to be a plural wife, what it was to be female in fundamentalist society. Through their behavior, through their examples and traditions, and through their beliefs these women taught their daughters to continue on the path they believed was the one sure way to salvation. Young polygamous women learned from their mothers' examples.

Vera Black attested to this continuation of teaching and tradition in her testimony before the court. In answer to the question, "Now that principle [plural marriage] was taught in the home, in your home, while you were a young lady?" Vera answered, "Well I don't know what you mean exactly, if anyone lives the situation, why they naturally get it in their lives." Vera's testimony continued along this same line:

Q. It had the sanction of your parents, didn't it, your father and mother?
A. I presume it did.

Q. And were you opposed when you proposed to become a plural wife of Mr. Black, were you opposed by them?

A. I guess I had my free choice.

Q. You sought their counsel. I am sure. Didn't you?

A. Well, they never stopped me.

Q. They rather encouraged it did they not?

A. They didn't have too much to say about it, they gave their children their free agency.

Q. It was discussed in the home?

A. Well that is what I mean, I was along enough in years that I had knowledge enough to think for myself, I had my own head.

Q. Do you feel like you would be willing to continue to violate the laws of the State of Utah by living as man and wife with Mr. Black in the future?

A. It would be a pretty hard thing to do, to give anybody up after you have lived with him as I have. I couldn't live without him.[52]

At least in this case, it could be postulated that Vera Black internalized polygamy as a child and that that later formed her expectations as an adult. Plural marriage could provide a powerful emotional connection between a man and a woman, in this case Vera and Leonard Black, who were bound together by their faith.

Thus, paradoxically, it could be maintained that fundamentalist women triumphed by accepting limitations. The patriarchal order stressed a woman's need for male guidance and support. The exaltation of her fertility locked her into the primary role of mother. These very limitations led the courts to deal with fundamentalist women as dependents, like children, unable to take care of themselves and in need of protection and intervention on their behalf. But in safeguarding their motherhood, the courts also gave them the cradle in which they would continue to nurture fundamentalism.

Howard Pyle
and the Raid of 1953

The fundamentalist colony of Short Creek, Arizona, continued to grow during the late 1940s and early 1950s, despite the repeated absences of many of its leading male citizens. The population of Short Creek doubled every decade between 1935 and 1955, largely due to natural increase. Moreover, the communal nature of the fundamentalist colony also attracted new members inspired by the work. By 1953, the population had reached 39 men, 86 women and 263 children. The little town now had a sawmill, a shingle mill, a cannery, an automobile repair shop, a fruit drier, and a carpentry shop. Every year the men built new homes to house an ever-increasing number of fundamentalist Saints. At times there was a housing shortage—some families lived in makeshift shacks or unfinished basement homes—but basically the community thrived.

Outsiders watched the growth of polygamy in the quiet shadow of the red butte that sheltered Short Creek and were alarmed. The Mormons carefully monitored their temples, wards, and mission systems as they watched the movement of the polygamists in the Colorado Plateau area. Zion Park Stake officials visited the small town to identify for excommunication proceedings those involved in any way with the group. Increasingly, however, Arizona's government and the Mormon Church focused attention on the town's women and children. More than any other factor, it was the "plight" of these "victims" that led to the third and most socially devastating raid on the fundamentalists of Short Creek on 26 July 1953.

This concern underlay the rhetoric of Governor Howard Pyle's radio message delivered that same day, which referred once to "insurrection within its own borders," but proceeded on with the language of protectionism: ". . . to protect the lives and future of 263 children. . . . the product and the victims of the foulest conspiracy. . . . a community dedicated to the production of white slaves. . . . degrading slavery." Pyle continued:

> Here is a community—many of the women, sadly right along with the men—unalterably dedicated to the wicked theory that every maturing girl child should be forced into the bondage of multiple wifehood with men of all ages for the sole purpose of producing more children to be reared to become mere chattels of this totally lawless enterprise.
>
> As the highest authority in Arizona, on whom is laid the constitutional injunction to "take care that the laws be faithfully executed," I have taken the ultimate reponsibility for setting into motion the actions that will end this insurrection.[1]

An understanding of Howard Pyle's personality is very important in comprehending not only what happened but why. For most of Arizona's thirty-nine years of statehood, it had elected Democratic governors. That year, Pyle became the first Republican in twenty-five years to be elected to the state's highest office. In that year Arizona had 225,000 registered Democrats and 50,000 Republicans. At age forty-five, Pyle never before had run for political office, was not a cattleman or a military veteran, and was not backed by a substantial moneyed interest like the citrus growers, miners, or even the Mormon Church. At the spring convention of the Arizona Young Republicans Pyle delivered an old-fashioned western hellfire and brimstone speech using the rhetoric of evangelical Christianity to promote patriotism. Not a candidate at the time, he soon became one. In fact, the group was so moved by his remarks that they called for his election on the spot. The Young Republicans of Arizona took credit for his nomination, but it also was rumored that party strategists were using him to test the Democrats' strength. Their real interest lay two years ahead in 1952 when they planned to pull an all-stops-out campaign to elect Barry Goldwater, the attractive, popular ex-Hump flier and member of Arizona's premier mercantile family. "You might say this Pyle was a sacrificial lamb," explained one political strategist in 1951. "After his defeat we planned to autopsy him for hints that would help Goldwater later on."[2] Nevertheless, Goldwater was Pyle's strongest and most loyal ally. The morning after Goldwater heard about Pyle's success at the Young Republican convention, he visited him at the radio station to offer his congratulations and support. He later wrote: "The news had come over my car radio the previous night. On hearing it, I'd driven straight back from the desert, where I'd been shooting photos. I was so excited that I hadn't gone home to shave or change clothes."[3]

The *Arizona Republic* enthusiastically announced the partnership. Goldwater is a young man, the paper said, "full of enthusiasm as well as sound ideas, and should add a great deal of strength to the already formidable movement to give new life to the party in Arizona. . . . Both are young businessmen, with a fresh viewpoint and progressive ideas."[4]

Pyle's opponent, state auditor Ana Frohmiller, was easily one of the best-liked Democrats in the state and seemed to be a sure bet. By 1950 Frohmiller had been successfully elected fourteen times—twice as Coconino County treasurer, and twelve times as state auditor.[5] Her campaign slogan attempted to capitalize on those many years of experience: "I offer the voters experience, not an experiment." Pyle rebutted by suggesting that experience should "likewise be evaluated. Frankly, I wouldn't trade my experience in public affairs in this state, my personal, first-hand, acquaintanceship with the problems of this state, my knowledge of the needs of the people of this area, for my opponent's 35 years on the public payrolls—all of it confined to the walls of the capitol building."[6] Pyle, a radio announcer, could count on two assets—a rich, resonant bass voice and his moral fervor. Both had already secured him a place in the hearts of housewives across the state. Pyle had a second advantage. The Republicans threw all their forces behind him. By the end of the campaign, Pyle had spent $11,428 to Frohmiller's $875.[7]

KTAR billed Pyle as "The Golden Voice of America," and featured his popular interview show, "Arizona's Nearest Neighbor." He often reminded his audiences, "Laws are not enough: we must have a spiritual awakening." He used the same idea for the title of perhaps his best-known speech, "Laws Are Not Enough," delivered 19 November 1953 to the Los Angeles Bar Association—an address which at least partially provided justification for the raid: "It takes more than laws, however well written and justified, to make men and nations responsible. Beyond them we must build in men a desire to keep the law because it is right that they should, right as David believed it to be right when he added these words to the Psalms—'I delight to do Thy will, O God, because Thy law is within my heart.'"[8]

Howard Pyle was pleasant, well liked, and respected. Even more important, he was in touch with his times. Pyle epitomized what the decade of the 1950s was about for most Americans—a conservative turning back to American traditions. He came by his moral fervor naturally. Born in Sheridan, Wyoming, he grew up in Oklahoma and Nebraska, the son of an ordained minister of the Baptist Church. Young Howard Pyle didn't party or go to dances. He had strong beliefs and he acted on them; he was not particularly rigid—just sure of himself and his principles. As a young man he worked as a timekeeper for the Southern Pacific Railroad, as a real estate salesman, as secretary of the Tempe Chamber of Commerce, and as the Tempe correspondent of the *Arizona Republic*.[9] When the *Arizona Republic* acquired KFAD and changed the call letters to KTAR, he began a career in radio. Over the next twenty years Pyle progressed from staff announcer to vice-president of the company. During World War II he served in the Pacific as a war correspondent.

The press pegged him "The Bald Eagle" because his hair had dwindled to a wisp on the top of his head. He also had an uncanny resemblance to Dwight Eisenhower, both physically and ideologically. As a political missionary not too much different from Senator Joseph McCarthy or the young Senator Richard Nixon, he was on the alert for the anti-Christ or anti-American (often considered the same thing at the time) behind every sagebrush or red sandstone rock. His search soon led him to Short Creek.

With victory an overwhelming unlikelihood, Pyle enlisted Barry Goldwater himself to be his campaign manager. Goldwater had no political expertise either, but he was going to need more experience for 1952, so he took the job. The two men made an unlikely but effective team. Conservative Republicanism was a religion to both men, and they campaigned with unexpected energy, flying all over the state in Goldwater's private plane to rallies of Republicans and Democrats alike, who gathered to hear Pyle's message of reform and to see Arizona's foremost war hero—Barry Goldwater. The two formed a warm and tender friendship. Both men were conscious of the contribution they could make, what Goldwater called in a letter to Pyle, "the heritage we leave our children."[10]

Goldwater said at the beginning of the campaign: "In this spontaneous action of the Republican Party of Arizona we may well be witnessing the start of a movement that will sweep America. A movement that will return morality to politics." Howard Pyle was, according to Goldwater, the answer to America's problems. "Today, . . . we find our nation treading on the threshold of socialism . . . our government being run by people who think one way and act another."[11] Ironically, in light of his later confrontations with the fundamentalists, one of Pyle's oft-repeated campaign statements was, "Arizona is a state where refugees from oppression can come."[12] Goldwater occasionally would climb onto the podium to make his pitch, promising audiences across the state that good times were ahead. Other meetings were more informal. "Pyle and I would go into a bar and shake a few hands. I'd say, 'Just put the governor's drinks up here on the bar.' I called Pyle 'governor' to get a little respect and let folks know we meant business. . . . I introduced Pyle to the twenty-four hour day," Goldwater would remember. "He was glad when the campaign was over, but I was just getting my engine warm."[13] Pyle's powerful speaking style and Goldwater's incessant energy carried them through the campaign. It was a close election—Pyle won by just 2,991 votes—but the surprise was that he won at all.

In 1952, the *Saturday Evening Post* featured him in a lead article suggesting that such a "charismatic" westerner might one day be presidential material. His charisma manifested itself largely in his interests, enthusiasm, and affability. He generally made friends, not enemies. People trusted him. As governor, Pyle did not isolate himself behind his desk in the silver-domed Arizona State Capitol Building, but instead worked hard to win over both his opponents and those who had not yet made up their minds about him. In an ironic way, it was in part his desire to please others that led him into the political fiasco of Short Creek.

The fundamentalists in Short Creek had steadily acquired political enemies. The area's cattlemen and other taxpayers resented them because of the burden their huge broods of children placed on the tax base through school taxes. In November 1953 thirty-six cattlemen from both Utah and Arizona initiated legal action designed to close down Short Creek's school, a move that Jonreed Lauritzen described as proof that the 1953 raid was "not so much a moral issue as a matter of taxes."[14] The Mormons of northern Arizona and southern Utah resented their blatant practice of plural marriage, by now morally repugnant to socially conservative mainstream Mormons. Their open and successful challenge to the authority of the Church also bothered

Mormon ecclesiastical officers in Arizona. But possibly no one resented them more than Mohave County Superior Court Judge Jesse W. Faulkner.

Louis Barlow in May 1954 described this period of "planned persecution" as "bitter and poisoned" by years of division over the issue of plural marriage. "People were quick to re-tell the stories of a weird and disgraceful way of life, of forced child marriages to long-bearded criminals. Of course those who knew any of the Short Creek people through business dealings or having visited Short Creek just laughed at such stories, supposing that their fantastic nature would make them detectable to any thinking person." However, it was, according to Barlow, "through such fantasy and the school tax complaints that Judge Faulkner of Mohave County became intoxicated with an obsession to annihilate the community."[15]

Faulkner lived in Kingman, the seat of Mohave County, in a substantial native-stone house separated from the street by a neat row of well-groomed cypresses. Those trees also marked a clear boundary line between the sanctuary of his private life in his home and his public life with its absorption in issues of right and wrong, justice and injustice. His opinions, like his sharply chiseled profile, were clear cut. He dressed simply: plain rimless glasses, white shirt, and dark suit. Like good Mormons, he never smoked, drank, or swore, and he was offended by dirty stories. When one juror showed up for duty drunk and incoherent, the outraged Faulkner called him to the stand and sentenced him to three days in the county jail for contempt of court.[16]

In 1950 when Pyle was elected, Faulkner had already been a superior court judge for a number of years. The judge liked order and control. The very existence of Short Creek was offensive to him. In March 1951, during Pyle's second month as governor, Faulkner took a hefty file of evidence to Phoenix and laid it open. According to the *Arizona Daily Star*, "Judge Faulkner complained to the attorney general's office that the population of Short Creek had risen to several hundred, that most were children of plural marriages, and that girls no more than twelve and thirteen years old were being given in marriage to men fifty and more years old."[17] The county welfare department had documented that an increasing number of women from the town were petitioning for support for an alarming number of dependent children; many of them listed the same man as their husband; several were underage. Faulkner would later refer to the situation as a "taxpayer's emergency" in his county that was too big for him to handle.[18] He continued: "They have dared to demand expanded school facilities, yet they pay no taxes whatsoever. They claim exemption because of a community plan which they claim exempts them from taxes.[19] He expressed fear that the group was multiplying rapidly and that the whole thing was getting out of control.[20] The prisoners of the 1944 raid were back in the community as leaders, missionaries, and martyrs. At the time Faulkner concluded: "I believe a grand jury investigation is in order."[21]

Arizona State Attorney General Fred Wilson had reservations about a grand jury investigation but liked the idea of a two-state raid. He insisted, however, that first "we must have more information—proof beyond a shadow of a doubt." Wilson asked the legislature for money, ostensibly to gather information about insect control in Mohave County. The legislature responded with $2,500 from an emergency appropriation fund of $10,000. Few legislators knew the actual proposed use of the funds.[22] Pyle agreed to the plan, and sent his personal speech writer to Short Creek. "He went up to that place," recalled Pyle with evident distaste, "and he discovered to his horror that eighth-grade kids were going home from school to nurse their babies under circumstances that to him were just horrendous."[23] Pyle's fourteen-year-old daughter Mary Lou was in the eighth grade; another daughter, Virginia Ann, was ten. He could not help thinking of them in a similar situation, and he was outraged.

Because fundamentalists did not register their plural marriages or the births of children to their plural wives, Pyle also felt some concern that it was "impossible to keep accurate statistical records for the state—marriages, births, deaths, the whole package of vital statistics."[24] Pyle knew that Utah, had tried twice to deal with the colony and had failed both times. Drastic measures might be necessary. He had heard many stories about Short Creek, some outrageous, some probably not far from the truth. He related one that would probably fall into the first category: "They [the fundamentalists] had these structures on skids; and if you came after them from the Utah side, they would put chains on them and drag them over the line; and every time you went at it [law enforcement] from either side, you got this switch when you got there. They were all in another state."[25] The fundamentalists maintained that this was folklore. The same type of story first circulated during the media hype surrounding the 1935 polygamy trials.

Pyle, Faulkner, and Wilson took the next step together. Pyle remembered, "I called in the legislative leadership, discussed it with them at length and of course the state was in an awkward position. Here was a legitimate appeal from the Superior Court Judge. Therefore the next order of business was to find out how much truth was in the charges that were being made and the substance of the appeal itself."[26] In March 1951 the legislative leadership appropriated $10,000 for a full-scale investigation.

In April 1951 Pyle hired the Burns Detective Agency of Los Angeles to gather evidence to be used against the people of Short Creek. He loved the ingeniousness of their cover. Pretending to be a movie company looking for locations and extras, they packed movie equipment into the town and photographed every adult and child in the community. The polygamists, uneasy but courteous, posed for their pictures, meanwhile cautioning their children to stay nearby.

"When they brought the facts back, photographic and otherwise, we realized that the judge was right, we had a problem." Pyle continued, identifying one of the irregularities: "We had an electric power plant attached to the school, which was a tax-supported enterprise; but in various ways the power output from that publicly owned power operation was being wired all over the little community and taxpayers were paying for it." He also identified a variety of other "so-called miscarriages of tax funds for private purposes [which] constituted the fundamental reason for the appeal through the court and finally to the state."[27] The photographs the detectives brought back showed, according to Pyle, that the fundamentalists were living like animals, "in absolutely filthy conditions, some in old abandoned cars, in unfinished shacks, and generally in subhuman conditions."[28]

According to Pyle, Wilson's hopes for a two-state raid foundered when Utah's governor J. Bracken Lee responded, "You do whatever you have to do but we're not going to become involved."[29] After Pyle telephoned Lee, Utah's governor consulted with his new chief of the highway patrol, Superintendent Marion A. Snow, a retired FBI man involved with the 1944 raids on the polygamists. According to Lee, the chief advised him not to pay attention to Pyle: "Don't get involved. We got the dickens beat out of us by the press and everyone else with the polygamy raids. It simply was not worth it."[30]

Nevertheless, Wilson and Utah State Attorney General Clinton D. Vernon corresponded throughout 1952 about the investigation into polygamy in Short Creek, sharing information and pledging cooperation in the gathering of further evidence.

Wilson informed Vernon of the proposed raid on Short Creek in a letter dated 26 February 1952: "In accordance with our several conversations in regard to the existence of law violations on the Arizona and Utah borders near St. George, Utah and Short Creek, Arizona, and specifically as per our telephone conversations of yesterday, I am writing you to give you the details of the plans developed by this office for prosecutions in that area." He continued:

> It will be necessary, because of the number involved, for us to process as many of them as possible on the ground, and for that reason we are going to arrive prepared to do so. Under the Arizona law our Judges of the Superior Court can sit as committing magistrates and our Supreme Court has held that each County Superior Court is a unit of the State Court and therefore they have jurisdiction to act in any county in the State. In accordance with these provisions we are arranging to have three Judges sit together and handle these matters as committing magistrates, and because of the children involved, we are having the best representation possible from a juvenile standpoint.[31]

Obviously, the plan was already clearly conceived; Wilson then described it in more detail. We will, he said, "converge upon this area at an early morning hour—surround each dwelling with at least four officers; keep the occupants in the house until the house is searched and the occupants identified and then attempt to process at least one charge upon each of the adults and to place the children in the custody of the Juvenile Court."[32]

By the spring of 1952, Wilson felt he had enough evidence of unlawful cohabitation to secure convictions against most of the adult members of the community. With or without Utah, it was time to move. The raid was planned for mid-June. Wilson's idea was to transfer the entire population of the community to Kingman where parents and children would be secured in barracks constructed for the purpose. Wilson acknowledged that these were drastic measures, but that this was "the only possible method as all other methods heretofore have only served to advertise and increase the popularity of the movement, to the extent that where ten years ago there were from twenty-five to thirty children—now there are over a hundred and this of course is the principal concern. This of course is the principal evil of this practice and primary concern of the effort."[33]

Judge Faulkner would later claim credit for originating the idea of the raid. "Now in my opinion there are just two remedies, two ways of stopping polygamy: one is to go right down the line and prosecute and convict and sentence every man and woman guilty; and the other is to take the children of these bogus marriages and turn them over to a proper department for placement in juvenile homes or for adoption."[34]

Secrecy was essential to the success of the raid. House Bill Number 235 had first appeared before the Arizona House of Representatives on 20 February 1952 in the guise of an appropriation for the control of grasshoppers. A group of Pyle's loyal Republican supporters sponsored the bill. These men, primarily from rural counties, included Representatives Cook, Bloomquist, and Morris of Cochise County; Pulsipher of Apache County; McBride of Graham County; Simms of Greenlee County; Burton, Ewing, Hardwicke, Martin, Riley, and Willis of Pima County; Bartlett and Miles of Pinal County; Brown of Santa Cruz County; Bisjak of Yavapai County; and Johnson of Yuma County.[35] Through its second reading, its appearance before the committees on Judiciary, Appropriations and Rules, the bill met with no opposition and was adjudged both proper and constitutional. House Bill 235 was added to the calendar of 6 March 1952 along with bills creating an egg code, amending traffic control signal legends, calling for the registration of sex offenders, and creating an underground water commission.[36] The House recommended that it pass and sent the bill to the Senate where it surfaced as Senate Bill 82.

Pyle and Ross Jones, the new attorney general, met in secret in July 1952 with leaders of the House and Senate appropriations committees.[37] During ten tense and arduous days, Jones outlined the plan for the proposed raid. Originally, the intent had been to ask for an appropriation of $30,000, but Senator Harold Giss of Yuma and Representative Nielson Brown of Nogales upped the total to $50,000. The appropriation bill that passed through the Senate and House, ostensibly for grasshopper control, bore the nickname "Operation Seagull," an allusion to the seagulls which had miraculously saved the Mormon's cricket-threatened crops in the 1840s. Senate Bill 82 read in part: "Section 1. APPROPRIATION. The sum of fifty thousand dollars is appropriated to the governor of the state of Arizona. Section 2. PURPOSE. The purpose of this appropriation is to control such infestations of grasshoppers and other insects in the agricultural and grazing areas of the state as shall be deemed a menace to the welfare of the state by the governor of the state of Arizona."[38]

Embedded in a general appropriations bill, the raid funds were assigned to the governor as "emergency funds" and the legislature as a body did not know their true purpose.

House Appropriation Number 1–106–000–1300 (as it was officially designated) covered virtually all expenses of the raid. According to Pyle, one-fifth of the $50,000 was earmarked to pay the salaries of four men: Kent A. Blake, Paul W. LaPrade, Carl Pryor, and Alfonso Nyborg, who was deputy sheriff in Short Creek and a key source of information for the prosecution.[39] LaPrade, Pryor, and Blake were assistants to Attorney General Ross Jones and were assigned the overall planning of the raid—not only the legal case to be developed against the fundamentalists but the physical arrangements of the raid itself.

Another $6,000 would pay travel expenses for possibly up to one hundred individuals—probably to travel by car but possibly by airplane. Food for the prisoners and government personnel would account for another $8,000. The raid would ultimately involve every law enforcement body in Arizona as well as numerous others—more than a hundred public welfare workers, matrons, doctors, medical assistants, police officers, highway patrolmen, and National Guardsmen. They all had to be fed and housed during the raid, which might last as long as a week. More than $6,000 was earmarked for food and provisions for the fundamentalists during a three-day "holding" period. These would be primarily women and children, since the men would be taken away for incarceration as soon as they were arrested. It originally was planned to "airlift" the women and children out of Short Creek to destinations across the state.

LaPrade, Pryor, and Blake started intensive planning in July 1952 with the target date now chosen as 26 July 1953. The earlier plan for a raid in 1952 failed to materialize for a number of reasons, not the least of which was that Howard Pyle was shocked by the logistical problems involved. Utah's refusal to cooperate also sobered him. Perhaps the upcoming election for both he and Lee in the fall of 1952 was a particular consideration. They assumed that the public would favor strong action against the fundamentalists, but they weren't sure. Pyle would later echo Wilson's concern: "Before a single complaint was drawn, or a single warrant prepared, or the first preliminary order for today's action issued, we had to be certain beyond the last shadow of doubt."[40]

According to Wilson, the raid was canceled because of a supposed "leak" to the International News Service in Salt Lake City. The fundamentalists later said that they had indeed heard about an intended raid but did not camouflage their lifestyle or otherwise try to avoid the projected raid. Furthermore, there was not enough money available for a raid of the scope proposed by the attorney general's office.

But the idea did not fade away. Arizona State Senator Earl Cook and Representative Robert Morrow, under pressure from cattle interests, joined Judge Faulkner in pressing Pyle for action. Politically, fundamentalism was a pressure cooker about to explode. If its present growth rate was any indication, reasoned Faulkner, the fundamentalists soon would control the voting balance of Mohave County. Also, more and more fundamentalist women would be going on public relief, many simply donating their welfare checks to the communal pool.

The United Effort Plan also alarmed outside observers. Its board of directors, many of whom were members of the priesthood council, seemed to have extraordinary community and financial control. They arbitrated all internal problems, decided who could join the trust, and even determined whom other community members could marry. Pyle viewed every member of the United Effort as a co-conspirator against the government. In a time when the fear of communism was running rampant, a communal order was particularly suspect.

A grim vision of the future finally pushed Pyle past delay. He was quoted after the raid as saying, "It is easy to see from this rapid expansion that in another ten years the population of Short Creek will be in the thousands, and an army will not be sufficient to end the greatest insurrection and defiance of all that is right."[41] What Pyle saw as blatant evidence of abuse and neglect of women and children, fraud, and the presence of an economic system that smacked of communism combined to make the raid necessary from his point of view.

Pyle, Jones, and Frank Porter, the sheriff of Mohave County, were filled with personal anguish during the next few weeks as they wrestled with difficult questions about the nature of the raid, possible human rights violations, constitutional guarantees, as well as the emotional stress involved. For them the raid had to be "bloodless." Pyle insisted that "every precaution must be taken to prevent anyone from being hurt. I accepted personal responsibility for anything that went wrong with the raid and I held my breath and kept a constant prayer with me in anticipation of the worst."[42] The best way to insure that the raid would be nonviolent, he felt, was for the numbers of officers to be overwhelming. "What I envisioned," he recalled, "was a police action in the role of the Good Samaritan."[43]

The Utah Attorney General's office continued to gather information about the fundamentalists after the raid was canceled in 1952.[44] Utah Attorney General Clinton Vernon proceeded to cooperate with the Arizona Attorney General's office. In an effort to involve the FBI, he enlisted the United States Attorney, Scott Matheson, as well as attorney John S. Boyden, Washington County Attorney V. Pershing Nelson, and District Attorney Ellis J. Pickett in the search for additional information.[45]

In December 1952 Scott Matheson reported to Vernon the results of the federal investigation into allegations of Mann Act violations. "It is apparent from evidence disclosed in the report that immorality, if any, indulged in by the parties was merely incidental and did not constitute the primary purpose of the travel."[46] It was determined that there would be no further FBI investigations and "therefore, of course, no Federal prosecution."[47] It increasingly appeared that Arizona was going to have to proceed alone.

While the planning was going on, Pyle made a series of strategic phone calls. He himself informed the Federal Bureau of Investigation in Arizona of the plans. Although Utah would not officially join Arizona in the raid, J. Bracken Lee and newly elected Utah Attorney General E.R. Callister offered their support in preventing fundamentalists from crossing into Utah.[48] Callister and other representatives of the attorney general's office met with Ross Jones in a series of meetings during the next few months in Salt Lake City and Phoenix.[49] According to Ogden Kraut, himself a fundamentalist, Governor Lee called FBI director J. Edgar Hoover asking him whether or not he should join Pyle in the raid. Hoover responded, "Heavens no, I have made a personal policy of never touching anything to do with religion. It's too much of a hot potato."[50] That confirmed Lee's opinion; however, Utah would cooperate in extradition proceedings.

Governor Pyle also telephoned Mormon Church headquarters. During the final days of preparations, he made daily contact with a Church leader, usually Apostle Delbert L. Stapley, to keep the

Church posted on every step of the process. Stapley "was a very prominent local citizen and he and I had been very close friends for a number of years," Pyle explained. "We didn't make a single move that we didn't clear with the Council of the Twelve. They were one thousand percent cooperative, a hundred percent behind it."[51] Pyle had no question, even in retrospect, of the unofficial but positive ecclesiastical support and approval at the highest levels. "They were heartily in favor of any effort that might be made officially" because this was the perfect opportunity once more to officially and publicly disassociate the official Church from the polygamists. "They wanted it understood that this [polygamy] was something they did not approve of."[52]

While Pyle, LaPrade, and Blake were planning the raid, at Pyle's request Mormon bishops and Relief Society presidents in Arizona quietly began to solicit volunteers who would house the children seized in the raid.

Operation Seagull called for a tent "command post" and commissary to be set up in the center of town. It would have its own mobile power unit and a radio transmitter for communication between "Rathole Number One" (Short Creek) and "Rathole Number Two" (headquarters in Phoenix).

Pyle was particularly sensitive to the possible accusation that the government was waging military action against the community, so he had the army insignia on each National Guard vehicle temporarily painted out. Guardsmen were to be paid out of the same emergency fund as was everyone else.[53] Despite Lee's vow not to become involved, Utah guardsmen also came across the border from St. George to conduct the extradition of Utah citizens.[54]

Ross Jones asked Paul LaPrade and Kent Blake to prepare evidence for the polygamy cases. They researched the latest case law on conspiracy, cohabitation and trusts. LaPrade inquired in a letter of 23 April 1953 about Utah's laws that had a bearing on the United Effort Plan: "1) Do the laws of Utah provide for a common law trust? 2) If so, has the 'United Effort' complied with such laws? 3) If so, are there any signed documents on file that may be admissible as admissions of membership to said organizations?"[55] LaPrade also asked for information used in the trials resulting from the Boyden raids in the 1940s,[56] as well as for birth certificates,[57] suggestions for witnesses, and other valuable information to be used in the prosecutions.[58] At one point, LaPrade considered the idea of calling Joseph Musser, Guy Musser, Marion Hammon, Rulon T. Jeffs, and other fundamentalists from Salt Lake City as witnesses.[59]

LaPrade and Blake prepared 122 warrants for the arrest of thirty-six men and eighty-six women who had been identified in the preliminary investigations. The arresting officers would also have several "John Doe" and "Jane Doe" warrants. Within weeks those warrants would be served.

Short Creek, 1935. The town's dusty streets were lined with simple homes in a
stark and beautiful setting. Photos courtesy of Utah Historical Society unless
otherwise noted.

The Albert Edmund Barlow families, including four wives and eighteen children. Date of photo unknown.

Barry Goldwater and Howard Pyle in 1951 during the latter's campaign for governor. Photo courtesy of the Arizona Historical Foundation.

Short Creek, 1953.

Short Creek in 1953, at the time of the raid.

The simple dwellings of the town sat peacefully in their picturesque setting in 1953.

Unidentified house in Short Creek at the time of the 1953 raid.

Another unidentified dwelling at the time of the 1953 raid. Like all communities, there was a disparity among the dwellings of the townspeople of Short Creek.

Joseph S. Jessop, 84, is supported by his son Tom (right), and George Justige at the time of the 1953 raid. Photograph used by permission of the photographer, Ralph Camping.

The fundamentalist adults, detained in the fenced-off yard of the schoolhouse, must have wondered what the government had planned for them.

Young Alvin Barlow (to the left) was one of the adolescent boys left behind when the buses took the adults and smaller children from Short Creek in July 1953.

Soon after they arrived, government forces served breakfast from a makeshift kitchen in a tented central command post.

Another view of the officials and fundamentalists near the tent set up in the first hours of the raid.

Viola Broadbent and her four daughters in front of their home at the time of the raid. Note the number placed above the doorway by officials for identification purposes.

Mildred Barlow posed with her sister wife, Sara Barlow, for officials at their home in July 1953 before being taken off to jail.

These three unidentified sister wives reluctantly stood in front of the number identifying their family home.

A simple and clean interior from an unidentified home raided in 1953.

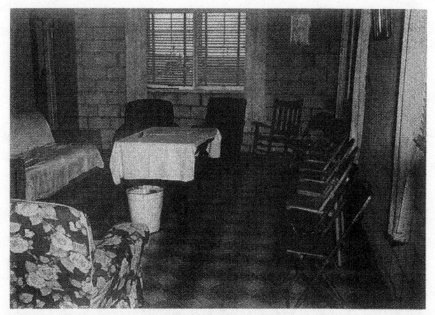

Another interior view of a Short Creek dwelling—clean and simple with no frills or other ornamentation.

A car labeled at the time of the raid; officials said it was a habitation while fundamentalists claimed that it was only a play area for their children.

A larger family group photographed at the time of the 1953 raid.

This group of fundamentalist children posed for the official photographer on the porch of a home amid the tools of a rural household.

Margaret Hunter Jessop and her five children had already said a tearful good-bye to their husband and father before posing for this photograph in front of their frame house.

Clearly unhappy about posing for this photograph, the ages of these unidentified four sister wives vary greatly.

The look of horror on the face of Vera Black's youngest daughter at the sight of the cigarette held by the officer sitting at the family's kitchen table speaks volumes about the clash of cultures of the fundamentalists and the outside world. Photograph courtesy of Ralph Camping.

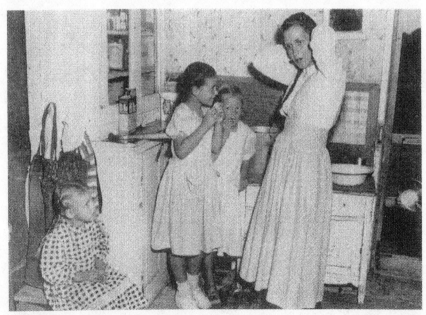

Vera Black and three of her children in their kitchen at the time of the raid. Photograph courtesy of Ralph Camping.

Vera Black and her six children in their official photograph from the raid.

Within hours after the raid began, Short Creek's streets were virtually deserted: one little girl on a dusty street caught in a conflict beyond her understanding. Photograph courtesy of Ralph Camping.

Political cartoonists found much to inspire them throughout the controversy. This cartoon from the *Arizona Republic* appears to sympathize with the fundamentalists in the face of the threat by the Utah courts to take away their children.

The Hot Potato

By Reg Manning
Arizona Republic Staff Artist

Cartoon by Reg Manning from the *Arizona Republic* satirizing the political hot potato that the polygamy issue became in the minds of Arizona politicians, even after Governor Pyle had left office.

The People Speak

The "Capture"
of Short Creek

The day chosen for the raid, Sunday, 26 July 1953, was the same weekend as Mormon Pioneer Day, a state holiday in Utah. The twenty-fourth of July held great significance for the Mormon people and their unwelcome closet cousins, the fundamentalists. It marked the day of the Mormon pioneers' official entry into the Salt Lake Valley.

Along the Arizona Strip, Friday, 24 July was hot and dry. Even farm animals lingered in the shade beneath the few trees that lined fields and streets in Short Creek. The weekend's festivities began with an evening social held in the schoolhouse, the only building in town large enough to seat a sizable group of people. The room was crowded with enthusiastic citizens singing patriotic and religious anthems including "The Star-Spangled Banner" and the Mormon favorite, "Come, Come, Ye Saints." After the school orchestra performed, the town patriarch, eighty-four-year-old "Grandpa" Joseph S. Jessop, whose son Tom had recently returned from the Korean War, rose to entertain his audience with stories of his youth in Utah. He also warned them of rumors of an impending raid. His listeners chuckled and exchanged disdainful glances. The threat of another raid seemed insignificant compared to the two years many had already spent in prison for the cause.

On Saturday night, the locals gathered beneath the stars for a dance that, like all their socials, opened and closed with prayer. Again, a major topic of conversation was the threat of a raid.

Mothers, sobered by even the remote possibility of arrest, returned home and told their children that if they were ever separated that they would find them.

Earlier that day, while Short Creek had been preparing for its evening dance, the forces of the raid had gathered at Williams, Arizona, 125 miles to the south, in the handsome red sandstone high school. Its auditorium on the second floor boasted fifteen rows of permanent seats. The room quickly filled with perhaps sixty or seventy Arizona Highway patrolmen, deputy sheriffs, national guardsmen, and liquor control agents.[1] Many, like fundamentalist Tom Jessop, also were returned veterans eager to reenlist in the work of making a better America.

The remainder of the room filled with civilians, attorneys, and social service workers. Townsfolk had crowded out onto their front porches, amazed at the parade of patrol cars that streamed into town. The official rumor spread that Superintendent of the Arizona Highway Patrol Gregory Hathaway had called a special traffic school.

The briefing began. Paul LaPrade and officers from the highway patrol outlined the plan to the men and women, who had come to Williams wondering why they were there. Maps from the air national guard showed what the Short Creek area looked like from the air. One map pinned to a blackboard at the front of the stage detailed the route for each separate unit. Roadblocks at the west and east entrances to town would prevent other traffic from interfering. One group would travel through Fredonia, cross the Grand Canyon at Navaho Bridge, and converge on the town from the east, while the second would drive through Las Vegas and pass through Hurricane, Utah, thereby giving the illusion of support from the Utah government. Both units would reach Short Creek at the same time. Each patrolman received a map with a red circle around the house of the family for which he would be responsible. He was likewise assigned a number that corresponded to a family. Officers Hodgson, Diebner, and Rogers would photograph the raid for the state's permanent records.[2]

Although they described the basic plan, much information was withheld from the participants. Secrecy was still the rule and was not easily surrendered. Each participant learned only as much as was needed for his part in the efficient execution of the plan. Therefore, rumors ran high among the raiders as they did in the town of Short Creek itself.

Paul LaPrade's office had leaked just enough information to the press to whet its appetite. Reporters were to wait at Fredonia where they would join the convoy as it crept down the winding road toward Short Creek. When Ralph Camping, photographer for the *Arizona Republic*, left his home late Friday afternoon he told his wife Trudy that he would not be home that night. "In fact," he said, "I do not know when I will be home." Ralph apologized for not being able to tell her more, but told her not to worry.[3]

The cars pulled out of Williams in the late afternoon and moved forward with what *Time* magazine would call "the ponderous secrecy of an elephant on a skating rink."[4] At Fredonia, the press cars fell in at the rear; there were nearly as many photographers and reporters as there were government agents.

As dusk fell, the lights of the first group could be seen fifty miles away like a trail of fireflies winding through the undergrowth. After descending from the Kaibab Forest and passing through Fredonia, the convoy turned out its lights, moving ahead cautiously by moonlight. Ralph Camping would remember how very dark it was traveling that night.[5] An eclipse would occur at 4:30 A.M., making the darkness absolute except for starlight.

As most of the children of Short Creek slept, the government forces were traveling along the more than four hundred miles of dark roads with less secrecy than they had supposed. Advance notice of the action purposely leaked to Salt Lake City newspapers by the attorney general's office was telephoned to Short Creek. Long before they doused their lights, lookouts on the red butte above Short Creek spotted the caravan coming from the Kaibab Forest, like a streak of fire moving along a spill of gasoline. Among the lookouts were David Broadbent,[6] and two sons of John Y. Barlow, Joseph and Dan Barlow. Dan, at age twenty-one, was already the husband of three women and the father of several children, including a brand new baby girl.[7]

One of the men scratched a match. It flared in the inky darkness, lighting their calm, clean-shaven faces. They lit a stick of dynamite, lobbing it up and out. It cracked in the sky like lightning in a summer storm, warning the families waiting below that their government had arrived.

After the tension, there was a certain amount of relief. In fact, the Johnsons, Barlows, Jessops, and Broadbents welcomed martyrdom. The idea of persecution for their religious beliefs had always hallowed and made more endurable their suffering.

The caravan of "good Samaritans" swirled into Short Creek at 4:00 A.M. with lights flashing and sirens blaring—announcing to the world that they had, indeed, arrived. They found many of the people of Short Creek—men, women, and children—standing behind the picket fence that encircled the schoolhouse. They had assembled an hour earlier, dressed and well groomed, to sing while they waited. Unlike their singing two nights before, however, the music was intermittently broken by nervous gasps, tears, and whispers moving through the crowd like waves upon water.

When Sheriff Fred Porter climbed out of the lead car, Leroy Johnson, wearing a clean white shirt, necktie, dark pants, and dark blue suspenders, stepped forward with quiet dignity to meet him. He told Sheriff Porter that they had run for the last time and were going to stand and shed their blood if necessary. Porter responded, saying that no violence was wanted. He raised his voice slightly so that it carried over the waiting congregation when he continued by saying that they were in Short Creek to do a job and that they were going to get it done.

As it turned out, the warning stick of dynamite was the closest thing to force exhibited by either side. By 4:30 A.M. the town of Short Creek had been "secured" by the combined forces of the State of Arizona. The deputy sheriffs fanned out through the crowd with 122 warrants for the 36 men and 86 women named in them. Within eight minutes they had served the warrants for all the adult fundamentalists on the Arizona side of town; thirty-nine of the warrants were for men or women whose primary residence was on the Utah side of town. Some of these 122 would choose to avoid arrest or extradition and flee to other regions of the state or out of the state altogether. Utah Governor J. Bracken Lee pledged his support in extradition proceedings.[8]

Five adult members of the community were in no danger of arrest: Mr. and Mrs. Jonreed Lauritzen, the son and daughter-in-law of Jacob Lauritzen; the town's lone bachelor, Don Covington, who lived in a white house in the center of town; and Mr. and Mrs. Alfonso Nyborg.

As soon as the officers began serving the warrants, Leota Jessop slipped out of the crowd and headed home.[9] Two officers followed her down the street and tried to stop her. She pushed past them, but one put his hand on her forearm to restrain her. "He asked my name," she recalled; "I refused to tell. I went to my room where several children were supposed to be sleeping. I lit the lamp and found my daughter, Dianna, awake, shaking with fright. Her face was pale and terror was in her eyes. The other children were awakened and very frightened. My oldest boy pretended to be asleep."[10] Unlike the majority of officers involved in the raid, this officer was more than willing to share information with Leota. He told her that the husbands and fathers were to be sent to jail; that the women would be allowed to go with their children, who were to be placed in LDS homes where "they could live a proper and normal life"; and that "Short Creek was to be exploded with dynamite and burned to the ground."[11]

The charges against the fundamentalists included rape, statutory rape, carnal knowledge, polygamous living, cohabitation, bigamy, adultery, and misappropriation of school funds. The information later filed in the superior court for the preliminary hearing accused certain members of the group with having "encouraged, advised, counseled and induced their minor, female children under eighteen years of age to actively participate in said unlawful conduct."[12] The information further accused the United Effort Plan of being dedicated to the "mutual and common end of establishing an isolated community, communal in nature, wherein the members of said United Effort Plan could actively practice polygamy, plural marriage, and polygamous cohabitation."[13]

However, Arizona officials staging the raid clearly believed that it was intended to "rescue 263 children from virtual bondage under the communal United Effort Plan." According to Assistant Attorney General Paul LaPrade, who prepared the case, "The principle objective is to rescue these children from a life-time of immoral practices without their ever having had an opportunity to learn of or observe the outside world and its concepts of decent living."[14]

After the officers served the warrants, Judge M. S. Gibbons of Apache County convened a magistrate's court in the schoolhouse and held all the male adult residents of the community under bond for a preliminary hearing on 31 August 1953 in Kingman.[15]

The highway patrol quickly strung a makeshift barbed-wire fence around the schoolyard and put the adults who had been served warrants behind it. Some had their children with them, others had left their children at home in bed asleep. Until late afternoon, none could leave to attend to their children or to the animals that roamed hungry in the fields or stood patiently in the barns.

Patrolmen also set up tents for the command center and a kitchen, and soon began serving heaping piles of bacon and eggs to the prisoners and their jailers. The fundamentalists refused coffee. They adhered strictly to the Mormon "Word of Wisdom," which forbade "hot drinks"—a stricture long interpreted among Mormons to apply to tea and coffee.

Edson Jessop recalled that first meal as a humiliating, degrading experience. "We had to hunker down on the ground, in the sun and the flies, eating tasteless food brought from Phoenix—within sight of our own homes, stocked with fresh garden vegetables, milk, eggs, home-baked bread and the civilized comfort of chairs and white tablecloths."[16] Under the emergency program set up by the Arizona National Guard, the raiders were prepared to feed the community for a period of from one week to ten days.[17]

The white schoolhouse housed two Mohave County Superior Court judges, Lorna Lockwood and Jesse Faulkner, who took jurisdiction over every child, including the juvenile wives, and made them wards of the court. According to the *Salt Lake Tribune*, among the twenty-nine Utah women accused of conspiracy was one fifteen-year-old with a four-month-old baby and another fourteen-year-old wife.[18] The judges reviewed information gathered by social workers who visited each of the fundamentalists' homes.[19]

The chair of the Utah Welfare Commission, H.C. Shoemaker, had come to Short Creek from Salt Lake City to handle welfare cases involving Utah residents.[20] Utah Juvenile Court Judge David F. Anderson began custody proceedings early the next week in a tent on the Utah side of Short Creek to decide whether or not the children should be left with their mothers or be given foster care.[21] Besides Shoemaker and Anderson, Utah welfare workers included John Farr Larson, director of Children's Services; Aubra Cartwright, field supervisor for southern Utah; and K.D. Williams, Washington County welfare director.[22] John Henley Eversole, Chief Assistant Attorney General of Arizona, acted as the liason between the two groups, conferring daily with Shoemaker and E.R. Callister, Utah Attorney General.[23]

On the second day, the judges themselves visited several homes and interviewed children of polygamous parents.[24] Twenty-four-year-old Viola Broadbent, the first wife of David Broadbent, sat all day with the other women on folding chairs in the center of the schoolyard. Fanning their faces with their aprons and shading their babies with their hands, the women waited, chewing the state's sandwiches and drinking sodas. That same day Pyle made a statement disclaiming any further participation in the proceedings: "My part in the operation has been concluded. The matter is now in the hands of the courts."[25]

Some reporters roaming Short Creek's streets were alarmed by what they saw. James Cary, a writer for the Associated Press, described Short Creek's lonely streets: "Dirty, ramshackle buildings, starkly etched against the faded red backdrop of the vermillion cliffs, cluster along this dusty road. Hordes of children play quietly in the pink sand that stretches for miles around in a dreary, monotonous wasteland. The stamp of poverty, deep and warping, is everywhere."[26]

Another reporter noted, "Not one of the houses I was in had either window or door screens and none had plumbing. Sleeping conditions obviously were crowded. . . . I saw no evidence of an adequacy of food—certainly not of balanced diet—and many of the children had peaked faces that indicated a shortage of body-building foods."[27] An editorial in the *Arizona Daily Star* spoke of the town's lack of an "adequate education carrying with it respect for the laws of the state and nation in which they live."[28]

Walking down the deserted streets was for photographer Ralph Camping a heartrending experience. He was struck by the poverty, the sacrifice of these people living beneath the cliffs of the Arizona Strip country, and he was moved by their plight. He asked one child, "Who is your father?" The little boy indignantly spat into the dust at his feet and ran away to hide from this stranger.[29]

By 3:00 P.M. most of the women and children had been released to return home for an unspecified length of time. They would wait three days. At about 3:30 P.M., the men were allowed to return home to prepare to go to jail and to say good-bye to their families. At 4:00 P.M., in a scene that was repeated all over town, a young officer knocked on Edson Jessop's door and read the arrest warrant to him. "It hit hard to have my children hear their father accused of 'unlawful and notorious cohabitation,' 'bastardy,' 'rebellion' and 'insurrection,'" he recalled. "It hurt until I had to blink [back] tears when my little girls, scared and bewildered, clung to my legs and cried and kissed me good-by as I climbed into the deputy's car to go to jail in Kingman."[30]

That afternoon when a deputy sheriff led Dan Barlow out of his simple frame home where he lived with his three young wives Elnora, Edith, and Lorna, Dan fully believed that he might never see his six-day-old daughter Madeline again. In the few minutes Dan was home, he and his wife Elnora inspected the baby, searching for a birthmark or some other distinguishing characteristic that might help them recognize her.[31]

By 4:00 P.M. all thirty-six arrested men had been put in patrol cars to be driven to Kingman along with eight women who were either childless or whose children were grown. These women were Millie (Mildred) Barlow Johnson, then twenty years old, Fawn J. Broadbent, Elvera Olson Zitting, Josephine Ford Johnson, Helene Ethel Woodruff, Myrtle Cooke, Rachel A. Balmforth, and Fern Loraine Shapley Jessop, a minor whose marriage to Jerry Jessop was annulled at the request of her parents. Fern later returned to her husband and family in Short Creek. Permilia Johnson Jessop came to Kingman later in the week.

The Kingman County Jail, where the fundamentalists arrived at 11:00 P.M. that night, thoroughly disgusted them. Mildred Barlow Johnson remembered that the walls were crawling with bugs and that the space was filthy—unbelievable conditions for human beings. The eight women immediately demanded clean sheets, hot water, and soap. Before they ever slept in their cells they had thoroughly scrubbed the walls and floors. But they couldn't seem to wash away what they felt was the the filth of what had happened to them. Transferred to another section of the prison the next day, they began to scrub again. They also prayed and began to fast.[32]

On the twenty-eighth and the twenty-ninth of July, a court photographer and a deputy sheriff photographed each home and each wife with her children. They also photographed outbuildings and junked, rusting cars that the children played in, incorrectly labeling such cars as "dwellings" for some plural families. Later, the fundamentalists would mention among their resentments the added indignity of being linked with this image of slovenly indigence.

The officers also searched the homes of the polygamists in great detail for evidence. Among the books confiscated from virtually every home were the usual Mormon scriptures—the Bible, the *Book of Mormon*, the *Doctrine and Covenants*, the *Pearl of Great Price*—as well as *Celestial or Plural Marriage* by Joseph Musser, the fundamentalists' second bible on the doctrine of plural marriage. *A Leaf in Review* by Byron Harvey Allred, a historical defense of plural marriage, was the second most popular work in town. The officers gathered up past issues of *Truth*, as well as sales slips, pads, and copies of trade agreements with the United Effort Plan or the Short Creek Community Supply. Marriage licenses, birth certificates, blessing or baptism certificates, and wedding anniversary cards were carefully placed in labeled folders to reappear as evidence in future trials.[33]

Besides confiscating physical evidence, police officers questioned the fundamentalists about their beliefs and lifestyle. Understanding the legal implications of testimony to the contrary, most would not admit they were involved in plural marriage. According to an article in the *Salt Lake Tribune*, "They maintained that they belonged to the 'real' Mormon Church, that they believe in the Prophet Joseph Smith and are following the laws revealed to him." Thirty-two-year-old Spencer Johnson called the raid "an outrage, an invasion of religious freedom."[34] One of the victims of the raid, Jeremiah Charles Jessop, recently returned from fighting in the Korean War, said, "This raid is one of the most flagrant, dramatic acts ever performed. If Governor Pyle had wanted us to be at a certain place at a certain time we would have been there."[35]

Shocking stories abounded. One woman had allegedly moved to Short Creek with her two daughters, embittered by an ugly divorce in Salt Lake City. After they joined the fundamentalists in Short Creek all three women married the same man and lived as sister wives.[36] One seventeen-year-old told the officers that she "had been a prisoner in Short Creek all her life. "I was told I had to marry a seventy-year-old man," she said; "I told them they could kill me first."[37]

Women like Millie Barlow Johnson and Elizabeth Sara Barlow adamantly defended their beliefs during questioning. "Our women have more freedom of choice with their mates than those of the outside world," they claimed. "We marry the man we want. Our girls pick their own husbands."[38] They refuted statements given by two fifteen-year-old girls to the *Star* in which the girls described their elementary school education in Short Creek as leading toward indoctrination in the principle of plural marriage and in which the girls had said: "The only books that were pressed on us were books about celestial marriages. We weren't much liked by the rest of the town when we objected to marrying men with a half-dozen wives."[39]

"We each want 10 children," Sara and Millie maintained. "What else is a woman for but to have children." According to the *Daily Star,* the women believed that

> the poverty that forces them to feed their large broods on homemade wheat bread and potatoes for many months a year is forced on them because of oppression by outsiders who don't understand, they said. The dirt-covered wooden floors in their homes, the empty cupboards, the thousands of flies that swarmed through the unscreened rooms, the too-thin bodies of the children; all these meant nothing, the women said. "We wouldn't think of raiding another town and telling the people there how to live. Why must they oppress us, we who are obeying God's will?"[40]

Several of the women named in the indictments lived on the Utah side of town. One such woman, Verena Cooke, testified in a sworn affidavit of her extradition to Arizona: "On July 29, 1953, Antone Prince, Sheriff of Washington County, also an Arizona officer and Welfare worker from Arizona came to the door of my home which is in Short Creek, Utah, and demanded that I let them enter, and told me I must sign an extradition waiver permitting them to take me into Arizona for arrest, or else be taken to jail at St. George."[41] Others refused to identify their children, lending some confusion to the raid.[42]

Verena, the legal wife of Jack Cooke, refused to sign the extradition waiver and was taken against her will into Arizona and placed in the custody of the Arizona state welfare workers. One official of the attorney general's office commented in the *Kane County Standard* that despite this resistance, "every effort is being made to keep mothers and children together in this community and the huge operation of carrying out charges of conspiracy to commit statutory rape, adultery, bigamy, open and notorious cohabitation, marrying the spouse of another and various other crimes in the faraway location has many unforeseen angles that may take months and months of legal work."[43]

At 9:00 A.M., Saturday, 29 July, an officer appeared at Gwen Balmforth Johnson's front door and told her to pack for a journey, not specifying for how long or how far. A strong woman, Gwen and her husband Leroy Johnson had two children.[44] Furthermore, after the death of John Y. Barlow in 1949 following that of his wife Mattie in 1944, Leroy and Gwen Johnson took in six of the Barlow orphans and became their foster parents. Gwen was intelligent, serene, and dignified, inspiring love and respect not only in her home circle but among the other women of the community. Seven months pregnant with her third child, she was especially worried about three of her foster children, seventeen-year-old Truman, sixteen-year-old Sam, and fifteen-year-old Alvin, who would surely be left at home without anyone to care for them. She scrambled to pack for her own two children, Stephen and La Mar, and the three youngest foster children, Ada, Veta, and Nephi Barlow.

Less than an hour later, Mrs. Johnson and her children gathered up their suitcases and joined other women and children who were walking up the street to the schoolyard where five big Commercial Trailways buses waited. Many left canning or cooking projects behind—bottles still sitting in pressure cookers on burners that had been hastily turned off, counters heaped with ripe fruit that would soon rot, loaves of baking bread left to char or sour in the cooling ovens. Stories later were told of the haste demanded by the officers, such as demanding that mothers pack for a three-day trip for them and their children in ten minutes. Resistance was met with threats of force.[45]

At the school, state welfare representatives explained to the fifty-six women that the government was taking custody of 153 of Short Creek's children. Of the town's total of 263 children, ninety-nine were children of plural wives living on the Utah side of the creek; these and the ten children of monogamist parents were not taken into custody.

Officials then herded the women into the fenced-off portion of the schoolyard, separating them from many of the older children. Some children, believing that their mothers were being taken away to jail, screamed and cried, stretching their arms through the barbed wire. The women could not nurse their babies in privacy or attend to the children wandering outside of the fence.

Six-year-old Colleen Barlow, her five-year-old sister Martha, and their mother Leta Barlow, who lived on the Utah side, had climbed the hill north of Short Creek that Tuesday, weeping as they saw their friends, aunts, and sister wives climb into the buses. They did not know if Utah's government was planning similar action against them. Uncertain and afraid, within days of the raid, some women on the Utah side moved out of the area.[46]

Rain poured down on the sandy red earth of Short Creek as the women and children were loaded onto the bus at 2:00 P.M.[47] Because of the confusion of dealing with so many disraught women and children, it was almost 5:00 P.M. before they were all finally aboard to begin the treacherous drive down the canyon to Phoenix. It was a long and arduous trip. One bus became stuck in the muddy road between Short Creek and Fredonia and had to be towed out. On the steeper grades the buses often moved forward at only fifteen miles per hour. The drive would take seventeen miserable hours. It was not until 7:00 A.M. Wednesday that the buses arrived at their destinations in Phoenix and Mesa.[48] As they convoyed the buses, twelve patrol cars periodically sounded their sirens, adding to the drama of the journey.

The state provided sandwiches, sodas, baby formula, evaporated milk, and boiled water, but the ride was horrendous. The children cried and fidgeted in their seats. The bus drivers had been instructed to refuse to stop for any reason. The buses had no built-in toilet facilities, and the only provision was a single portable child's potty chair in the aisle of each bus. In addition to the children's needs, many of the women were pregnant. The bus drove on. One pregnant woman, close to her delivery date, went into labor as the bus twisted and jolted; she refused to tell the officials on board or ask them to stop. Marjorie Holms's six-year-old daughter Susie, already sick when they boarded the bus, was feverish and dehydrated by the time they reached Flagstaff four hours later. Holms implored the matron on board to let her take the child to the hospital, but the matron, suspecting a trick, refused. The girl eventually died from complications of this illness.

Behind them, Short Creek was unnaturally quiet as shadows lengthened into evening. Truman, Alvin, and Sam Barlow were left behind to fend for themselves and divided up the responsibility for the homes left vacant in Short Creek. They worked hard into the night, emptying ovens, washing dishes, closing windows and doors, and rounding up and tending the dogs, chickens, and cows left roaming through yards.

Jonreed Lauritzen, writing for the *Arizona Daily Star*, later described deserted streets, empty houses, and the disruption of community life. "There is no sound of voices or laughter now. Inside, the desks are in disorder, and tables and chairs are as judges and clerks and officers had left them after the hurried hearings and the final order to evacuate. A few discarded legal papers still lay on the tables and benches where two weeks before the older boys and girls had worked from early morning to late at night, happily shaping tomahawks to fill an order from a novelty dealer."[49] The thirty plural wives on the Utah side of the creek redoubled their efforts, canning the fruit, tending the animals, taking care of the ninety-nine children, and helping the few remaining men in the fields.

In Utah, Washington County sheriff Antone Prince arrested five women Wednesday, July 29, on Arizona warrants. The next day, Thursday, July 30, he released them to return to care for their children.[50] Not knowing what was planned for them, on Friday night, 31 July 1953, 125 of the married women and children who remained in Short Creek attempted a mass escape on foot through the hills and into the canyons north of town. Three teenage boys led the group four miles through driving rains before they were turned back by Washington County deputy sheriffs. Sheriff Prince and Deputy Sheriff Israel Wade searched the steep cliffs for any stragglers.[51] A second escape attempt a few days later was aborted by police who discovered a truck filled with forty-one women and children fleeing to the north.[52] Paul LaPrade, learning of the various escape attempts in vehicles and on foot, sent officers into the hills to track the escapees down. "Some of them had hiked 10 miles into Utah before we caught up with them, . . . and a bunch of hungrier, more miserable, tired children, I've never seen," he said. "For their own sakes, we took them into custody." [53]

However, by Saturday, 8 August, Utah juvenile authorities found that most of the eighty Utah children involved in the case had disappeared from sight. Late Friday afternoon Judge Anderson notified Shoemaker that only a few summonses had been served successfully. "Most of the children and some of the parents cannot be located, he reported."[54]

On August 11, Utah Secretary of State Lamont F. Toronto, acting in the absence of Governor Lee, ordered the extradition of those Utahns facing charges of unlawful cohabitation in Arizona.

Rumors reached Mormon Church officials in British Columbia that a group from Short Creek was headed to Creston, a mountain town near the Canadian border already home to fundamentalist Mormons practicing plural marriage. However, immigration officials said that no application had been received from members of the Arizona colony for entry into Canada.[55]

The *Daily Star* described negotiations between Leroy Johnson and the remaining individuals still being sought by the state of Arizona on charges related to the raid. "Aaron Kinney, attorney assisting in the defense of the Short Creek residents arrested in a July 26 raid, said in Phoenix that Leroy Johnson, 65, a spiritual leader of the settlement, was attempting to get the fugitives to give themselves up."[56] It was predicated that extradition of the entire group would be waived if the voluntary procedure was successful. By Friday, August 14, Washington County Attorney V. Pershing Nelson announced that about half of the twenty-two women and five men named in writs of extradition and arrest warrants had agreed to voluntarily return.[57] The remaining fundamentalists, including nine already arrested and brought before Fifth District Judge Will L. Hoyt in special hearings on the Utah side of Short Creek, were expected to soon follow suit. Because of this development, additional hearings originally scheduled for Thursday morning by Judge Hoyt were cancelled. An attorney representing the defendants, identified in the record as a "Mr. Nelson," said "it must be made clear that the return to Arizona was being made strictly on advice of cult leaders and defense counsel and not because of any suggestion by Utah officials."[58]

Twenty-seven of those served warrants in Utah waived extradition and appeared before Superior Court Judge J.W. Faulkner on 20 August 1953 at Kingman's Mohave County Courthouse.[59] They were released on their own recognizance with instructions to appear on 31 August for a preliminary hearing on the conspiracy charge. Eleven warrants for Utah polygamists were still outstanding.

By the end of a week, Leroy Johnson had raised $43,000 to release on bail all thirty-six men and eight women. Bail for Charles Zitting and Leroy Johnson was set at $2,500 each. Bond for each of the other men was $1,000 and $500 each for the women.[60] The remaining teenage boys from the Utah side of town drove trucks down to Kingman to pick up some of the released prisoners; others flew back to Fredonia in a private plane, then hitchhiked home from Kanab.

Returning just over a week after their arrest, Dan Barlow and Spencer Johnson were the first two back. The court assigned a Mohave County deputy sheriff to drive them back home. The deputy had not had a full night's sleep since the beginning of the raid and traded off driving with the two fundamentalists until they pulled the car off the road so they all could get a couple of hours' sleep, the law officer obviously trusting the two "lawbreakers."

They returned to a virtual ghost town on the Arizona side of Short Creek. It was empty of women and children. A reporter from the *Arizona Republic* visited Jerold Ray Williams, a monogamist schoolteacher described by one fundamentalist as having happened to "be teaching in the wrong town." "Sometimes," Williams said, "the loneliness is unbearable." Thumbtacked to Williams's dusty bookshelf was a note carefully written in childlike printing. "Dear Father," it said, "I love You. We went to Encanted Park. We had fun. I surely do miss you. Love, Roger." His seven-year-old Roger would live for the time being in Phoenix with his mother. This scene was not uncommon. The men were fathers without children, husbands without wives. The legal ordeal lay ahead.[61]

At 7:00 A.M. on Wednesday 29 July the buses arrived at their separate destinations in Phoenix and Mesa. Some went to the National Guard Armory, others to the YMCA. The YMCA's parking lot was crowded with women in bright summer dresses—LDS Relief Society women whom the state had designated as foster mothers for the fundamentalists' children. Social Services housed six of the women with their children in the Y itself instead of assigning them to foster homes. Ester LeBaron Spencer, ironically the only wife for the moment of Floyd Otto Spencer, was pregnant with her eighth child. After a few days, most of the women and children left the armory and were distributed to foster homes throughout the Mesa area, and in Snowflake, St. Johns, and St. Davids.

A week after the raid, Arizona highway troopers, struggling to reconcile their images of enforcement officers with the human tragedy of disrupted families, staged a picnic for the fundamentalists' children in Mesa's Encanto Park. Their wives baked cakes and prepared salads; the troopers paid the pavilion rental themselves. They didn't want the children to always remember them with fear and resentment, and they worked hard to melt their terror, playing with them, teasing and joking with them, tossing the little ones into the air. One trooper was said to have wept at the grievous irony that his "protection" had inflicted such pain on the children.

Eight women and their children were placed in rooms at the Evans Rest Home at 5255 N. 43rd Avenue in Phoenix. After the novelty of the modern conveniences in the building—indoor plumbing, air conditioning, radios—wore off, the children became bored and restless. When one reporter visited the home he heard the whining voice of a little boy chanting, "I wanna go home. I wanna go home." His small shrill voice was soon joined by a chorus of other voices picking up the chant.[62] One pregnant plural wife admitted they were getting enough to eat, were well treated, and had new clothes from the welfare department, but insisted that "this wasn't home." She continued in a matter of fact voice, "We have always been persecuted. We always will. We learned to accept it. In the end, we know God will take care of us."[63]

From the government's point of view, the raid provided Short Creek's children with their first glimpse of civilization. "It left them wide-eyed and enthused and their 'liberators' convinced of the wisdom of the mass evacuation from the polygamous Arizona border town. The looks on their faces told me it was worth while," said Highway Patrol Lt. Robert Brown, who helped coordinate the trip out of the isolation of Short Creek and into modern society.[64]

The children, as wards of the court, received state welfare aid. Some fundamentalist women also solicited welfare assistance for themselves.[65] By 1955, the cost of supporting the children and their mothers in their foster homes for twenty-four months had reached $110,000—more than the annual budget of Mohave County.[66] Foster care arrangements varied considerably. When Marjorie Price, Mormon Church Phoenix Stake Primary President, called for volunteers willing to open their homes as foster mothers, a primary board member from Glendale came forward. Delas White and her husband Coy opened their home to a polygamous woman and her children for the next twenty-two months.[67] A willingness to help was the only criteria for selection. Some of the fundamentalist women and children were well provided for in nice surroundings; others faced more difficult, less adequate housing situations. Alyne Bistline Jessop and her three children were ushered into a room with clean towels and a rocking chair.[68] One woman led a mother and four children to a toolshed behind her Mesa home. It contained only four single beds, no chairs, dressers, or toilet facility. When the mother burst into tears, the foster mother commented, "If you break the law you have to accept the punishment," then turned and walked back to her own home. The family stayed there seven months.[69]

When the bus carrying Margaret Hunter Jessop, sister wife to Alyne Bistline Jessop, reached the armory, her first priority was getting her children to the restroom, but instead they were all shepherded into a large gymnasium. She noticed that there was a woman watching her. The woman came up and said that she wanted to take

Margaret and her family. Bewildered, Margaret and her children followed her out of the building. As they were driving down the street, the woman spoke kindly that it was going to be quite an experience for all of them and hoped that they would be comfortable.'" The home was a brand new house on a quiet dead-end street where the foster mother's husband was waiting to meet them.

Margaret felt that she and her children were treated well, but was appalled to learn that the woman they were staying with had selected her family because she wanted to adopt another child. Margaret refused to even consider the idea but believed that a number of different people came to look her children over for possible adoption. She vividly remembered how people followed them around, they were so hungry for a child.[70]

The woman, Margaret recalled, had been told that their lifestyle was sort of prehistoric, and she was surprised that they weren't the backwoods type of people she had supposed. In fact, when told to transmit an ultimatum from the authorities that Margaret would, the next day, have to choose either to renounce her faith or give up her children, the woman broke down and cried. Fortunately, this forced choice never materialized, and the foster mother eventually helped the family find a comfortable apartment. She also gave Margaret a washing machine, her mother's sewing machine, and paintings of her mother's, also enlisting her sisters to help collect furniture and decorations.[71]

Even the fundamentalist women who were treated well and lived comfortably were haunted by fears of losing their children to arbitrary government action. Many of them spent hours walking through their neighborhoods, gradually finding each other at parks, in shopping centers, or on the streets. The policy toward the polygamists was still in constant flux. There were those in control who still supported the idea of permanent separation of the women and their children. Even six months after the women had been placed in their own apartments, they had limited mobility. The Arizona state social workers with whom they had regular contact kept them separated from other members of the group, refused to provide any information about their husbands, refused to tell them where their sister wives were, and gave them no information about how long they must stay where they were.

Viola Broadbent found that a number of Short Creek women were living in apartments near her own. Soon they would meet each afternoon in the park. One day she noticed a man standing at the fence of the park watching her children. After a while he approached her, squatted down before her baby Lydia and said that he and his wife would like to adopt her daughters and give them a good life in a Mormon home. Recoiling in horror, Viola quickly swept Lydia up in her arms and, dragging her other child, ran all the way back to her apartment. She never returned to the park and never felt safe until she returned to Short Creek.[72]

Social Services assigned one fundamentalist woman to a rest home, "The Schmidt Haven of Rest," in Mesa for a number of months with her two children and eight other children, including five children of Leroy Johnson whose own mother had been bedridden and couldn't make the initial trip. Exhausted from the journey, she had to spend the first three days in bed. During the next few weeks, the effort of caring for so many children further depleted her energy.

The birth of her son two months later was a further ordeal. She reluctantly went to the hospital with the nurse assigned to her case, longing for the Short Creek type of birthing, at home with a midwife, a woman. It felt strange dealing with a man, a strange man at that. She had only seen the doctor once before having her baby. As she entered the hospital, the nurses kept bringing in papers to sign, and she was so groggy and in such pain that she didn't read them carefully. After she had signed the papers, she burst into tears wondering if she signed adoption papers to give her baby away. During labor she went to the front desk and asked to see what she had signed, protesting that she didn't want to sign away her baby. They reassured her that the papers were simply admittance papers to the hospital. After ten days she returned to the rest home and the many children under her care. The older children, including a twelve-year-old girl and fourteen-year-old girl, had tended the younger children.[73]

Another woman claimed that hospital personnel would not let her see or nurse her newborn baby. On the third evening of her stay a social service matron tried to persuade her to place the baby for adoption so that it could be raised in a more settled home environment. She refused and eventually was permitted to leave the hospital with her baby.

Attending public school was a strain for many of the children. The raid had been front-page news for weeks. Even little children had to be soldiers for the cause, and sometimes that was a heavy burden to carry when their parents were held up to them as criminals. Classmates could be cruel, teachers insensitive.

Some classmates found the children's "modest" mode of dress amusing, their attitudes outdated, and their circumstances shameful. But often the children were proud of their differences and viewed the events as challenges given by God to test them. When one girl bought her mother some lipstick thinking she didn't wear it because of their poverty, her mother told her that they were different because they *wanted* to be. That was the point; and many children soon learned and accepted it.

For Marie Jessop Darger, age six, Mesa was an ordeal in fear. She was afraid every time she went to school that they would take her mother away while she was gone. Even after their return to Short Creek, she was always afraid of strangers, even strangers among them. She later confessed that she had always felt like the raid was her fault, since she had been taught that if she was good, if she was righteous, the Lord would protect her. She knew that she had occasionally been disobedient and reasoned that this was the reason for the raid, that God was punishing all of them for her sins.[74]

After six months in Mesa, social service workers moved Viola Broadbent, her four daughters, and another plural wife and her children to a small town outside of Flagstaff. This was part of a state policy to redistribute the mothers and children to small towns throughout Arizona, again hoping to permanently destroy the community.

Sometimes lonely poems passed back and forth between the men and their wives. This body of verse testifies to the bonding that occured within the framework of polygamy, and to the emotional upheaval felt during this bewildering series of events. It connects the polygamous men and women to other separated lovers of all times.

"Exiled"
Phoenix—1954
by Aunt Fern

When shall I see you, husband dear;
And fold in fond embrace,
To bridge the gap and span the tide,
Since last I saw your face?

I long to tell you all my woes,
Cause you will understand.

And tell you too the joys I've had
Since kidnapped from that land.

Our trials-true, are many
And our burden often great;
But the peace of God is with us
On our mission up to date.

Distant my camp may be from yours
And letters hard to write,
But my thoughts and prayers and love
Are with you day and night.

One year after the raid, the Arizona Welfare Department conducted an updated study of the circumstances of various fundamentalist women and their children. Dan Barlow's pregnant fifteen-year-old third wife, Lorna Allred, had been released into her father's (fundamentalist Owen Allred) custody. Rather than be placed in a foster home in Mesa, Lorna traveled to Salt Lake City and spent the next two years with her parents.[75] Her sister wife Elnora Barlow expressed her hopes to shortly return to Short Creek. Dan's third wife, Edith Black, the daughter of Leonard and Verna Black, gave birth to a baby, Vivian, while waiting the outcome of the hearings. Several of the mothers expressed their concern about the "undisciplined children in the neighborhood," the bad influences their children were facing. Nevertheless, Marjorie Holm, Margaret Hunter Jessop, Josephine Balmforth and others said they were happy that their children were doing well in school. Her caseworker credited Marjorie with "keeping them [her children] contented," but claimed that "Marjorie makes no friends outside the Short Creek families. Shows no desire to."[76]

After twenty-two months, Viola Broadbent's case finally was resolved and her husband, David, came for her in an old jalopy of a truck that many of the men shared to retrieve their families. Most of the other women also returned over the next few months. The ordeal of separation from their community was over.

All of the women returned to Short Creek when they had the chance. A few stayed in Phoenix for as long as four years before they returned; however, it was not because they didn't want to but because their cases were more complicated and took longer to resolve. They had not been broken. The principle of plural marriage, in their way of thinking, had not been tainted by the accusations, the arrests, and the legal action.

The Legal Experience

Reactions to the raid varied. In general, the news was warmly received in Utah. Leroy Johnson would later teach his people that the Mormon Church supported the raid financially. "They answered to the tune of $50,000 to assist the state in carrying away the women and children of this people."[1] In another sermon he said that the Church provided $100,000 and that the legal costs incurred by the polygamists were $50,000.[2]

Johnson also told a story about a visit made by Church President David O. McKay to Mesa, Arizona: "President David O. McKay was in that conference and he made this statement, 'I want the people to know that the Church of Jesus Christ of Latter-day Saints is in full harmony with the actions of the state of Arizona in the Short Creek episode.' What did it mean? Wait and see. It isn't over yet, and I doubt very much if the persecution of this people is over."[3]

A *Deseret News* editorial praised the raid:

> Law abiding citizens of Utah and Arizona owe a debt of gratitude to Arizona's Governor Howard Pyle and to his police officers who, Sunday, raided the polygamous settlement at Short Creek and rounded up its leaders for trial.... Again, we commend the Gov. for his forthright efforts. We have full confidence that the rights of the innocent will be protected, the accused will be given a fair trial, and we hope the unfortunate activities at Short Creek will be cleaned up once and for all.[4]

Governor Pyle thought this type of solid public support was typical; but he was somewhat mistaken. Four days after the raid, he wrote Goldwater expressing his irritation about certain criticism of the raid, particularly by some members of the press. "Of course you have heard about Short Creek and perhaps you have read Gene Pulliam's insane editorial. It's a long, long story with opinion running about three to one in our favor. Can't imagine what has happened to Gene."[5]

Although the *Deseret News* seemed blind to violations of civil liberties and praised Howard Pyle for his ingenuity, other newspapers including the *Los Angeles Times* and the *Arizona Republic* (both of which ran front-page stories on the raid) saw instead the face of totalitarianism in Arizona. The *Arizona Republic* also condemned the action as a "misuse of public funds," describing it as a "cloak and dagger raid, typical of Hollywood's worst product."[6] Public opposition began to increase. In fact, by 1954, public sentiment against the raid was nearly unanimous. Pyle would later predict: "When I die, I know I will be remembered for Short Creek far beyond anything I did in office."[7]

In a 1974 address entitled "The Hazards of Public Life," given before the 15th Annual Arizona Historical Convention, Pyle reflected on his life in public service. "If there is one thing certain about public life, it would be that you can never be certain about the way it's going to turn out. If you step into public life from the business world where you have been accustomed to some measure of efficiency, you are very promptly stuck with some large-size disappointments."[8] Pyle expressed regret about the public criticism of the raid but he continued to believe that the raid was based on legitimate concerns. He did concede, however, that "it was neither the time nor the place to do what we did."[9] Every one of the accused men were released by Judge Tuller, a man he himself had appointed. The state legislature had never created statutes to prosecute violations of the anti-polygamy clause in the Arizona constitution. He felt somewhat isolated and betrayed by the system. "You get killed quicker in government doing your duty than turning your back."[10]

Jonreed Lauritzen, the son of Short Creek's founder, Jacob Lauritzen, and a non-polygamist resident of the town, was quickly disillusioned at the failure of the operation to meet its objectives. In an article that appeared 31 December 1953 in the *Southern Utah News* he wrote:

> We who have sat unwilling and embarrassed in the bleachers of the Short Creek arena have been bewildered by the difference between

what we saw and what we heard on the loud speakers. First the Governor's radio speech the morning of the raid puzzled me, for he seemed to be reading from the wrong script. He was not talking at all about the characters we knew in the show. Then after the thunderous overture and fanfare the show began to fall apart. The players seemed not to know quite what to do next. Who ever had the script seemed to have disappeared in the confusion and there was nobody to do any prompting.[11]

The Arizona Young Democrats assailed the raid on Short Creek, describing the manner of conducting the raid as "odious and un-American." The club accused Governor Pyle of seeking national publicity to enhance his future political career and called the conduct of the raid "circus-like."

> This criticism is not based on the fact that allegedly unlawful practices were brought to a halt but rather on the method and expenses used to achieve the above end. It is not necessarily a prerequisite for the successful enforcement of law that the governor of a state call a press conference of national magazines, papers and newsreels a week prior to the raid made merely for the purpose of insuring the governor nation-wide publicity for his own benefit.[12]

Judge Faulkner, however, was satisfied with the results of the raid. "Looking back over it now, there probably were some things that might have been done differently," Faulkner conceded; however, he maintained, "The manner in which the raid was conducted is not as important as the decisions to come. The men and women at fault will face trial. Their children are away from them at last. For once," he concluded, "the children are safe."[13]

Within days, members of the Arizona House of Representatives questioned the legality of the raid. Representative L.S. "Dick" Adams addressed the issue of the appropriateness of the appropriation funding the raid in a letter to state auditor Jewel W. Jordan, which was reprinted in the *Arizona Daily Star*: "Because the state financial code imposes a liability on the state auditor for auditing and approving claims against the state not authorized by law, I desire to call your attention to the fact that no legislative authority has been granted for 'Operation Short Creek.'"[14] Continuing his own personal investigation of the raid, Adams asked Greg O. Hathaway, Superintendent of the Arizona Highway Patrol, to what extent patrolmen participated in the raid, how they were paid, how long they were away from their law enforcement responsibilities, and how many of them were involved. Adams would argue that a constitutional amendment approved the previous fall made it illegal for the highway patrol to use highway funds for non-traffic enforcement purposes.[15] Furthermore, he suggested that the hours the sixty-eight patrolmen spent on the raid represented 319 man-hour days, or the equivalent of $8,759.25 in wages. Adams labeled the entire action an abuse of discretionary powers by Governor Howard Pyle. He very tellingly argued that the "raid could not have been an emergency if it had been planned for 26 months."[16]

The manner in which the government funded the raid was a matter of particular concern. Theoretically, the $50,000 legislative appropriation was to have covered all costs. Actually, however, this amount only satisfied part of the debts incurred. An editorial in the *Star* suggested several ways in which the incidental costs of the raid spread throughout all branches of government: "None of this money can be used to repay the highway patrol for the use of the 60 patrolmen and 30 cars involved. Nor can it be used to repay the department of liquor licenses and control for the 12 agents borrowed there. And it cannot be used to compensate the attorney general's office for the regular deputies involved, to repay the Maricopa County superior court, or to repay the expense to Mohave County except for the special deputies used."[17] The appropriation was targeted exclusively for transportation costs, food, special deputies, and other special services.

Attorney General Ross Jones, himself a key player in the raid, ruled on 14 August that "highway department funds can be used legally to pay highway patrolmen's salaries for the time they were used in the state's recent polygamy raid at Short Creek."[18] Howard F. Thompson, special assistant to the attorney general, read the following statement to the press: "It is clearly apparent that the duties performed in this operation were authorized in their capacity as peace officers."[19]

Letters to the editors of Arizona papers expressed a variety of opinions, ranging from passionate outrage to complacent support of the governor's actions. They focused on constitutional questions, such as freedom of religion and privacy, on the way the raid was conducted, its size and scope, and on the plight of the children. A letter from one M.E. Lindsay typifies the attitude of many people who were confused by the government's decision to break up families in this extraordinary way:

> That the welfare board in Phoenix will decide which children in Short Creek a mother is to be permitted to keep and which will be put in foster homes is a violation of personal liberties that makes everything pale in comparison. These women have shown spunk and will power in every action of defiance; and in pictures, the young girls are neatly dressed with carefully braided hair, which belies the implications that these women are spineless "slaves" and victims. They are raising their families under severe economic and pioneering conditions, but they seem quite capable of raising their own children and want to do so![20]

Within a few weeks of the raid, the Mormon Church moved to discipline those fundamentalists who had maintained their membership in the Church. Apostle Mark E. Petersen had long encouraged the Zion Park Stake presidency to actively identify and confront any suspected violators of the prohibition of plural marriage within stake boundaries. However, before the autumn of 1953 they had failed to do so. Petersen called the new stake president, Leo Reeve, not long after the raid and said, "Now is the time." Eager to fill the measure of his new calling, Reeve told Petersen that he and his assistants would do what they could. Petersen cautioned Reeve to have in hand sufficient proof of cohabitation before he and his counselors proceeded. According to Reeve, the most difficult part of the procedure was serving the summonses. "When we went into town to serve the summons [for the high council court] they would run and hide and do everything they could to avoid us. And when we finally held the court they would plead and cry, begging us not to do it."[21] This surprised Reeve because he knew that the fundamentalists taught that the Mormon Church was misguided. Members of the group answered this seeming contradiction by saying: "The Savior is going to come and put it right and we want to be in."[22]

Long-time opponents of the fundamentalists in the Arizona Strip country, thirty-six cattlemen sought an injunction in November 1953 against payment of salaries to Short Creek's four teachers on the grounds that the community no longer had a need for the school.[23] The issue of the fundamentalist schoolteachers would soon escalate into a full-blown lawsuit.

Regardless of public opinion, the raid on Short Creek was front-page news. In fact, "Operation Seagull" was rated in December 1953 as Arizona's top news story (receiving 492 out of a possible 500 votes).[24] The *Arizona Daily Star* ran stories on Short Creek throughout the next two years, giving it constant and thorough treatment. The *Arizona Republic* gave it careful attention for six months and then dropped off its coverage significantly as the hearings proceeded.

It is interesting to note that Utah papers treated the raid on Short Creek like it was merely an Arizona local interest story. Never reaching the front page of the *Deseret News*, the raid quickly fell from public attention. Although the *Salt Lake Tribune* covered the story more completely than did the *Deseret News*, it basically dismissed it as of limited interest, resulting in several single-column stories over six months.

On 31 March 1954, eight months after the police arrived in Short Creek, adjudication was still in process. State Senator Jim Smith addressed the Arizona Senate that day, demanding that justice be given to "all citizens of the state," including those in Short Creek. "I have chafed for many months wondering what would be the outcome of this the most infamous publicity stunt ever perpetrated on a group of American citizens," he stated. "There has never been an injustice in the annals of American history equal to the deportation of the women and children of Short Creek since the disbursement of the Arcadians in the 18th century."[25] To that date, although many senators had privately criticized the raid, none had so publicly and forcefully denounced the governor's action.

Smith pointed out that six of the thirty-six men taken in the raid were, in fact, monogamists and unjustly accused. Jerold Williams, D. Lynn Hunter, Orval Johnson, Spencer Johnson, Lorin Broadbent, and Floyd Spencer had filed a complaint the month before, on 19 February 1954, protesting the violation of their constitutional rights and privileges. The document listed a number of abuses that had resulted from this false arrest: their wives and children had been taken to Phoenix and placed under state and county welfare jurisdiction; their children had been made wards of the state; their homes had been unlawfully searched without valid search warrants, and their property possessed without due process. Their final complaint was simply, "We were denied freedom of worship."[26]

Smith pled for a dismissal of the men's charges, reminding his colleagues: "These men were not financially able to go into a long-drawn-out lawsuit against their own state (which should have been their protector). Therefore, they pled guilty to a crime of which not one of them was guilty with the understanding they would get a suspended sentence and with the hope that their wives and children would be restored to them."[27]

Smith then asked the president of the senate to call a special session of that body to discuss how to protect the constitutional rights of even the state's most remote citizens "before the sun sets today on this Capitol." Despite his impassioned remarks, his attempt failed and no such session materialized.

Leroy Johnson, who was the leader and spokesman for the men of Short Creek in the series of hearings and trials that spanned the next two years, was unwaveringly courageous. His zeal and conviction helped to unite and inspire them, helped them to stay faithful, beat back discouragement, and led them to their legal victory. Just weeks after the raid, in response to a request to encourage his people to surrender to the court, he wrote in reply: "I cannot accept your request to lead these innocent women to the slaughter house and betray them with a kiss. That you might stick a dager [sic] in their hearts and drawing [sic] their lifes blood by persuading them to deny their testimony, in order for them to retain the custidy [sic] of their children. These people believe that Jesus is the Christ and that Joseph Smith is a Prophet of God. And that God Commanded that the Law of Celestial Marriage (together with all the other Laws he gave) must be lived in order to gain their salvation."[28] Clearly, though his command of writing skills was not great, his belief was, and Johnson believed the fundamentalists were martyrs for truth.

With the exception of the eight plural wives without direct responsibility for children, no women were arrested because, according to Judge Lockwood, "the best interests of the children will be served by leaving them in the custody of their mothers under certain conditions."[29] As reported by the *Star*, Judge Lockwood suggested that "Rehabilitating the women and children of the Short Creek polygamy colony will take time and work but 'nothing will be left to chance.' . . . 'The families won't be torn apart, hasty decisions will never be made.'"[30]

However, in responding to a motion in October 1953 to dismiss custody proceedings involving the children, the Mohave County Superior Court ruled that the mothers could retain custody only on four conditions:

1. The mothers shall not return to Short Creek,
2. They shall refrain from teaching their children to violate the laws of Arizona,
3. They shall not consort with the father of their children, and finally,
4. They shall subject themselves to the supervision of the State Department of Public Welfare.[31]

Maricopa County Superior Court Justice Lorna Lockwood heard individually the cases involving each child. The fifty-year-old native of Douglas, Arizona, had been raised in the shadow of her father, who also was a judge of the superior court. Lockwood had begun her career in Arizona's juvenile court, where she was known for her innovative and effective techniques.

A decade later, in response to a letter, Lockwood explained how she saw the state's involvement: "The theory of our Juvenile Court laws under the constitution and statutes of Arizona is that when children are in trouble, through their own fault or the fault of others, it becomes a matter for the court to handle. I have always believed that the Juvenile Court, as well as every other court, has a two-fold purpose—to protect human rights and to enforce human responsibilities." Lockwood's part in the decision to allow the fundamentalist mothers to accompany their children after the raid became obvious as she explained:

> The Juvenile Court should consider not only the best welfare of the individual child brought before it but should also consider what is best for other persons including parents and society with which the child may be in conflict. I have always felt that parents bear a great responsibility, and the court should always attempt to make a Juvenile Court proceeding a truly family affair, involving not only the child but also the parents. . . . *Future religious practices* on the part of these defendants contrary to the laws of the land are very improbable in view of the fact that to do so will result in the loss of physical custody of their children.[32]

On 6 August 1953, in an interview published in the *Mohave County Miner* in the midst of the complicated hearings on the welfare of the children of Short Creek, Lockwood praised the women and children of Short Creek as "kind and gentle and courteous. Except for their marriage beliefs, the women are excellent in character. They are good mothers to their children. They believed they were doing what was right. I respect their religious convictions even though I disagree with them."[33] After meeting with the women, she concluded that they would most likely not be persuaded to change. The *Salt Lake Tribune* reported her comments on the subject: "I personally believe that we won't be able to convert any of the adult women to single-married beliefs. They seem perfectly content to lead the kind of lives to which they were subjected. It will be our duty to teach their children the laws of God and the state."[34]

Dan and Elnora Barlow appeared before Justices Lockwood and J.W. Faulkner to determine the future of their children: four-year-old Susanna, two-year-old Daniel, and two-week-old Madeline on 29 July 1953. The Barlows listened to the court's condemnation of the fundamentalist lifestyle and its determination that the children were neglected under the state's juvenile code. Arizona assumed temporary custody of the children until a hearing could be held because, in the opinion of the court, "the morals of said children are endangered, and they are in danger of becoming law violators if they are permitted to remain in said community and in the custody and control of their said parents."[35]

The juvenile court proceedings were all filed in Mohave County and bear numbers assigned by the clerk of the superior court in that county. Some of the cases were argued in Mohave County; however, others were argued in Maricopa County. The cases were heard for a period of up to two years, beginning 29 July 1953.

Each of the children taken into the custody of the court at Short Creek was first placed under the supervision of the chief probation officer of Mohave County and later placed in the temporary custody and control of the Arizona State Department of Public Welfare. Whether or not the child remained with its birth mother, its welfare became the responsibility of the state.

Although each case reflected a unique set of circumstances and personalities, the Jessop case can serve as an example of the group. Edson Jessop and his wife Alyne Bistline Jessop were sworn in and testified before Justices Faulkner and Lockwood on 3 September 1953 and again at a second hearing on 29 August 1954.

The central issue in each of these hearings was whether or not the child in question was "neglected, dependent, or delinquent." The court had the commission to judge whether or not the parental rights should be permanently "divested and terminated." Social service workers, matrons, and other interested officers were present at the

Jessop hearings but all declined to comment. The court judged that no one had presented sufficient information to justify removal of custody of the Jessops' child from his parents; therefore, the court ruled that "the right to the companionship, presence and association with the child remained with the parents." Furthermore, on 3 March 1955, the Superior Court of the State of Arizona ordered that the necessary steps be taken to return all the children of Short Creek to their respective parents.[36] After each of the separate juvenile court hearings was resolved the fundamentalist parents of Short Creek had a formal written judgment regarding their own cases in their hands and had returned to their homes.

In August 1953 the Mohave County Court brought Maricopa County Judge Little from Phoenix to preside over the preliminary hearings of the men of Short Creek, with the aim of insuring some sort of impartiality. However, some fundamentalists claimed that, most unprofessionally, Little telephoned Faulkner, possibly the most prejudiced man in the state on the issue, to discuss the case. On 27 August, the preliminary hearing was postponed so that it could be heard in Phoenix. A new date was to be set by Superior Court Judge J. Smith Gibbons of Apache County after hearing defense motions on 28 August.[37]

Judge Gibbons rejected both defense motions—a request for a bill of particulars and a motion to quash the cases—that would have potentially dismissed complaints against 107 residents of the fundamentalist community. He set the date for the preliminary hearing for 28 September in Maricopa County Superior Court.[38] Kent Blake and Paul LaPrade represented the state at this hearing.

A second hearing was waived by the defendants on 22 September and information was expected to be filed soon after in Mohave County Superior Court. Paul LaPrade and Aaron Kinney, a Phoenix defense attorney, announced the waiver. All parties involved expected the case to be moved to Phoenix.[39]

The trial itself was held in Phoenix on 7 December 1953 before Judge Robert S. Tuller of the Superior Court of Pima County, which had original and complete jurisdiction because there were no courts of appeal. Tuller dismissed ten of the cases for lack of evidence in any of the rape and statutory rape charges. The fundamentalists would later detail the processing of bargaining with the prosecution for a plea of guilty on the conspiracy charges.

After the first week in November, through our council, a representation was made to me and to my codefendants, coming from the
prosecuting officers of this state, that if we would enter a plea of
guilty to a conspiracy that our homes would be returned to us; that
all women in the community would be relieved of charges and permitted to return to their homes; that our charges would be treated
as a misdemeanor; and other representations too numerous to set
forth herein.[40]

The fundamentalists agreed to the plea bargain and pled guilty to
a charge of conspiracy. Sentencing came on 7 December 1953, the
same day as the trial. Tuller directed the twenty-six accused polygamists to stand in the jury box during sentencing. He asked, "Do any
of you gentlemen desire to address the court before sentence is
passed?" There was no response. Tuller quietly continued, "Well,
most of the clamor and outcry have died away. In this remote corner
of this remote state, in this quiet courtroom, the time has come for
you gentlemen to face up to the majesty of democratic government,
to the dignity of the law, and to the power of the people."[41] Tuller had
pondered long and hard on the matter. His was the voice of Arizona.
The judgment was made in the name of all those who had so carefully planned the raid, had assisted in its execution, and watched its
denouement. He soberly continued:

> You, yourselves—and the few score or few hundreds who stand for
> your same principles—are a small segment of the people; and we in
> official position serve you even as we serve all. Your voices may be
> heard in the halls of the legislature or in the streets equally with
> those of your fellows. The law treats all alike. . . . It is not my desire
> to cause you humiliation. No crime deserves that. I do not preach to
> you. No one is without sin, and certainly not your judge; but my
> failings may not be yours, nor do mine justify [yours]. . . . Although
> fanaticism flourishes in ignorance, I find among you gentlemen
> keen intelligence, extensive formal education, broad travel, sophis-
> ticated outlook, heroic service to your country, pleasant personal-
> ity, industry, humor and optimism.[42]

What would be the function of punishment imposed? Tuller summarized three possibilities: to avenge society, to rehabilitate the criminals (though he considered the polygamists impossible to change);
and to deter others. For this last purpose, he maintained, the women
and children of Short Creek had been physically separated from their
men and made wards of the court.[43]

He announced a year's probation; sentence would be suspended until 1 December 1954. During that period the convicted men were to violate no laws; were to report to probation officer Charles F. Adams monthly by letter or in person; were to report all changes in address before moving; and were to cease to practice, implying cohabitation.

Tuller concluded: "Gentlemen, you are now on probation. You take with you my fear that you will fail; my hope that you will succeed; my hatred of your crime; my love of you as my fellow men."[44]

The probation period was to end at midnight 30 November 1954.

Denouement:
The Black Case, 1954

The raid on Short Creek did not end plural marriage, nor did it prevent elderly men from marrying young girls. The denouement of the raid took almost three years to play out. During those years, the fundamentalists lost some of their most beloved brethren—Joseph S. Jessop died on 2 September 1953, Joseph W. Musser died on 29 March 1954, and Charles Zitting on 11 July 1954.

There were no more raids, but the governments of Arizona and Utah continued to gnaw at the community in other ways. Less than a year after the raid, the Arizona State School Board attempted to revoke the teaching certificates of Clyde Mackert, Louis Barlow, and Jerold Williams, all residents of and teachers in Short Creek. All three were fundamentalists, although only Barlow and Mackert had plural wives at the time.

The Arizona State Board of Education first heard the matter on 20 February 1954. At that board hearing attorney G. W. Shute represented Mackert, Barlow, and Williams. In addition to the testimony presented by the three men, evidence was produced that led the board to call for the revocation of their teaching certificates. The fact that the three had pleaded guilty to the charge of conspiracy to commit open and notorious cohabitation figured prominently in the proceedings.[1] Moreover, the evidence included three other issues: that the men had fathered children by women to whom they were not lawfully married, that they had violated their oaths of office; and that they had engaged in the practice of polygamy in violation of Article 20 of the Arizona Constitution.[2]

The Board provided them with one alternative—the possibility of signing an oath promising that they would not practice polygamy in the future. The three refused. In fact, Clyde Mackert, the thirty-three-year-old graduate of Arizona State College at Flagstaff, angrily denied accusations that his pupils failed to receive even a rudimentary education in the battered wooden schoolhouse operated by the fundamentalists.

Louis J. Barlow, who was also principal of the Short Creek school, similarly condemned the action. His letter to the school board detailed the unique problems he faced in Short Creek incidental to the issue of polygamy.

> The five years I have been at Short Creek have been full of challenges. I accepted the responsibility of administration of this small school the first year and set out first to inspire the children to enjoy school and enjoy learning. Along with all the duties of an administrator of a small school...I had the responsibility of teaching full time with fifty-four students in four grades and at as many different levels of achievements as there were children. There were not enough desks or chairs for all the class to sit down at one time. There were not enough books of any course in any of the four grades for each child to have an individual book. The operating budget was almost the smallest in the state. The buildings were run-down and unpainted. The children often had to wade through deep mud in the school yard to reach the creaking frame school house.[3]

In short, they faced many of the same sorts of problems endemic to rural communities, in this case exacerbated by the inordinately large number of children. In 1954, according to the *Mohave County Miner*, there were sixty-five children in school from the Arizona side and forty-one from Utah.[4]

To Louis Barlow, this was clearly a political issue incited by local cattleman who resisted the idea of funding local educational programs. The battle had begun decades earlier in the debate over land use. Cattlemen needed the area as a corridor through which to drive their herds to the open fields to the north of the Grand Canyon; and they frequently drove their cattle through town, much to the annoyance of local residents. "The brazen cowmen bluntly demonstrated their prejudices by exaggerating the unpopularity of the religion of some of the Short Creek residents," Barlow wrote. "Other residents of Short Creek who send their children to the local public school, but who are not Fundamentalists, have also reaped the rancor of the cattle barons and their employees."[5]

For Jerold Williams, another of the defendants, the constitutionality of what he called an "extraordinary religious test oath" was the issue. "Who is going to be sufficiently wise and have pure motives sufficient to be the judge of these moral questions?" he queried. "Does the chairman who influenced the highly educated members of the board to require this oath from the three Short Creek teachers think himself sufficiently clean to make the first judgment? Has not he learned his lesson from previous presumptive attacks on the innocent people of Short Creek?"[6]

Williams further accused the state of failing to live up to its commitment in the case against the polygamists decided in December 1953, writing: "The state authorities did not keep their word. We were promised that all other charges would be dropped; the 'offense' would be called a misdemeanor, and the sentence would be suspended. We were to retain all our rights and privileges as citizens. We reasoned this plea would help the state authorities out of an embarrassment, free us from heavy legal expense defending our many cases in the courts, and open the way for the return of our wives and children."[7] Williams saw the present conflict as yet another attempt of the government to end the practice of plural marriage.

To orthodox Mormon officials the Short Creek Mormons were heretics stemming from protestors who would not "wisely adjust their beliefs" when the main body of the Church abandoned their practice of polygamy in order to stop persecution and gain statehood for Utah.

As a member of the state board of education and governor of Arizona, Howard Pyle was apprised of each step of the process, and he expressed his approval and support to board members challenged by the unwillingness of the fundamentalists to acquiesce.[8]

The refusal of the teachers to sign the "blank oath" complicated the case enormously for the state board of education. It raised the question about the constitutionality of requiring such an oath for one category of citizens and not all. The board questioned the attorney general's office about what to do next. The response counseled them to wait until the deadline—31 July 1954—had been reached and then revoke the licenses based on the power endowed upon the board by the state constitution "to revoke all certificates or life diplomas for immoral or unprofessional conduct, or for evident unfitness to teach."[9] This was the procedure followed by the board.

The three fundamentalist teachers brought suit against the Arizona School Board of Education in October of that year.[10] Several of the issues argued by the plantiffs involved abuses of the constitutional concept of rule of law, particularly the concept of generality. It was claimed that the anti-polygamy oath was clearly an effort to create a law designed to punish a rebellious element in society. Furthermore, prescribing a penalty for one who pled guilty to the charge of conspiracy to commit open and notorious cohabitation violated state statute. The Superior Court of Arizona ruled on 31 July 1954 that the Arizona State Board of Education did "not have statutory authority to increase, alter or in any way change a penalty prescribed by the legislature.... Such action by the Arizona State Board of Education is beyond its statutory jurisdiction and is, therefore, invalid, void, and beyond its jurisdiction."[11] The superior court dismissed the board's action as "in excess of the powers granted it by law."[12] Barlow, Mackert, and Williams resumed teaching at Short Creek.

By April 1955, the unanswered questions of freedom of religious practices, social perniciousness, and the sexual exploitation of teenage girls that lay behind the raid had attracted enough national attention to inspire a U.S. Senate hearing. Once again, Short Creek was front-page news in Arizona.

Mohave County Attorney Bernard T. Caine took the case to the Committee on the Judiciary when it met in Phoenix beginning 28 April 1955. The Subcommittee to Investigate Juvenile Delinquency of the Committee on the Judiciary convened in the state capitol building in Phoenix for four days of testimony, in which they heard from virtually every person involved in the planning or the execution of the raid. Senator William Langer, a Republican from South Dakota, presided over the hearing. Caine told Langer that in its forty-three-year history the Arizona legislature had failed to implement the constitutional prohibition on polygamy through statutory law. "The last session of the Arizona legislature," Caine said, "had for consideration a bill introduced by Representative Rutherford of Mohave County defining and establishing penalty. It passed the House but was buried in the Senate."[13] Caine bemoaned the fact that Mohave County had no financial resources to pursue an investigation.

On the night of 2 May, Senator Langer, Bernard Caine, and

members of the senator's staff, Peter M. Chumbris and Lee McLean, traveled to St. George and on to Short Creek the next morning to conduct hearings in the community's schoolhouse. Members of Langer's staff were asked to drive in cars with either Utah or Arizona license plates—not their United States government licensed cars—to maintain the secrecy of the operation. Utah and Arizona deputy she-riffs cordoned off the entire town and summoned many of the com-munity's adults to appear. That day, the fundamentalists were mourning the death of a mother who had died giving birth to twins.

That fact didn't interrupt the hearing. Langer heard testimony about family relationships, religious doctrine, and the marriages of juveniles. After hearing nearly identical stories from eight witnesses, he dismissed the others. Langer found a situation quite different from his expectations, and was quoted as saying, "I was impressed by the sincerity of every one of the witnesses."[14]

In the official records, a letter of the alphabet shielded the iden-tity of the "ladies" invited to testify. Mrs. A., Mrs. W., and so forth were asked a series of questions about their beliefs, the environment in which they had been raised, their family relationships, and what they had observed about the marital relationships in other families. For example, Mr. Chumbris asked Mrs. A.: "'Do you know Mrs. D. very well?'...'How old a person is she?'...'Were there any other women there at the time?'...'And you of your own knowledge know of no other wife that Mr. D. has but this lady you just referred to, is that correct?'"[15]

Much of the fundamentalists' testimony was intentionally vague and unclear. The hearing took place at a time when many of the sister wives and children of these women were still in Phoenix in the cus-tody of the state. The fundamentalists had little reason to trust the state and therefore hedged and circled each question, skittish about giving truthful answers that might be used in court against them. Many, believing they were protecting their children, simply refused to tell the truth.

The transcript of these hearings provides the most definitive source of information about the raid but still did not deal with the important constitutional and legal questions raised by that action.[16] And certainly the raid had little impact on the commitment of the fundamentalists to the institution of plural marriage.

During the five years between 1953 and 1958, the Mormon Church quietly continued its policy of surveillance and excommunication of the fundamentalists, although Church officials rarely mentioned the subject of plural marriage in public meetings. The pursuit of the polygamists continued to fall under the special jurisdiction of Church President David O. McKay, who conducted the work with a personal passion.

C. LaVar Rockwood of Lindon, Utah was one of several Church leaders called to the work of apprehending known violators of the prohibition against plural marriage. Sometime around 1956, according to his recollection, Rockwood was invited to attend a meeting at the St. George Mormon Temple for all priesthood leaders in the southern part of Utah. A stake president identified the men as they entered the temple doors. Two of the twelve apostles stood at the bottom of the steps and touched the men as they were approved for entry to the assembly hall on the top floor.[17]

The First Presidency and members of the Quorum of the Twelve sat in the seats that stretched across the front of the assembly hall. The audience, who sat grouped together in wards and stakes, received the sacrament before listening to instruction about the perniciousness of the practice of polygamy among the fundamentalists. President McKay "was very clear in his dynamic, charismatic manner as to what the problem had been in the area. He indicated some polygamous people were sending their children to Primary, Sunday School and Priesthood meeting. He very clearly outlined Church policy that when there was the slightest indication or suspicion of a polygamous lifestyle the parents of the children [were] to be called in and before witnesses admit as to being the mother and father of the child."[18] Thus, despite the official silence on the issue of polygamy, there were still "very commanding instructions to affirm the absolute dissolution of any support of any polygamous ideas within the leaders' department."[19]

The parents' nightmare in the aftermath of the raid occurred not only in Arizona but also in Utah. The Utah Juvenile Court further tested the constitutionality of removing children from polygamous parents by attempting to permanently remove the children of one family by placing them for adoption, thus materializing the worst fears of all fundamentalist parents. It was an ordeal for the family of Leonard and Vera Black, but all fundamentalists feared, mourned, and hoped with them.

Immediately after the July 1953 raid, Arizona's attorney general, Ross Jones, telephoned Judge David F. Anderson of Utah's Sixth

District Juvenile Court in St. George, Utah, to inform him that the Arizona Juvenile Court was concerned about neglect among the children of polygamists. He reminded Anderson that approximately one-third of the community, including about eighty children, was actually living in Utah.[20] The two men would continue to correspond extensively throughout the episode.[21]

Anderson gathered Washington County's juvenile probation officer, sheriff, and welfare representatives to organize an investigation and evaluate whether the Utah Juvenile Court should take some type of action. Utah's efforts to deal with the polygamists would, like Arizona's, involve several different government agencies from throughout the state.

Since 1907, the Utah Juvenile Court had been a court of original jurisdiction regarding the interests of children, who were treated differently than were adults. Thus, matters of the neglect, dependency, and delinquency of children under the age of eighteen were resolved under the special provisions of juvenile court law, which sometimes suspended certain procedures seemingly guaranteed by the Constitution. In this way, the government attempted to protect this class of citizens unable to care for themselves.

Paul LaPrade informed Anderson early in September 1953 that Arizona was considering dismissing criminal charges against the women defendants, "inasmuch as if the juvenile order sticks it will be much more effective than any criminal proceedings would ever be. In addition, we would not be up against a situation of convincing the jury that young girls in their early twenties are guilty."[22] Anderson considered this a wise move but was personally more willing to work with the families of the fundamentalists on an individual basis, suggesting he would "take all possible steps to protect the children from growing up to be polygamists."[23]

Anderson held a series of meetings with the fundamentalists and their attorney over the next two months. He postponed a meeting scheduled for 23 October because the fathers of the Utah polygamy families were in Idaho harvesting potatoes trying to make enough money to carry them through the winter.[24] He acknowledged doubts about possible resolutions to the problem in a letter dated 23 October 1953 to the director of the Utah Bureau of Services for Children, John Farr Larson. "These families are the extreme opposite of the ordinary family that is broken up by Juvenile Court order. It is plainly evident that there would be no hope of getting the cooperation or understanding of either the parents or the children in making a foster or adoptive home placement."[25]

Increasingly, during October Anderson said, he had begun questioning the way the Arizona attorney general's office was dealing with the polygamy cases, particularly the advisability of allowing the fundamentalist women to stay with their children. "From the information I have," he wrote, "it is my opinion that it is purely wishful thinking to assume that the children can be left with their mothers without being indoctrinated with the plural marriage belief. If the Juvenile Court is to go ahead and handle these cases, I believe that the only practical solution would be to take the children from their parents and place them in an entirely new environment. It is the advisability of this step which I seriously consider."[26]

It was obvious to Judge Anderson that the fundamentalists would not cooperate with permanent foster care or adoption proposals. Also, he felt that "because family ties are so strong, it looks to me as though it would be virtually impossible for most of these children to make a satisfactory adjustment in other homes." Aggressive and effective prosecution of the fathers of these children was in Anderson's opinion the only way to effectively resolve the issue, basically by preventing future polygamous marriages through such harsh punishment. "I can't escape the feeling that going ahead with these cases will do more harm than good to the children, and will amount to punishing the parents through the children."[27] Anderson considered it more advisable to dismiss the petitions unless cases of dependency emerged.

H.C. Shoemaker, the chair of the Utah Public Welfare Commission, responded to Anderson's concerns on 29 October 1953. "We think that a trip to the Capitol is in order for you . . . at which time we shall pretty definitely have determined upon what we have no right to dictate whether these cases shall be dismissed. We do, however, wish to give you our viewpoint in the matter."[28]

The proceedings were recorded in a memo dated 9 November 1953. The commission proposed an approach to polygamous dependency cases that would insist that if parents wished to retain custody of their children they must first "refrain from teaching the children anti-social behavior such as to inculcate the idea that the religious tenets of the organization are more binding than the law of the land." It also suggested that the work commence immediately and that prosecutions begin for two or three polygamists each month.[29]

The Utah Public Welfare Commission considered Anderson's recommendations and discussed with Paul LaPrade Arizona's continuing efforts to prosecute the polygamists. Anderson scheduled a meeting with the fundamentalists and their attorneys on Monday, 23 November.[30] As a result, the cases were continued until 25 January 1954 based, according to Anderson's understanding, on the voluntary agreement of the parents that "as soon as possible all juveniles of the age of eleven years or older would be placed in non-polygamist homes approved by the court and that all juvenile wives would forthwith leave their polygamist husbands and return to their parents."[31] These juvenile wives included Adaire Stubbs, Verena Black Cooke, and Eva Jessop. But more importantly, this meeting helped to dispell any reservations Anderson had about removal of the children from their parents.[32]

In December 1953 Anderson filed twenty separate court petitions alleging that the eighty Utah children were neglected in the sense that their parents had failed to teach them proper moral principles and persisted in teaching them the doctrine of plural marriage. At the 25 January meeting Anderson informed the fundamentalists that each family would be judged on an individual basis, that parents would be given the chance to submit sworn statements to the court expressing their willingness to discontinue the practice, and that each home would be visited by public welfare investigators. Furthermore, welfare officer Shoemaker wrote to the parents of Short Creek: "If any home is proved to be unfit, judgment will be entered awarding the right of custody of the children concerned to the Utah State Department of Public Welfare."[33]

During the next several months, Anderson called in representatives of the United Effort and their attorney, Horace Knowlton, for depositions, and asked if they would comply with the law.[34] The fundamentalists affirmed that plural marriage was their religious duty and that it therefore superseded the law of the land.[35]

Anderson decided to make a test case of Leonard Black, who had fathered twenty-six children.[36] Black married his first and legal wife, Verna, sometime between 1925 and 1928. They had twelve children before 1953. He had eight children by his second wife, Vera Johnson Black, who was thirty-six in 1953. John Y. Barlow married Leonard and Vera Black at a religious marriage ceremony in Hurricane or Short Creek, Leonard Black could not remember which.[37] Lorna, his thirty-one-year-old third wife, had seven children by 1953. Five out of Black's six married children were already living plural marriage. Verna and Lorna had homes on the Arizona side of Short Creek, while Vera had a home a half-mile away in Utah. The children in question ranged in age from two to seventeen. They were Spencer, Orson, Lillian, Elsie, Francis, Emily, and Wilford Black. Custody of the baby was not challenged—Vera was allowed to keep it.

Anderson visited their home in early 1954 and found their standard of living low compared to his own but admitted that they had adequate food and clothing to meet the children's minimum physical necessities.[38] This evaluation was critical, since neglect was the central question in the investigation. Neglect was defined in part by Section 55–10–6, Utah Code Annotated, 1953 as follows: "A child who lacks proper parental care by reason of the fault or habits of the parent, guardian or custodian.... A child whose parent, guardian or custodian neglects or refuses to provide proper or necessary subsistence, education, medical or surgical care or other care necessary for his health, morals or well-being. A child who is found in a disreputable place or who associates with vagrant, vicious, or immoral persons."[39] The court saw in the Blacks' lifestyle and beliefs evidence to support an accusation of neglect.

St. George Juvenile Probation Officer, Jay R. Huntsman, filed an amended petition on 19 March 1954 alleging that the eight Black children were "dependent, neglected children contrary to the provisions of the statutes in three respects: that the parents provided inadequate clothing, food and medical care; that the parents taught the children that polygamous relationships were proper even though illegal; and that the parents actually lived in a polygamous marriage."[40]

The next day, 20 March 1954, the court conducted a hearing on the matter. Anderson heard extensive testimony including evidence from the probation officer that the couple refused to obey the law prohibiting polygamy.

When questioned about his daughters' plural marriages, Black showed the same type of evasion that typified testimony in the Langer hearings.

Q. Let's, just for the sake of clarification Mr. Black, who are the two daughters?
A. Cleo and Leta.
Q. Are they married to the same husband?
A. It is common knowledge.

Q. Do you know whether they were living as husband and wife up
until July 1953, and holding themselves out as being husband and
wife?
A. It was more or less a known fact.
Q. Were they married to anyone else?
A. No.
Q. Do they have any children?
A. I think so.
Q. And as far as you know is the father of the children Joe Barlow?
A. Yes.[41]

The pivotal issue about Leonard and Vera's worthiness as parents was their membership in a group that practiced polygamy and
their belief that they should teach the doctrine to their children. It
was the singular and persistent practice of plural marriage that made
the Blacks offensive parents in the opinion of the court. For the
Blacks, however, plural marriage was ordained of God.

At the hearing on 20 March the court heard Knowlton defend
Leonard Black's character:

> Mr. Black is an industrious man of high moral character and integ-
> rity. He has never been sued on a bill. He is not now on relief and
> has never been on relief except five years ago when he had a heart
> attack. He has never been arrested prior to this recent action; has
> never been charged with any violation, even to parking or any other
> ordinance. His children—26 in all—have never been charged with
> any delinquency.[42]

Washington County Attorney J. Pershing Nelson probed Black's
involvement in the United Effort Plan. Black admitted being a member of the trust, saying, "I turned in my property several years ago
with the idea of helping build up the country. That was my intention,
so I joined it to help build up the country."[43] The Blacks' own homes
were very simple—two to four rooms each with no running water or
indoor bathrooms. Vera Johnson's frame home included a kitchen,
general utility room and two bedrooms. The families' boys and girls
slept in different rooms but in the warmer seasons often slept out-
doors.

After testimony from Leonard and Vera Black, the court heard
from their two oldest children, Orson and Lillian, and from Jonreed
and Verda Lauritzen (longtime non-fundamentalist residents of Short
Creek). Seventeen-year-old Orson testified after his parents. Nelson

pushed Orson to recount his indoctrination into the faith. In common with all other members of the family, Orson attended church meetings with his parents in Short Creek's schoolhouse or in private homes, and he had recently been ordained an elder in the priesthood. Clearly, he had absorbed the fundamentalist viewpoint. When asked whether he would choose to obey his church or his government, he responded: "Well, it depends on whether the law of God is higher than the law of the land."[44] His sister, Lillian, herself only twelve years old, knew her parents were polygamists but had not decided whether or not she would be a plural wife.[45]

Jonreed Lauritzen, son of Jacob Lauritzen, characterized his fundamentalist neighbors as industrious, honest, reliable people. Having lived with the polygamists his entire life, Lauritzen had developed the opinion that theirs was a worthy experiment. "I think there is room in our United States for an experiment such as Short Creek. I believe that they might perform a public service by continuing on with that and developing a way of life that is a little different from ours. We experiment with plants, we experiment with diseases, why shouldn't we experiment with social interrelations."[46]

Judge Anderson truly believed that "the only way that the children of these polygamous families can be prevented from going into polygamy is by permanently separating them from their parents at a fairly early age, so that they will not be exposed to the fanatic religious teachings."[47]

As was stated in a later appellant brief regarding the case, the court failed to find "evidence that any of the children were destitute and without proper sustenance, clothing or medical care." Nevertheless, the court concluded that the Black home was an "immoral environment for the rearing of the children," because of their advocacy of the doctrine of plural marriage."[48]

On 11 May 1954, Judge Anderson decreed that the children were neglected within the definition of the laws of Utah[49] and ordered the Utah Department of Public Welfare to place the children in foster homes for a period of one year.[50] During that time, the parents could cease their practice of polygamy and thus prevent the permanent adoption of their children. The court issued nineteen findings of fact established through the hearing.

Anderson gave Leonard and Vera Black thirty days to sign an affidavit of intention to comply. They refused. Therefore, he awarded custody and control of the Blacks' children to the Utah State

Department of Public Welfare. He notified the Blacks in a letter dated 31 May 1954 that representatives of the Utah State Department of Public Welfare would come to Short Creek on the morning of 4 June 1954 to take custody of their children. The court's probation officer, Jay Huntsman, arrived at Vera Black's door early on the morning of 4 June. He told Mrs. Black that he had come for her children and that she needed to come out onto the porch to talk to the welfare officers about it. Historian Juanita Brooks, moved by the story of Vera Black, waited with Vera for the officers who came to take seven of the eight children to their assigned foster homes in the Provo-Orem area. Brooks encouraged the already feisty Vera to fight the order and insist on riding to St. George with her children. This Vera did, and in fact continued on with the children to Cedar City, where she was finally ousted from the vehicle by a judge's order.[51] There the Iron County sheriff delivered the children to Lamar Andrus, Child Welfare Consultant, Utah State Department of Public Welfare. The state then placed the children in foster care.

In early June 1954 Vera and Leonard Black sued for a writ of habeas corpus from the Utah Supreme Court. Later that same month, Justice William Stanley Dunforth of the Fourth District Court in Provo, Utah, held a hearing on that writ and ruled that Judge Anderson's initial judgment was unconstitutional because it violated the freedom of religion and freedom of speech clauses of the United States Constitution. He ordered the children returned to their home, pending the couple's already filed appeal to the Utah Supreme Court. They were returned within a week.

Vera and Leonard Black had appealed Anderson's decision; however, on 30 December 1954 the Utah Supreme Court upheld the decision of the juvenile court.[52]

The Blacks' appeal to the Utah Supreme Court, prepared by their attorney Horace Knowlton, centered on five points of concern: 1) the obstruction of constitutional rights to freedom of speech and freedom of religion; 2) the fact that the children were taken from their natural parents without due process; 3) that these efforts expressed an overextension of the doctrine of *parens patria*;[53] 4) that the conclusion of law finding the children "neglected children" was unconstitutional in that it was vague and uncertain; and 5) that the findings were not supported by evidence. Vera and Leonard Black lost their appeal and temporarily lost custody of their children.[54]

In answer to this appeal, the Utah Supreme Court issued a unanimous decision on 16 May 1955 deciding against the Blacks on all points. Justice George M. Worthen's twenty-five-page opinion employed the harshest language used in anti-polygamy judgments since the nineteenth century judicial crusade. According to Worthen, plural marriage trapped children in a condition of perpetual sexual immorality. He also maintained that it was "inexcusable for these parents to hide behind this religious cover." He resurrected *Reynolds* v. *United States, Davis* v. *Beason,* and *State* v. *Barlow et al.* to disclaim any use of the religious freedom clause in the First Amendment.[55]

Clearly, the court looked at the Blacks as a test case, but even more importantly it chose to use them as an example to all fundamentalists of what would happen to the children of polygamous unions if parents did not conform to the dictates of the state. Worthen wrote: "The Juvenile Court was too lenient on these parents.... The practice of polygamy, unlawful cohabitation and adultery are sufficiently reprehensible, without the innocent lives of children being seared by their evil influence. There can be no compromise with evil."[56] Regardless of the benefits of being raised by their natural mother, Worthen continued, "it would be more desirable that they be brought up as law-abiding citizens in righteous homes. The price is too great to require these children to continue under the same influences that they have been exposed to."[57]

During December, it all finally came to a head. On 3 December 1955 Vera Black received a letter from John Farr Larson, Director of the Bureau of Services for Children for the State of Utah, advising her that "representatives of this department will call at Shortcreek on Tuesday, January 10th 1956, at 9:00 A.M. for the purpose of carrying out the court order."[58] The letter continued, "It will be greatly appreciated if at that time you will have the children prepared with their personal belongings to leave your home."[59] Interestingly enough, this was pursuant to the order of the Sixth District Juvenile Court issued on 16 May 1955. They had waited six months to act. Perhaps they decided to act at this time to put additional pressure on the Blacks.

A week later, on 12 December 1955, the Blacks received the final blow when the United States Supreme Court denied their request for a writ of certiorari. The Court agreed that the seizure of the children violated the First and Fourteenth amendments to the Constitution, which forbade seizure of property without due process of law, but that it was within guidelines set for juvenile court proceedings. Furthermore, the law stated that "The [juvenile] court may conduct the hearing in an informal manner and may adopt any form of procedure in such cases which it deems best suited to ascertain the facts relating to such cases."[60]

The Utah court ruled that the Black children should be restored to their parents only upon three conditions: the parents were not to continue a conjugal relation, the children must remain in Utah, and the children were to report periodically to the juvenile court. It was acknowledged, however, that polygamists did indeed have Constitutional rights and protections, no matter how repugnant their practices might be to their larger society.

Among the most noticeable supporters of the Blacks were Utah writers Juanita Brooks and Maurine Whipple. Both women were moved by the plight of Vera Black and her children; they had taken up the Blacks' cause as a personal crusade and had invested considerable energy in the legal battle. Quiet support also came from others who saw injustice in the way the courts had treated the Blacks. In one letter dated 21 December 1955 to the editor of the *Salt Lake Tribune*, Norman C. Pierce articulated the following viewpoint:

> The judicial department of the State of Utah can now justifiably strike hands in full fellowship with the Russian government because of the stand they take toward thousands of inhabitants of this state.
>
> I do not criticize them for trying to enforce the law that is on the books in the case of the Fundamentalists, but I do severely criticize them for the method they employ to enforce it.
>
> Demanding a monthly affidavit from these parents that they have paid lip service to a law they detest with a penalty that deprives them of their children if they do not give this lip service, is going far beyond the constitutional rights of any American court.[61]

The drama of 10 January 1956 staged on the front lawn of the Blacks' Hildale, Utah, home played out like a scene from a tragicomedy. Vera Black was fortified in her resistance by a circle of friends and associates who had gathered to meet the representatives of the state. This group included Vera's brother, Spencer Johnson, as well as Clyde Mackert, J. Huntsman, David Bateman, Jerold Williams, and eighteen-year-old Sam Barlow. Juanita Brooks and Maurine Whipple were also there.

The confrontation was entirely one of words—words carefully chosen to express both the emotion and the injustice of this action. The sheriff, Ray Renoif, as the agent of the government, was almost a passive member in this dialogue. He had a very specific job to perform and if he failed to do so, someone would surely fill in where he had not. At one point the sheriff said, "I don't know anything about it at all. I just came along. I would hate to see them taken. If it was me, I would sign the thing."[62] Nevertheless, the polygamists, as well as Brooks and Whipple, were prepared to try to persuade him to refuse to seize the children and return empty-handed.

Maurine Whipple carefully recorded the dialogue at the Black house when the officers arrived to take custody of the Black children. "Our rights are at stake," Louis Barlow emotionally asserted. "We can't just pass those things off with a shrug and say, 'Well, this is a different age, a different time.'" [63]

"It is not just a few remote people of Short Creek who are concerned. It is a crusade against the American home," Williams added. One child, Wilford, was a particular concern of Juanita Brooks but was, nonetheless, taken by the sheriff and the officer of the court. His brother Vaughn had whooping cough, so LaVar Andrus (an officer of the court) backed down and said that they would not take Vaughn at that time.

Sam Barlow asserted the unconstitutionality of the court's actions. "Do you think the Constitution of the United States hangs on whether you do this? There is one point that is significant. Here is a family trying to live its religion. Here is a law officer trying to uphold the laws. What is more important, that the sheriff uphold the court order or these people maintain their religious rights?"[64] The juvenile probation officer, Jay Huntsman, and Sheriff Renoif answered that it was up to the court.

Juanita Brooks tried to intimidate Huntsman, asking, "Are you the man who goes in and gets them?" Huntsman pointed to Andrus and said, "He is." "You don't like it too much, do you?" she continued. "I don't like it at all," he answered.

Clyde Mackert then remarked, "The time they were taken before, even though it was only a week, had a lasting effect on those children."[65] The conversation continued for another hour and a half along somewhat the same lines.

At one point Louis Barlow said, "We want to be a respectable community. I am willing to go into the service again. Out on the front lines, you are somewhat removed from the ideals of the Constitution, but here you are fighting for something that is real."[66]

Eventually, petite Vera Black read a statement she had released earlier to the press. A quiet, soft-spoken and somewhat timid woman, her voice trembled as she strained to be heard and, more importantly, to be understood.

> Ours is a nation of equal rights before the law. Why should I be required to sign an unconstitutional loyalty pledge or any oath of any kind in order to keep the children I have honorably born, unless all mothers in our state be required to sign an oath?
>
> I will gladly sign an oath to support and sustain the Constitution of the United States, and obey all the laws of the State of Utah which conform to the spirit and letter of that great document.
>
> I am ever willing to teach my children the laws of Utah concerning marriage when they grow old enough to understand such laws.[67]

It came down finally to a confrontation on the issue of whether or not the Blacks would give up the children on any grounds. After Vera Black had refused repeatedly to allow the children to be taken, Maurine Whipple protested, "As a free American citizen, I give you my opinion. If somebody went to take my children they would have to take them by force. Any mother on earth would say that. Any mother wouldn't let her children go except by force."[68]

Vera concluded, "I still make that same statement. We won't give these children up willingly." Unwilling to use force to remove the children, the officers left without them. They returned two days later with strengthened resolve. They placed the children temporarily at the state hospital in Provo, and a few days later in a foster home in Orem. The children stayed there until 13 June 1956. One child, Wilford, was allowed to stay with his mother.

Juanita Brooks wrote to Mrs. Elsa Harris of the Utah County Welfare Office to plead that Wilford be treated with special consideration.

> You may remember me as the woman who talked to you in St. George the day the Black children were taken first in 1954. You will recall that my chief concern was for the one child, Wilford, because I had observed him the day before and sensed his mortal terror. Only a mother who has nursed along such a frail, sensitive child, could realize what that experience did to Wilford, and how deeply and irreparably he is being injured by this one. . . . I pray you not to separate this child from either his older brother, Orson, or his younger one, Francis, with whom he has slept every night as long as he can remember. . . . To me, no teaching of children under

the age of ten can justify tearing them out of a home where they have love and security to scatter them and make them public charges.[69]

Juanita Brook saw a photograph in the *Daily Herald* on 13 January 1956 of Vera Black and her children weeping and holding each other. In response to that and an article in the *Deseret News* on Saturday 28 January entitled "Stamp Out Polygamy," she responded with a series of indignant letters to the editor and welfare officers in Provo. In one she wrote: "That the official organ of the Church of Jesus Christ of Latter-day Saints should approve such a basically cruel and wicked thing as the taking of little children and babies from their mother strains the faith of many, many of us. . . . In trying to stamp out one evil, let us not commit another so black that it will shame us for ages to come."[70]

No testimony offered in any of the court cases either asserted or established that Vera Black was an unfit mother in any way except for her religious beliefs. The court left room for negotiation. If the Blacks were willing to denounce their lifestyle and religion, the court would recognize the gap between legal technicalities and social realities and return the children to their parents.

After their children had been taken away, the Blacks traveled the next day, on 14 January, to Salt Lake City to appeal personally to Governor Lee for intervention on their behalf. They failed. Vera Black was finally persuaded she had absolutely no recourse but compliance. At a press conference staged in Provo, Vera told reporters that she would continue to fight for custody of her children. "I just couldn't sign that document," she passionately maintained. "It was against my conscience and my religion. God help me to regain my children."[71]

That same month of January 1956, Utah's six juvenile court judges formulated a policy for dealing with cases involving custody of the children of polygamous families. The decision, following what was already the tradition of the juvenile court, was to consider each case individually. Later the same day, on 26 January, the six judges met at the Utah State Capitol Building with Utah State Welfare Commission officials and Utah Attorney General E.R. Callister.

As reported by the *Tribune*, Callister told the judges that future efforts to eliminate polygamy within the state of Utah must be marked by cooperation between the separate agencies. "These people," he said, "are teaching their children to break the law. It is analogous to prostitution. In many cases, girls 14–16 are being married off, some of them to men of 60." H.C. Shoemaker, the chair of the public welfare commission, criticized the "soft-hearted and soft-headed thinking" by many people on the subject of polygamy. "Polygamists," he said, "are breaking the law, and the state must not throw up its hands in the face of growing lawlessness."[72] This same *Tribune* article estimated that there were 5,000 polygamous families in Utah in 1956.

Before the afternoon was over, the judges met with John Farr Larson, director of the Welfare Commission Bureau of Services for Children, to discuss other procedural problems. The Black case threw the agencies involved into disorder, forcing them to reexamine both procedures and attitudes about the problem.

The case was never far from the public eye. On 8 March 1956 Salt Lake County Attorney and future United States Senator Frank E. Moss called for the cooperation of Attorney General Callister in calling for a grand jury to push further the drive to wipe out the practice of polygamy in Utah. Moss said, "I plan to confer with the attorney general Friday regarding the report that has been completed in his office on plural marriages and seek his co-operation in calling a grand jury for its consideration of the offenses of polygamy so indictments can be issued." A grand jury would allow his office to better "prosecute alleged cases of polygamy because the grand jury can direct the issuance of subpoenas."[73]

That same day, Moss noted that he had received a letter from Shoemaker which informed him that "within a short time a representative of the attorney general will call on you and give the names of families in Salt Lake County we believe represent the best opportunity for prosecution."[74] The census showed that by their own admission, about 1,600 polygamists lived in Salt Lake County. However, despite plans for future prosecutions of polygamists, few ever materialized; for the moment the spotlight was on the Blacks.

Once again the polygamists had been confronted with superior force and had no choice but surrender. Vera and her children were finally reunited in June 1956 after Vera agreed to sign an oath on 31 May 1956 renouncing her belief in polygamy. Vera and Leonard Black testified before Juvenile Court Judge Durham Morris of Cedar City at a final hearing on 11 June 1956. Both said that they had not lived together as man and wife since the 1953 raid and that they would teach their children to obey the laws of the land. Vera began crying when the court asked her if she would be happy to be reunited with her children. "Oh, of course I would," she said.[75] The reunion two days later was predictably emotional. Vera continued to feel that justice had not been served and she returned to life in plural marriage after her children were returned to her.

The psychological effect was great. *Black* v. *State* immediately acquired mythic significance in the minds of many polygamous parents and their children, who saw in it an example of the loathing in which their government held them and its willingness to destroy their families.

Conclusion

Perhaps the most basic yet compelling questions that emerge from the story of the confrontation between the fundamentalists of Short Creek, Arizona and the government are, *how* and *why* did this happen? This series of events seems in many ways to contradict what Americanism represents. But as Michael Kammen so convincingly argues in his book *People of Paradox*, the dualities in our culture identify us as a people as much as do our points of unanimity. This story highlights the contradictions between the right to privacy and societal convention, between American individualism and group cooperation, and between religious and secular lifestyles.

The vigor and direction of the crusade against polygamy in the 1940s and 1950s was unprecedented even in the state of Utah. In a broader context, however, it is possible to read anti-polygamy sentiment as analogous to nativist discrimination against foreigners and ethnic groups which has plagued America since at least the early nineteenth century. The raid of 1944 took place in the midst of a global war which had devastated and demoralized nations. Later, the invention of the atomic bomb created the ominous possibility of total global annihilation. The war in Europe and following Cold War had seriously challenged the security of the American people. Perhaps some Utahns expressed this anxiety by trying to gain control over the lives of at least one small part of the "enemy"—in this case a religious sect with beliefs outside those of society's mainstream. To its attackers, polygamy seemed to threaten the basic moral fiber of the American people, although no one did, or perhaps could, specify just how this might happen. Also, in a time when everything communal was

branded red, the communal nature of Short Creek was particularly
suspect.

The raid on Short Creek in 1953 shared the front page with news
of the Korean War armistice. Both similarly magnified the anti-
communist paranoia that had seized the public consciousness after
World War II. Both were defined by outsiders as threats to the democratic experiment. The McCarthy era was a conservative reaching
back to American traditions; it could be found not only in the United
States Senate but in an Arizona governor's office. The communist,
the anti-Christ, and the polygamist threatened or seemed to deny that
nebulous something that made America great.

Paradoxically, considering the worst fears of the orthodox, the
fundamentalists of Short Creek were some of the most patriotic
people in the state of Arizona. The rhetoric of patriotism was part of
their religion. Perhaps most perplexing, the fundamentalists failed to
become bitter about the treatment they had received, but almost
seemed to love America the better for it.

For the fundamentalists, the constitutional guarantee of freedom
of religion was the central issue. For the government this was a moot
point. Perhaps more to the point in understanding the government's
attitude toward the fundamentalists is the concept of *parens patriae*,
or paternal government. This idea centered on the concept that the
government existed in part to protect those citizens unable to care for
themselves.

The Constitution can be viewed as a sort of contract between the
individual and the social group—individual rights are proclaimed
and guaranteed until and unless they threaten the security and stability of the group as a whole. Laws are made to try to regulate this
commerce; the courts then interpret the laws in their specific applica-
tions and in their adherence to general constitutional principles. The
laws thus often subordinate the interests of the individual to the general interests of society—an organizational structure of relationships
and services. In the same way, the rights of the individual were qualified to preserve the good of the body politic. It is not possible to un-
tangle totally the interests of the individual from the interests of society as they are so closely woven as to present a constantly changing
pattern. The Constitutional guarantee of religious freedom itself assured that no single religion could dominate to prohibit the practice
of less powerful groups.

The government's attitude in 1953 toward the governance of

women and children was an inheritance from the Progressive Era, a time when reformers began to speak of the rights of children and to predict the future of society on the basis of the protection of the interests of its youngest members. Increasingly, middle America recognized that children had a moral and legal right to receive parental love and affection, discipline and guidance, and to mature in a home environment that would help enable them to develop into responsible and stable adults. The reformers of the Progressive Era took it upon themselves to insure that they did, even if it meant being at times coercive or endeavoring to legislate morality.

They were joined by state and federal governments and, even more importantly, by the courts. Judgments of the Supreme Court soon created extraordinary constitutional protections to safeguard child-parent and other important family relations. This emphasized the assumption that family relationships were important both to individuals and to the society at large. Problems in domestic relations had traditionally fallen under the jurisdiction of state law and were considered matters of civil legislation based on common societal assumptions about morality. In many ways, laws relating to the family reflected the roots of the political system because patterns of behavior, relationships, and family structures generally perpetuate the attitudes and fundamental values of a society. Families provide a stable structure for the process of cultural transmission, which is perhaps their most important function as far as governments are concerned.

The family is significant to government because it is a teaching station. As such it is obligated to teach children principles of morality, citizenship, and common decency. According to Governor Howard Pyle, to Judge Jesse Faulkner, and to other critics, the fundamentalists had failed to satisfy their constitutional responsibility to provide for their children. In the eyes of the world outside, the children of Short Creek were living in substandard housing, were fed inadequate diets, and were being denied access to proper education. It then became the responsibility of the state to step into the vacuum and, in the tradition of coercive reform, remedy the situation. The raid was the grandest effort to date of the exercise of coercive reform in the name of the protection of children. It seemed to illuminate reformist principles with an unmatched moral fire.

Short Creek in 1992

The three raids on the fundamentalists did not wipe out the practice of plural marriage in southern Utah or in northern Arizona. In fact, the group continued to grow at the same rate as it had since 1930, doubling each decade. By 1992 more than 4,500 fundamentalists lived in the town known after 1962 as Colorado City/Hildale. Partly in reaction to negative opinion about the Black case and the raid itself, the Utah Attorney General's office assumed a position of ignoring the practice rather than actively prosecuting polygamists. This uneasy truce with law enforcement agencies throughout the state of Utah centered in part on the realization that the raids had backfired and in fact had served as a sort of crucible that forged a powerful bond for the fundamentalists.

Utah State Attorney General Paul Van Dam addressed this issue in a 1990 KUED television documentary, "A Matter of Principle."

> Every law enforcement officer in Utah knows there are tens of thousands of polygamists in the area, and they are clearly violating the law. Yet if we prosecute these men and women, we know from Short Creek that we will produce an incredible social disruption. Thousands of children must be cared for emotionally and otherwise, and that's a terribly expensive proposition.
>
> In addition, if you go after polygamists for illegal cohabitation, can you limit such a policy to polygamists, or do you pursue every couple in this state that is living together without benefit of a licensed marriage? And then, if you do make the arrests, where do you put these people in our crowded jail system? And finally, we know from experience that an arrest will not stop these people from

following what they consider to be a very important aspect of their religious faith.[1]

The Fundamentalist Family as Community

Legally, the practice of polygamy is still a felony in Utah but not in Arizona. However, the fundamentalists are no longer actively prosecuted by either state government. Because of this, the fundamentalists' policy of isolation has softened somewhat and intercourse with the world outside has increased. Yet when the fundamentalist does interract with outsiders it is from a family base.

The family traditionally has been defined as a group connected by consanguinity, place, economic responsibility, and tradition. The family is the unit of procreation and of the basic socialization of its children. Fundamentalist families most often fulfill the measure of each of these criteria and are in many ways more like a community— a series or group of families connected by place, economic interest, blood, and shared interests.

The majority of families in Colorado City/Hildale still believe in the principle of plural marriage, although statistics indicating polyga-mous households can be deceptive. In 1986, local officials estimated that there were 136 households living plural marriage. This figure does not include young people who have entered first marriages and are likely to eventually enter additional marriages, nor does it ac-knowledge the many family units that may cohabit in the same household. According to the 1986 special census of Colorado City/ Hildale, young people in the age group most likely to embark upon first marriages—20 to 29—represented 278 out of a total population of 3,467 (eight percent of the total population).

These communities are overwhelmingly youthful in their compo-sition: in 1986, eighty-three percent of the population was under the age of twenty-nine years compared with thirty-eight percent of Utah Mormons who were in the same age group (see figure).[2] Demographi-cally, Hildale and Colorado City were quite consistent in their age-group composition. Twelve percent of Hildale's population was be-tween the ages of thirty and forty-nine, while ten percent of Colorado City's population fell in this range.

Racially, virtual homogeneity marked the towns' population. Of a total of 2,099 people, all but three were Caucasian. Similarly, the

Utah Mormon population was ninety-eight percent white.[3] The communities boasted 261 houses, 229 of which were occupied. The population was almost equally divided between men and women—forty-nine percent were male and fifty-one percent were female, thereby discounting the belief that plural marriage offered a solution to a surplus of women. At least in this example there was a balance between men and women. The median age was 11.4 years, for males 10.5 years and for females 12.5 years.

The vast majority of housing units in Colorado City/Hildale were owned and/or occupied by members of the United Effort Plan. Out of 229 occupied units, members of the trust occupied 226. Twenty-nine of those houses were mobile homes or trailers. Only three of the units owned by the trust were rented to nine individuals outside the UEP.

The figures about household composition are also interesting. Eighty-seven percent of the people of Colorado City lived in households with more than one person. Only sixteen out of a total of 2,099 lived alone in non-family households. Groups of elderly sister wives often lived together in a household, a group arrangement peculiar to the fundamentalist people. Two hundred and sixty-five individuals lived in this type of family unit. An average of 8.1 persons lived in each household, and 8.5 people was the average family size. Considering that the families are in a state of flux and often not complete as to their final composition, the figure of 6.5 children per couple is a very rough estimate of the typical size of the fundamentalist family. Utah Mormons during the same time period had an average of three children per family unit.[4]

Out of 1,437 children under the age of eighteen, 1,129 or seventy-eight percent lived in families headed by a married couple. Seventy-eight children lived in households headed by women with no husbands present; no children lived in male-headed households without a woman present. Thirty-six children lived with other relatives; only two lived with non-relatives.

The situation for the elderly in Colorado City seemed to be extremely favorable. Only one person over the age of seventy-five lived alone; one individual over sixty-five lived with a nonrelative. The remaining twenty-three adults over the age of sixty-five either lived with relatives or as a group. Demographically, it is clear that Colorado City was overwhelmingly family oriented. Individuals clearly lived their lives in some sort of family unit.

Community as Family

As is almost always true in rural Utah Mormon communities, political leaders of Colorado City/Hildale frequently are powerful ecclesiastical leaders as well. The towns' sheriffs, mayors and council members come for the most part from the religious elite; this is yet another indication of how religion permeates every aspect of the fundamentalists' lives.

Fundamentalist society continues to be patriarchal. Although occasionally a woman is elected to a city council or serves on the police force, most secular leaders are men. The line of authority drawn from God to the fathers of these families creates for the fundamentalist people a sense of order, direction, and purpose.

Fundamentalist women choose to accept this lifestyle. They are not victims but are actors alongside their husbands in the drama of community building. Women play the primary role in the socialization of children. It is their responsibility to perpetuate the group's values and beliefs, to inculcate religious values and beliefs into the minds and behavior of the youth.

In Colorado City/Hildale the differences between men and women are stressed and in fact celebrated. Because of this, male/female gender roles can be easily characterized. Ideally, because of their roles as mothers, women spend the majority of their time in the home. Their lives are domestic, private, and clearly revolve around the rhythms and seasons of the family.

Some wives live together with their husbands in a single home, others live in private residences with their children. The varieties of familial arrangements are many and reflect the distinctive requirements of each individual family. There are no community guidelines or restrictions on what families can or cannot do. Each family is an autonomous unit with its own particular set of economic and emotional problems. Clearly children raised in families with numbers of adults to sustain them have a different sense of community than do children in monogamous homes. The line between community and family in polygamous society is lightly drawn.

Ultimate responsibility for his families (be they one or many) falls to the husband. Those with separate residences for each of their wives usually have a complicated schedule of daily or weekly visits to each separate group. This can place enormous responsibility on the shoulders of the women who must then take on the role of mother and father in the absence of their mates. Although these families look like single-parent households, they are in very important ways different. Typically, however, efforts are made to recognize the authority of the father even in his repeated absences. One study observed: "Father is regarded as a special person, the head of the kingdom, whose wishes must be respected."[5] Since the chain of authority runs from Jesus Christ to the father and then to the mother of the family, ultimate authority in matters of discipline of the children and of the families' finances rests with the father, although in most families the mother has authority to make important decisions in his absence. In certain ways these women have more autonomy in their marriages than do many women in monogamous unions; however, they don't have the constant presence and support of an exclusive spouse.

Female friendships between sister wives are often different from any relationship outside of plural marriage. These women are connected to each other by their common husband, their children, their religious covenants and commitment, and often as well by a common residence and shared traditions. This often forges a relationship difficult for outsiders to understand. Of course, women also form female friendships in the traditional ways of compatible personalities outside of the deferential or familial organization. However, all these women are joined in what they consider to be the work of the Lord.

Besides their roles as mothers, these women, as is true of women in other rural communities, still play a vital role in the physical sustenance of their families. Again, women's work mirrors the seasons— canning fruit and vegetables throughout the summer months, sewing clothes and quilts for their family members, maintaining households, and always teaching and caring for their children. Although an increasing number of women work outside the home in the town's factories and industries, the ideal is still work at home. All the money brought in by family members usually becomes part of the common pot and is distributed by the father to the separate units. Although there is a growth of industry within the town, many of the men are employed outside of the area in construction, business, agriculture or cattle ranching.

The different treatment of the sexes begins in the home at an early age. As is true in families outside of fundamentalism, both boys and girls are taught to be kind, modest, obedient, and cooperative.

Although men play an important role in the discipline of the children, women take the primary role in the rearing of children. Babies are often spaced naturally by lactation, usually a one- to two-year period during which the baby sleeps in the mother's room. Until children are three or four years of age they are almost solely in the care of their mothers or older sisters.

The socialization of these children includes play and work at early ages that is gender differentiated. One study suggests that "The physical as well as the spiritual relationship between the little boys and their father is heavily stressed. Mothers often mention to their sons that they are built just like fathers and that they will grow up to be like him. Because they are males, they will have a special relationship to God that a female can never have."[6] Nevertheless, all children are taught from birth about God, about what He has given them, and about the importance of maintaining a relationship with Him through prayer. Moreover, the fundamentalists have a very earthy, pragmatic conception of the role God plays in their everyday lives. They acknowledge His hand in all that they do. They are particularly conscious of His role in their families.

There is a strong work ethic in Colorado City/Hildale. Children in these households are expected to participate in household chores and are given assignments appropriate to their ages in the house and in the gardens and orchards. Children join their parents in community cooperative work projects, learning in youth the value of united effort. Most fundamentalists in Colorado City/Hildale adhere to a modest dress code. Long hair for women and short, neatly groomed hair for men is the norm for both adults and children.

The primary role in religious instruction falls to the parents. Formal education is conducted in the public elementary, middle, and high schools. School superintendent Alvin Barlow oversees a school system that matches state standards and prepares an increasing number of young people for education at nearby colleges.

Sam Barlow, the town's former sheriff, is candid about occasional problems with local youths, particularly young men. Like teenagers in other rural Utah towns, their consumption of beer and alcohol plagues parents and town officials alike. For fundamentalist youth, as for Mormon teenagers, drinking is a very potent signal of rebellion. Parents are ultimately responsible for the discipline of their own children and try to maintain strict control over the activities of young people. Social activities, like Friday night socials, are attended by all members of the community regardless of age. Although young men and women do leave Colorado City, many return. They often find it difficult to live in a society they are so unaccustomed to.

Rites of passage and age-differentiated rituals are similar to those of Mormon youth. The series of blessings, baptism, and other ordinances mirror those of the Mormon Church. Sunday worship services are also similar to the mother church in terms of tone and rhetoric. However, the fundamentalists meet together to listen to instruction from their ecclesiastical leaders and then break into family units for religious instruction—the equivalent of Mormon Sunday School and Primary activities. On Sundays the town's worthy men meet together for priesthood meetings and to participate in partaking of the sacrament.

Community interaction includes more than church activities; numerous school and social functions foster the feeling of unity throughout the ever-growing group. The family is the key unit in the process of the integration of the individual into the community. The two communities are not formed by groups of individuals but by groups of families. Ideally, the people place the good of the group over private interests.

The process of courtship is circumscribed by the value system—a system of ideas and beliefs inextricably connected to their theology. Because there is minimal contact with outsiders, most young people find future mates among their own group at church, school, or at work in the community. Many marriages are based on romantic love, although more important is a sense of personal revelation or approval of one's choice from God. Regardless, the fundamentalists do not rush into marriage ill advised. The typical process is slow and thoughtful. Men and women might approach their father or the group's patriarch with a proposal, and after discussion can choose to accept or reject the advice they have been given. Rulon Jeffs, the group's ecclesiastical leader and patriarch in 1990, does not have absolute power over these important decisions; however, those men and women who ask him for advice most likely will take it.

One of the most criticized aspects of fundamentalist culture, centralized authoritarian leadership, has been an effective means of social regulation. Social sanctions—both rewards and punishments—are established and administered by parents as well as ecclesiastical and town leaders who share the basic religious beliefs and values.

The United Effort Plan

In the eyes of those who continue to support the concept, the United Effort Plan helps the fundamentalists deal with the political and economic challenges of the twentieth century. The purposes of the religious charitable trust continue along the same lines as they did when it was established in 1942. It is the entity set up by the fundamentalists that is designed to own land for the group's benefit; but, more importantly, it is viewed as a continuation of the Mormon law of consecration and stewardship. The fundamentalists believe that living a cooperative lifestyle under the United Effort Plan helps them to live righteous lives.

The UEP has evolved somewhat since 1942 to meet specific needs, but it remains reflective of Mormon theology. In a practical sense, the UEP helped the fundamentalists support their large families. However, families of thirty or forty can strain any communal system. As a result, during the 1980s many of the town's wives and mothers began to join their husbands in the work force, working in local factories, schools, and even in businesses in the towns of Hurricane, St. George, or as far away as Cedar City. In many ways a fundamentalist family is well suited to compensate for the absence of working mothers. In a family where two or three mothers leave each day for work, other mothers can fill in as surrogates, giving the children loving, careful attention.

More important, however, than increasing the number of working adults in the community is the recent dramatic change from a pioneer community to an organized town government and more fully developed lifestyle. The titles to the real property where many of the fundamentalists live are held in the name of the UEP. Members in good standing are allocated property according to their "just needs and wants" and can build whatever form of house they choose, adding to them according to their personal ability. No houses built on UEP property are encumbered by mortgages, which is one reason why additions to houses often take so long to complete.

Many of the men are employed in the building trades and are able to cooperatively raise homes, barns or public structures. Every home is built either through this arrangement or by the father of the family. The men build wings or additions to their houses as their wives' and children's needs develop.

Growth is perhaps the most striking feature of Colorado City in

1992. This clearly is a community that is expanding rapidly. The fundamentalists continue to manage this community development through cooperation. Men and boys regularly meet on Saturday mornings to join in community work projects. One morning the men met to move throughout the town fixing fences; another morning the group painted the kitchen walls of the Leroy S. Johnson Meetinghouse. When certain projects demand more attention, the group gathers on other days of the week to unitedly solve community work problems.

Particular attention is currently being paid to the quality of life in this isolated town on the Arizona Strip. A zoo is being built through donated labor on a lovely stretch of wooded land along the creek bed. Again with cooperative volunteer labor, a park is being landscaped at the base of Maxwell Canyon on land owned by Hildale City. Both projects are being developed in a similar manner although title to the land is on the one hand held by the city and on the other by the UEP. Regardless, the people have responded to the calls for help with the same energy and enthusiasm.

UEP projects vary according to the needs of the people. Considerable diversity in ownership and operations reveal a complicated system designed to facilitate growth and produce an environment conducive to righteous living. They include ventures where: 1) the UEP owns only the land; 2) the UEP owns the land and has a partial investment in the business itself; 3) the business and/or property is privately owned; 4) a privately owned business is built on UEP land; and, 5) enterprises are built on city land with cooperative labor.

Through these efforts and by maintaining the purposes of its originators, the UEP continues to satisfy the legal definition of a charitable trust, having objectives and purposes that fall within the proscribed parameters of a legally defined charity. In a very real sense, the UEP is a medium through which the fundamentalists can grow in temporal and spiritual strength. Failure to comply with the purposes of the UEP is considered a serious offense and is potentially punishable, according to the fundamentalists' interpretation of their scriptures, by eternal damnation.

Many fundamentalist church services are held in the Leroy S. Johnson Meetinghouse, a structure built on land donated to the UEP. Members of the group built this huge building—42,000 square feet—easily as large as two Mormon stake centers, with funds and labor donated entirely by members of the Fundamentalist Church, as it has come to be commonly called. The building is a lovely, although somewhat overwhelmingly proportioned, space—240 feet by 175 feet—built with donated labor and religious contributions for the use of the group, who meet each Sunday for religious instruction from their president. Also, Friday evening group socials fill the central chamber with musical presentations, theatricals or community dances. Besides general Sunday services, meetings of the elders, annual conferences, and the meetings of church-affiliated organizations, the Johnson Meetinghouse is opened for large-scale civic functions like high school graduation.

Besides trying to maintain a delicate balance between church and state, the fundamentalists are careful to distinguish between the "Church" and the UEP. The UEP helps the fundamentalists provide for families in need of special help. According to some, the UEP provides homes and homesites for many who come to the town because of legal prosecution, imprisonment of family members, or the general climate of persecution. Others, however, maintain that Colorado City provides a sanctuary for those ostracized for their continued belief in the principle of a plurality of wives. Besides caring for those who come to the area for protection, the UEP furnishes support to elderly women who no longer have families to take care of them.

The UEP in place in 1992 is a religious trust; it is technically not a corporation. If in the future the trust were to be dissolved for any reason, according to the bylaws property would then be equally divided between the members of the trust. Despite the fact that some local industries and properties are located on UEP property, most working men and women have jobs in private industry, or in companies of their own where they earn wages. They continue to contribute as they are able to the bishop's storehouse and in turn obtain from it some of their provisions. They buy other commodities they need with the money they have earned. The regulation and division of property is left up to the board of trustees of the trust.

The Fundamentalist Church provides medical care to its members in the form of an infirmary staffed by nurses and midwives. The infirmary is built on UEP land; however, the clinic is an independent entity, not a UEP-owned or -operated project. A town cooperative store, also under local management, purchases food in bulk and passes the savings on to the trust members. Families hold down their food expenses by growing the main part of their fruits and vegetables and by bartering goods and services with their neighbors and friends.

Land leased to the Colorado City Improvement Association by the UEP reduced the costs of building Colorado City's elementary schools. The CCIA uses these leases as collateral to secure construction loans for school buildings. Likewise, the UEP provides land for the Hildale and Colorado City offices, community parks and recreation facilities for community use.

Trust beneficiaries include all individuals who have benefitted in any way from UEP land operations. Obviously, no religious qualification could restrict incidental benefits felt by members and non-members alike. Anyone who enjoys a visit to the town's zoo will benefit from not only the UEP land but the generous offering of donated labor from members of the community. Membership in the trust, however, is limited to the faithful who, it is assumed, act out of a spirit of religious consecration.

Uncomfortable Relations: Polygamy and Mormonism

The Mormon fundamentalists of northern Arizona/southern Utah present an intriguing challenge to mainstream American values. How have they persisted so long? What is it that gives this culture its resiliency, its continued appeal?

To begin with, it must be realized that one cannot understand the fundamentalist people apart from their theology. To them, the hand of God is evident in all that they do. Every choice they make has religious implications. Their lives are imbued with a sense of mission, of eternal purpose. In a time when many in the world outside are floundering in efforts to find themselves, here is a people with an incredible sense of who they are, what they want out of life, and how to get it. The men and women of Colorado City/Hildale believe that it is only through living the commandments of God that one can be truly happy and receive exaltation.

The large families of fundamentalist culture often lend to individuals a stability and sense of shared responsibility that is too frequently absent in modern society. These people answer the scriptural question in maintaining that they are their brothers' keepers. This mindfulness of others functions as a social cement that binds the people together. The fundamentalist value system that stresses cooperation over individualism, the importance of the family, ethical leadership, and obedience and respect for authority has helped fundamentalism not only to grow but to thrive.

Finally, the relative isolation of this people has allowed them to take almost exclusive control over the socialization of their children and to control the exposure of their children to outside influences. Supervised interaction with outsiders holding other ideas and values has helped the fundamentalists solidify their values in the minds and behaviors of their young people. Social development has been encouraged in harmony with cultural values. Individual self-interest generally is tempered in the name of the community good. Whether one agrees or disagrees with this aspect of their culture, it is without doubt one element that has facilitated their survival and growth.

This ability of the fundamentalists to not only hang on but to grow at an extraordinary rate directly challenges the Mormon Church, which continues to excommunicate the fundamentalists as it discovers them. The stubborn tenacity with which the fundamentalists cling to their beliefs and their lifestyle is a direct affront to the authority of Church leaders.

After 1950, Church leaders rarely mentioned the subject of plural marriage in general conference sermons or in other public addresses to the Saints. When they did, as in a 1974 speech by Church President Spencer W. Kimball (another specialist in dealing with the fundamentalists), it was again to warn members not to associate with the various cults. Avoiding the subject rather than dealing with the questions it presented was one way to prevent confusion among the members or difficulties with the doctrine.

The official policy of the Church of Jesus Christ of Latter-day Saints toward the polygamists is essentially the same in 1990 as it was during the 1930s. Despite the confused and extended period of ambiguity that followed the Manifesto, during which many polygamous marriages were performed, after the 1930s the Church moved in a consistent and determined course of separation from the practice (and even the history) of Mormon polygamy.

As early as 1935, the Mormon doctrine of plural marriage was relegated to a position of relative obscurity as a hypothetical condition of the afterlife that should not be questioned, or necessarily understood, until another time.

The Priesthood Correlation movement of the 1970s severely restricted virtually all references to polygamy in official Church literature, lesson manuals, pamphlets, and public discourse. This omission was not backed by any written or official directive; it was more a general unspoken yet pervasive assumption that difficult doctrinal or historical topics, including polygamy, were not to be mentioned. One instance of purposeful removal of the subject of polygamy from official literature was the deletion of a group picture of proud jailed pioneer polygamists from the second edition of *My Kingdom Shall Roll Forth*.[7] In contrast to the fiery defense of the Principle in pioneer times, this quiet movement away from the topic has resulted in its almost complete neglect.

In the 1970s and 1980s polygamy was frequently in the news. Each time it made the headlines the Church pointed to its history of separation rather than of shared tradition. There was the notorious violence of the LeBaron clan which made headlines in 1977, and the 24 July 1984 Lafferty murders. The trial of the former Murray City policeman and polygamist Royston Potter, fired in 1982 for his polygamous lifestyle, again brought to the surface the troubling questions of freedom of religion which Mormon polygamy raises. The 1979 shooting of John Singer in Marion, Utah after years of his insistent flouting of state authority was evidence of the tension that continued between the polygamist and the state. The bombing of the Mormon Kamas Stake Center by John Singer's polygamous son-in-law, Adam Swapp, in 1988 demonstrated the explosive tension that exists for these people so willing to sacrifice all for their beliefs. In reaction to these events, each of which received national attention, the Church, as it had from the 1930s, quickly denied having any connection with polygamy, explaining that it had already dealt with these men and women in private Church courts.

One hundred years after the Manifesto, Mormons are left with the same unanswered doctrinal questions as were Church members a hundred years ago. The Manifesto suspended the practice of polygamy, but made no mention of the Principle itself. Successive presidents of the Church struggled with this inconsistency either by trying to make the Principle fit into Mormon theology or (more often) by avoiding the topic altogether. However, they spent most of their energy punishing offenders and trying to halt the practice—a policy which divided the fundamentalists from official Church society and identified the Church as a mainstream group which, like most of the rest of middle America, scorned the practice. Ultimately, the Church's accommodation to the world—the reaching out for recognition—centered on shared Christian experiences, and did not stress those practices or beliefs which functioned as too severe or harsh boundaries.

By 1990, orthodox Mormons no longer heard elaborations on the doctrine of a plurality of wives in conference addresses. Nor did they listen to amusing anecdotes about the intricacies of polygamous pioneer life. The polygamist Joseph Smith or Brigham Young was rarely acknowledged as such. It was as if the modern Church had divorced or separated itself from a large and important part of its historical past.

Polygamists continue to be excommunicated and denied both entrance into Mormon temples and into fellowship with the body of the LDS Church. These facts corroborate the incredible distance the two groups have moved in the seventy-year time period from 1920 to 1990. The lines dividing the polygamist from the parent church are both wide and deep, and probably unbridgeable. And it seems likely that among the challenges of the next century, Mormonism will continue to confront polygamy. It is even perhaps possible that the legal restrictions on polygamy will be lifted. Were that to happen, one can only speculate at the complications it would produce for Church and government leaders. However that may be, one can confidently predict that even if they merely continue in their present state, the principle of plural marriage and its fundamentalist practitioners will continue to present a challenge to Church and government alike.

Fundamentalist Families Involved in the 1953 Raid on Short Creek, Arizona[1]

Danny Barlow 21 (years of age in 1953)
w. Elnora Black 20
    Susanna 3
    Daniel 2
    Madeline two weeks
w. Edith 15 (daughter of Leonard Black)
w. Lorna Allred (daughter of Owen Allred)

Joseph Barlow 26
w. Clea Black 23 (daughter of Leonard Black)
    Maureen 7
    Joseph I., Jr. 5
    Milword 3
    Cynthia 1
    baby
w. Leta 22 (daughter of Leonard Black)
    Colleen 6
    Mattie 5
    Leonard 3
    Israel Yeates 1

w. Marian Broadbent 19
   John Leslie 2
   baby

Louis Barlow 27
  w. Lucy Johnson 25
    Bonnie 9
    Lehi 6
    Donald Nathan 3
    Metina Viola 1
  w. Isabell 24
    Judy Carol 8
    Louis Jessop 6
    Isabell 4
    Arden 2
  w. Adair 15

David Bateman 25
  w. Arleen Jessop 24
    April Dawn 5
    David Randall 4
    Coral Jane 2
    Connell Jessop 1

Lee Bistline 26
  w. Elaine Jessop 20
    Melanie 3
    Kerry Lee 2
    baby 6 months
  w. Naomi Zitting 16

Leonard Black 46
  w. Verna Colvin 45
    Clea 23 (Joe Barlow's wife)
    Leta 20 (Joe Barlow's wife)
    Beth 18 (Lynn Cooke's wife)
    Verena Cooke (Jack Cooke's wife) 16
    Edith 14
    Calvin 12
    Ralph 11
    Orlin 10

       Floyd Evan 9
       Mary 7
  w. Lorna Johnson 29 (daughter of Warren Johnson, Leroy
       Johnson's sister)
       Martin 11
       Louise 10
       Luella 9
       Emaline 6
       Issac 3
       Vernon Miles 1
  w. Vera Johnson 34 (daughter of Warren Johnson, Leroy Johnson's
       sister)
       Elsie 8
       Orsen 17
       Lillian 12
       Emily 6
       Wilford Marshal 5
       Ivan Francis 3
       Vaughn 1

Warren Black 52
  w. Ruth Walker 50
       Rachel 24
       Lois 22 (Spencer Johnson's wife)
       Viola 21 (Lynn Hunter's wife)
       Elden 19
       Leslie 16
       Shirley 15 (Spencer Johnson's wife)
       Ina 13
       Linda 11
       Gerald 9[2]
       Alice 8
  w. Esther Johnson 23 (daughter of Price Johnson)
       Isaac Clifton 6
       Theron Elvin 4
       Easton 3
       Sterling Allen 2
       Arvin Lee 1

David Broadbent 24
  w. Viola Johnson 23

      Fauneta 7
      Ester 5
      Kristene 3
      Lydia infant
  w. Fawn Stubbs 15
      infant
  w. Rula Kunz 15 (daugher of Morris Kunz)
      infant

Lauren Broadbent 22
  w. Lucille 19
      Louise Sherry 1

Jack Cooke 23
  w. Verena Black 16 (daughter of Leonard Black)
      baby—4 months
  w. Caroline Sope Zitting 17
      Robert Eugene 3 months
  w. Eva Jessop 14

Lynn Cooke 28
  w. Coleen Jenson 25
      Donavon Lynn 2
      two or three unidentified
  w. Beth Black 18
      Charlotte 1
      Clark Cordell 6 months

William B. Cooke 62
  w. Myrtle 60
      Older children over 18
      Alice
      Vera
      Erna
      Lynn
      Jack
      Richard 15
  w. Josephine Balmforth 41
      Dorothy 10
      Laura Adell 8
      James Fredrick 3

Reginia 1
Two others unidentified
Children by former husband:
Roger Nyborg 15
Dwight Nyborg 13
Noal Terry Nyborg 10
w. Rachel Balmforth 29
Thelma Rae 8
Charles Benjamin 4
Janice 2
Others unidentified
w. Alberta Balmforth 60
Josephine 41
Rachel 29
Stephen 18

Carl Holm 38
w. Margorie Morrison 33
Carl Jr. 11
Vickie 6
Susan Elizabeth 3
Marianne 1
w. Sharon Hunter 15
w. Florence Jessop 20
Con Mark 2
baby
w. Louise Jessop 18
baby
w. Esther Johnson Barlow 31 (daughter of Leroy Johnson)
by John Y. Barlow:
Warren 15
Edwin 11
Freddie 10
Esther 8
Linnie 6
Two unidentified
by Holm:
Paul Raymond 2
baby
w. Rachel Black (daughter of Warren Black) 24

Treena Ruth 5
Terry Nathaniel 2

Lynn Hunter 32
  w. Viola Black Hunter 21
    Bonnie Lee 4
    Duron Lynn 2
    Patricia 4 months

Dan Jessop 34
  w. Dorothy Norvell 23
    Dennis Calvin 5
    Dan Mathew 5
    Melissa Emma 1
    Two children unidentified
  w. Dorothy Elizabeth Woodruff 16
    Ethel 1

Edson P. Jessop 33
  w. Margaret Lucille Hunter 28
    Carol Lynn 7
    Margaret Lucille 5
    La Donna 3
    Nora Jean 1
    One more unidentified (older)
  w. Evelyn Camilla Fisher 26
    Lydia Marie 8
    Lorine 6
    One unidentified girl 3
  w. Irene Nielson 27
    Miriam 2
    Bob
  w. Lulu Alyne Bistline 30
    Shariel 7
    Sharene 7
    Val 3
    One son by Jay Jessop[3]
  w. Leota Dockstader 33
    by Jay Jessop:
    Joy L. 12

Diana 10
by Edson:
Jeffrey Porter 7
Brian Dale 5
Beck La Mar 3

Fred Jessop 46
   w. Lydia Johnson 35
   w. Parmelia Johnson 35
   w. Marriette Carling 35

Joseph Jessop, Sr. 80
   First and second wives dead
      Thomas 21
      Albert 19
      Willie 14
      Eller 14
      David 10
      Joseph 10
      Martin Hyrum 9
      Mable Annie 3
   w. Emma Norvel 50

Joseph S. Jessop, II 30
   w. Norda Johnson 20 (daughter of Warren Johnson)
      Meleta 1
   w. Rose Elise Hammon 20
      Rose Ilene 2

Richard S. Jessop 52
   w. Ida Johnson 46
      Jeremiah 24
      Billie 21
      Ray 17
      Annie 16
      Merill 15
      Loise 14
      Virginia 12
      Merlin S. 8
      Joann Marie 5

w. Lola 36
    Eva Jessop 14
    Johnny 13
    Frank Russell 9
    Irene 7
    Richard Glenn 1
w. Fern Carlson Shapley 33
    Fern Lorraine Jessop 14 (Jerry Jessop's wife)
    William 10
    Sadie 5
    Timothy Seth Jessop 1
w. Artemishie Johnson 20 (daughter of Warren Johnson)
    Ernest Randolph 2
    baby 1
w. Jennie May Bistline 45
    Bennie 18
    Dannie 16
    Jennie May Bistline Jessop (Dan Jessop's wife)
    Lee
    Alyne Bistline Jessop (Edson Jessop's wife)
    Three unidentified children

Leroy Johnson 64
w. Josephine Ford 60
    Orville
    Eda
    Parmellia
w. Mae Bateman 55
w. Gwendolyn Balmforth 24
    Stephen 3
    La Mar 1
    Foster children:
    Sam Barlow
    Truman Barlow
    Alwin Barlow
    Veta Barlow
    Ada Rae Barlow
w. Sarah Elizabeth Barlow 29
    John 11
    Ralph 10

      Ada 8
      Leona 6
      Sarah Elizabeth 2
      baby
   w. Wilma Black 44
      S. Morley 6
   w. Mildred Barlow 20

Melvin Johnson 39
   w. Ruth Nora Dean 34
      Rummell 16
      Stewart 15
      Freddie 12
      La Var Dean 8
      Mark Woodruff 6
      Rosemary 4
      Sterling Thomas 3
      Peggy 2
      Sylvia 1
   w. Hulenna Woodruff 25

Orvil Johnson 29
   w. Naomi Bateman 24
      Eleanor 8
      Orvil Leroy 5
      Anna 3
      Jeremiah Morgan 1
   w. Ada Ray Barlow 13

Price Johnson 67 (Leroy Johnson's brother)
   w. Helen Lucy Hull 43
      Ester Johnson 23
      Neta Johnson Dockstader 21
      Earl 20
      Eleanor Johnson Pratt 17
      Isabel 15
      Shirll 13
      Ann 10
      Joseph Lyman 9
      Alfred Alma 7
      Two more younger

Spencer Johnson 30
    w. Lois Black 22 (daughter of Leonard Black)
        Selma 5
        Violet 4
        Charles Spencer 2
        Larry 1
    w. Shirley Black 15 (daughter of Warren Black, sister to Lois)

Warren (Elmer) Johnson 62
    w. Viola Spencer 60
        Lorna (wife of Leonard Black)
        Vera (wife of Leonard Black)
        Artemishia (wife of Richard Jessop)
    w. Clela Stokes Cooke 31
        by Cooke:
        Billy 12
        Colleen 10
        Another boy
        by Johnson:
        Verl Merlon 7
        Nelda 5
        Owen Assel 4
        June 2
        baby
    w. Jeannine Stubbs 21
        Lillie 2
        baby

Floyd Otto Spencer 53
    w. Esther Le Baron 32
        Six children
        Pauline 3

Lawrence Stubbs 45
    w. Rhoda Olsen 37
        Fawn Stubbs 15 (wife of David Broadbent)
        David 13
        Rhodonito 10
        Ritchie Lamar 7
        Priscilla 3
    w. Genevieve Pratt 44

Jeannine Stubbs 22
Howard 19
Adair 15
Lowrana 16
Guy 10
Laurel 8
Lane Ritchie 7
Kimball Pratt 3

Jerry Williams 40
  w. Fayila Nareen Blackmore 33
    Rosalyn Marie 5 months
    Five little boys unidentified

Summary of Data

Total number of men: 31

Total number of individual family units: 90

Total number of living women: 88

Number of children per female: 3.27

Number of children per male: 9.1

Married women under eighteen: 15

Average age of males: 39.6

Average age of females: 26.9

Females with no children: 14

Excluding the sixteen women under eighteen years—32 women with average age at first birth under eighteen years

Average age at first birth: 17

Statement by Arizona Governor Howard Pyle

CONFIDENTIAL   CONFIDENTIAL   CONFIDENTIAL

The following tentative text of a statement by Governor Howard Pyle MUST be held in strictest confidence until the moment delivery begins on the combined radio networks, expected to be between 9 A.M. and 12 noon on *SUNDAY, JULY 26, 1953*.

IT IS EMPHASIZED THAT THIS TEXT MATTER IS SUBJECT TO CORRECTION AND REVISION BY RADIO FROM THE SCENE UP UNTIL THE ACTUAL MOMENT DELIVERY BEGINS. PLEASE FOLLOW BROADCAST FOR ANY NECESSARY REVISIONS, OR CHECK DIRECTLY WITH GOVERNOR PYLE AT HIS OFFICE IMMEDIATELY AFTER DELIVERY.

CONFIDENTIAL   CONFIDENTIAL   CONFIDENTIAL

STATEMENT BY GOVERNOR PYLE

Before dawn today the State of Arizona began and now has substantially concluded a momentous police action against insurrection within her own borders.

Arizona has mobilized and used its total police power to protect the lives and future of 263 children. They are the product and the victims of the foulest conspiracy you could possibly imagine.

More than 120 peace officers moved into Short Creek, in Mohave County, at 4 o'clock this morning. They have arrested almost the entire population of a community dedicated to the production of white slaves who are without hope of escaping this degrading slavery from the moment of their birth.

Highly competent investigators have been unable to find a single instance in the last decade of a girl child reaching the age of 15 without having been forced into a shameful mockery of marriage.

The State of Arizona is fulfilling today one of every state's deepest obligations . . . to protect and defend the helpless.

The State is moving at once to seek through the courts the custody of these 263 children, all under the age of 18. They are the innocent chattels of a lawless commercial undertaking of wicked design and ruthlessly exercised power. This in turn is the co-operative enterprise of five or six coldly calculating men who direct all of the operations and reap all of the profits, and are the evil heart of the insurrection itself.

It is no surprise that some of these vicious conspirators are former convicts.

Warrants were carried into Short Creek this morning for 35 men, many of them related, who include not only a hard core of plotters but a wider circle of fawning beneficiaries of this conspiracy that the State of Arizona is determined to end right now and completely.

As the highest authority in Arizona, on whom is laid the Constitutional injunction to "take care that the laws be faithfully executed," I have taken the ultimate responsibility for setting into motion the actions that will end this insurrection.

It should be clearly understood at the same time that so complicated an operation has required and has received the co-operation of many elements of our government . . . and has been undertaken only as a last desperate resort.

In many situations of the last few years I have reminded the people of Arizona that law enforcement is primarily a county problem—until such time as the counties themselves declare or by their actions prove that they are able no longer to fulfill their functions.

Mohave county appealed for state intervention to end this insurrection. The county's plea came to your governor from the Honorable J.W. Faulkner, Mohave county's highest legal authority as judge of the superior court there, in March of 1951, when I had been on duty only two months.

Judge Faulkner recited the almost incredible details of this conspiracy . . . details almost revoltingly incomprehensible at this mid-point of the 20th century. The sheer magnitude of the situation demanded immediate action, but even more urgently required proof beyond any possible doubt.

Hence it is that 26 months have passed since Judge Faulkner's first letter came to me. The investigation has been most thorough. Two attorneys general have participated. Appalled successive Legislatures have approved funds for every phase of the investigation . . . and it has been from the very beginning a disturbing undertaking.

It has been, frankly, the one and only real sorrow of my administration, intruding as it has on a hundred other problems of state, and occupying the time and energy of scores of men and women. There had to be absolute certainty that in the end the innocent should be as securely protected as the guilty were severely punished.

Before a single complaint was drawn, or a single warrant prepared, or the first preliminary order for today's action issued, we had to be certain beyond the last shadow of doubt.

All doubt is erased when it is realized that in the evidence the State has accumulated there are multiple instances of statutory rape, adultery, bigamy, open and notorious cohabitation, contributing to the delinquency of minors, marrying the spouse of another, and an all-embracing conspiracy to commit all of these crimes, along with various instances of income tax evasion, failure to comply with Arizona's corporation laws, misappropriation of school funds, improper use of school facilities, and falsification of public records.

The leaders of this mass violation of so many of our laws have boasted directly to Mohave county officers that their operations have grown so great that the State of Arizona was powerless to interfere.

They have been shielded, as you know, by the geographic circumstances of Arizona's northernmost territory . . . the region beyond the Grand Canyon that is best known as "The Strip."

This is a land of high plateaus, dense forests, great breaks and gorges, rolling arid lands, and intense color . . . a land squeezed between the even higher plateaus of Utah and the Grand Canyon of Arizona.

The community of Short Creek is 400 miles by the shortest road from the Mohave county seat of Kingman. Short Creek is unique among Arizona communities in that some of its dwellings actually are in another state.

All of the residents of Short Creek who live in Utah have been charged with the crimes they have committed in Arizona. We have neither enlisted nor encouraged the State of Utah to take action simultaneous with or parallel to our own, for it is a mass insurrection against the State of Arizona that we seek to suppress.

To the best of our knowledge and information, there are only five residents of Short Creek who are in NO way involved in this situation. They are Mr. and Mrs. Jonreed Lauritzen, Mr. and Mrs. Alfonso Nyborg, and Don Covington. They are old residents of a colorful part of Arizona who have found themselves surrounded by this conspiracy, and have given invaluable help in the elimination we have now undertaken.

Massive cliffs rearing north of Short Creek's little central street provide a natural rock barrier to the north. To the east and west are the sweeping expanses of dry and almost barren plateaus before the forests begin. To the south there is the Grand Canyon.

It is in this most isolated of all Arizona communities that this foulest of conspiracies has flourished and expanded in a terrifying geometric progression. Here has been a community entirely dedicated to the warped philosophy that a small handful of greedy and licentious men should have the right and the power to control the destiny of every human soul in the community.

Here is a community—many of the women, sadly, right along with the men—unalterably dedicated to the wicked theory that every maturing girl child should be forced into the bondage of multiple wifehood with men of all ages for the sole purpose of producing more children to be reared to become more chattels of this totally lawless enterprise.

Some of the boys have escaped this dreadful and dreary life. But the girls . . . no.

The very institutions such as the schools, upon which we all depend for the cultivation of the ideals that have made the nation great and Arizona great, have been perverted to the inculcation in our young of a devotion to this rank and fetid distortion of all of our basic rights and ideals.

The very operation of this insurrectional conspiracy, with its complete disregard of all decency and of all law, have served to expand the population of Short Creek until it is probably the second largest community in Mohave County.

Sixteen years ago it was nothing. You may recall at that time two individuals, who were almost all of the male population of Short Creek, were sent to the Arizona State Prison to serve terms for flagrant violations of the state's moral laws.

They had half a dozen wives.

But their prison terms ended...they returned to Short Creek... and now the two have expanded to the 35 men named in warrants today ...and their wives have increased from half a dozen to 85.

The criminally deadly part is that their children under legal age now number the 263 we mentioned earlier.

It is easy to see from this rapid expansion that in another 10 years the population of Short Creek would be in the thousands, and an army would not be sufficient to end the greater insurrection and defiance of all that is right.

Of the 120 persons named in warrants as being involved in this ever-growing conspiracy, 83 have their principal homes in Arizona. The rest base their operations in Utah, although a number of these have additional homes in Arizona.

Not all of the men for whom warrants have been issued have been arrested, but it is fully anticipated that they will be. Those who have crossed or subsequently cross the state line into Arizona during the course of the police operations will be jailed on the Arizona warrants. Those who elect to remain in Utah will be sought on warrants of extradition.

This may take days or weeks, but it WILL be done. It is regrettable that this action had to be undertaken on a Sunday, but there were a number of vital considerations. There has been a community entertainment the last day or two in Short Creek that has attracted the maximum number of those named in warrants. Today the maximum number of police officers have been free from other duties. And the situation they have moved against has been as godless as anything we have ever known.

It should be emphasized here that we have gone to almost unbelievable lengths to insure that the rights of no one are violated or even jeopardized in this action.

Moving into Short Creek right behind the officers with their warrants have been the courts. Superior Judge J. Smith Gibbons of Apache County has been acting as committing magistrate and has observed every legal propriety in holding the principal defendants to answer for trial in superior court as he also ordered these principal defendants to jail in Kingman, the county seat.

The defendants are being transported right now to Kingman to await release on bail for those who are able to provide it or who have it provided for them. These are the men and some of the more ardently involved women.

In the case of the unwilling wives and the children, the action has been parallel but entirely different. Juvenile judges have gone along with the other superior court judges.

Judge Lorna Lockwood of Maricopa county, whose understanding in juvenile matters is widely recognized, and Judge Faulkner himself, have started and for some time will continue a series of juvenile court actions through which the State of Arizona expects to be able to provide protection for the 263 children.

This protection is very inclusive. It is calculated, under Arizona's laws, to give these children every possible garment of secrecy so that in years to come, the action in which they are now involved cannot appear anywhere as a matter of public record.

Right along with the courts have gone trained social workers. A full staff from the state department of public welfare has gone along with the officers and the courts to take immediate custody of those children the courts decide should be brought under the protection of the State of Arizona.

There hasn't been and there won't be any hardship in all of this. Facilities, equipment, and supplies have been sent into the area to be prepared to feed every defendant and every innocent victim, and every officer and participating state official, as long as may be necessary.

There is a medical staff to guard against any health contingency, and facilities are provided to care for everyone. There has been and there will be NO invasion of homes or quarters, for our people have with them a complete miniature tent city which by now has been erected in unused community space, and will house the state's personnel for as long as such housing is necessary.

Representing the state department of law in the filing of complaints, the issuance of warrants, and the general direction of all legal phases of this operation, is the attorney general himself, Ross Jones.

He has with him two of his assistants, Paul LaPrade and Kent Blake. LaPrade and Blake are the men who have conducted the preparation of all the cases designed to shatter for all time this insurrection and the conspiracy that supports it.

To climax their work and beginning the conclusive phase of this operation, I signed an official proclamation on July first, declaring a state of insurrection to exist in Mohave County and in the community of Short Creek.

Secretary of State Wesley Bolin and State Auditor Jewell Jordan have co-operated fully in handling the transfer of funds, especially appropriated to the Governor's office for this purpose, to the office of the attorney general . . . and in the proper and orderly expenditures of sums from that appropriation.

As your governor, I have been at my desk since early this morning, ready to issue any order or authorization to meet changing plans or unforeseen circumstances. I have been in complete and almost instantaneous contact with the operation from its beginning, through my administrative assistant who is at the scene.

To the eternal credit of the press and radio of Arizona, none of this complex operation has been publicized in advance in any way, although representatives of all media have been full appraised of every development during the entire 26 months of preparation. The whole purpose of this operation would have been destroyed had any part of it been known generally in advance.

Now this most necessary cloak of secrecy is removed.

From here on out and no doubt for some time to come you will be hearing directly from press and radio correspondents whose names you know well and in whom you have implicit faith.

They have gone right along with the officers and the courts, to observe and report everything.

While we leave the rest of the details of this fantastic insurrection and its ending in their hands, it must be reiterated that the State of Arizona is unalterably pledged and determined to stop this monstrous and evil growth before it becomes a cancer of a sort that is beyond hope of human repair.

Even if the letter of the law didn't exist as it does . . . common decency demands this.

These children have the rights of all native-born Americans—the rights that were written into the Declaration of Independence. . . .

The right to life, liberty, and the pursuit of happiness . . . and as has so often been emphasized since, happiness of their own choosing. . . .

The State of Arizona is determined to insure that they have those rights for the remainder of their lives.

We could do no less than this.[1]

Notes

PREFACE
1. *Arizona Republic*, 27 July 1953.

CHAPTER 1
1. Mormon Apostle Orson Pratt remembered twenty-four years after Joseph Smith's death that in early 1832 "Joseph told individuals, then in the Church, that he had inquired of the Lord concerning the principle of plurality of wives, and he received for answer that the principle of taking more wives than one is a true principle, but the time had not yet come for it to be practiced." *Journal of Discourses*, vol. 13 (London and Liverpool: Latter-day Saint Book Depot, 1854–86), p. 192. As Mormon historian Max Parkin concluded, "It appears that polygamy was a secret practice in Kirtland in the 1830s and the Church, or rather the Church's Prophet, neither had the intention of making it a public matter nor at that early date making it a principle of the Mormon faith. . . . Within the Church, the conflict of the period was accentuated by the few who understood the new principle, and by others who mispracticed it." Parkin, p. 174.

2. Historian Lawrence Foster has emphasized the importance of the patriarchal foundation of plural marriage. "In some respects plural marriage may be seen as an outgrowth of characteristic American values, in particular, an attempt to restore earlier patriarchal patterns in marriage that were under attack in the period. At the deepest level, it was a fundamental protest against the careless individualism of romantic love, which seemed to threaten the very roots of family life and social stability. Lawrence Foster, *Religion and Sexuality: Three American Communal Experiments of the Nineteenth Century* (New York: Oxford University Press, 1981), p. 139. A plurality of wives facilitated the process through which Smith instituted the patriarchal ordering of society among the Mormons. In the plural union the male was the absolute center of the family, the nexus from which all authority, all direction flowed. Virtually as important was a quorum of sister wives united in their efforts to build both the family and

the kingdom. Thus, Mormons believed that both theologically and socially plural marriage helped them establish a more fundamentally sound social organization upon which the kingdom of God on the earth could be built.

3. See Valeen Tippetts Avery and Linda King Newell, *Mormon Enigma: Emma Hale Smith* (New York: Doubleday and Co., Inc., 1984); Davis Bitton, "Mormon Polygamy: A Review Article," *Journal of Mormon History* 4(1977): 106–11; Lawrence Foster, *Religion and Sexuality*; Richard S. Van Wagoner, "Mormon Polyandry in Nauvoo," *Dialogue* 18(Fall 1985):67–83.

4. According to historian Richard Van Wagoner, "Polygamy, a criminal act under the 1833 Illinois Anti-Bigamy Laws, was so unacceptable to monogamous nineteenth-century American society that Joseph could introduce it only in absolute secrecy." Richard S. Van Wagoner, *Mormon Polygamy: A History*, (Salt Lake City: Signature Books, 1986), p. 17.

5. See Robert B. Flanders, *Nauvoo: Kingdom on the Mississippi* (Urbana: University of Illinois Press, 1965); Marvin S. Hill, *Quest for Refuge* (Salt Lake City: Signature Press, 1989); and David E. Miller and Della S. Miller, *Nauvoo: The City of Joseph* (Santa Barbara: Peregrine Press, 1974).

6. Leonard J. Arrington, *Brigham Young: American Moses* (New York: Alfred A. Knopf, 1985).

7. *Deseret News*, 14 September 1852.

8. Gustive O. Larson, *The Americanization of Utah for Statehood* (San Marino: The Huntington Library, 1971).

9. Stanley Ivins, "Notes on Mormon Polygamy," *Western Humanities Review* 10(Summer 1956):229–39. Lowell C. Bennion in "The Geography of Polygamy Among the Mormons in 1880," an unpublished paper delivered at the Mormon History Association Conference held in May 1984 at Provo, Utah, and Leonard J. Arrington and David Bitton in *The Mormon Experience* (New York: Alfred A. Knopf, 1979), suggest lower figures than those in Ivins's 1956 study. Arrington and Bitton suggest that the figures differed for men and women. They conclude that 5 percent of Mormon males, 12 percent of Mormon women and 10 percent of Mormon children were from polygamous households. Jessie Embry in her study *Mormon Polygamous Families* (Salt Lake City: University of Utah Press, 1987) supports the estimate of 10 percent.

10. These included the 1862 Morrill Act, introduced by Representative Justin S. Morrill of Vermont, which prohibited plural marriage in the territories, disincorporated the Mormon Church, and restricted the Church's ownership of property to $50,000. The Utah Legislature asked Congress to repeal the act in 1867. Because of the Civil War and the isolated location of the Mormons the law was not enforced. In 1870, Illinois Representative Shelby M. Cullom introduced the Cullom Bill which called for greater federal control over Utah Territory and attempted to strengthen the Morrill Act. The bill failed to pass. The only anti-polygamy bill to successfully pass during the 1870s was the 1874 Poland Act, introduced by Vermont's Lake P. Poland, which gave district courts all civil and criminal jurisdiction and limited the probate courts to matters of estate settlement, guardianship, and divorce.

11. George Reynolds was the personal secretary to Brigham Young and was the husband to two Mormon women. He willingly surrendered himself to

federal officials in order to test the legitimacy of the laws restricting plural marriage. The court found Reynolds guilty. Although Reynolds lost his appeal before the United States Supreme Court, *Reynolds* v. *United States* would be of enduring significance for all religious citizens of the United States. Chief Justice Waite, on 6 January 1879 (when it was finally decided by the Supreme Court), spoke for the court when he said, "Laws are made for the government of actions and while they cannot interfere with mere religious belief and opinions, they may with practices." Waite further argued that allowing a religious organization to do whatever it desired in the name of religion would result in anarchy, allowing "professed doctrines of religious belief [to be] superior to the law of the land and in effect to permit every citizen to become a law unto himself. Government could exist only in name under such circumstances." Waite also noted that "In matters of opinion, and especially in matters of religious belief all men are free. But parallel with and dominating over this is the obligation which every member of society owes to that society; that is, obedience to the law." *Reynolds* v. *United States*, 8 Otto 145(1879), pp. 166–68. See also Orma Linford, "The Mormons and the Law: The Polygamy Cases," Ph.D. dissertation, University of Wisconsin, 1964.

12. John Higham, *Strangers in the Land* (New Brunswick, New Jersey: Rutgers University Press, 1955), p. 4.

13. Van Wagoner, *Mormon Polygamy*, pp. 158–72.

14. James B. Allen and Glen M. Leonard, *The Story of the Latter-day Saints* (Salt Lake City: Deseret Book, 1976), p. 396.

15. Ibid., p. 398. For further information about the underground period and the judicial crusade see also Martha Sonntag Bradley, "'Hide and Seek': Children on the Underground," *Utah Historical Quarterly* 51(Spring 1983): 133–53; Kimberly James Jensen, "Between Two Fires: Women on the 'Underground' of Mormon Polygamy," M.A. thesis, Brigham Young University, 1981; Gustive O. Larson, *The Americanization of Utah for Statehood*; Edwin Brown Firmage and Richard Collin Mangrum, *Zion in the Courts: A Legal History of the Church of Jesus Christ of Latter-day Saints, 1830–1900* (Urbana and Chicago: University of Illinois Press, 1988); and Orma Linford, "The Mormons and the Law: The Polygamy Cases," Ph.D. dissertation, University of Wisconsin, 1964. According to Larson, the Utah court convicted and sentenced three polygamists by the end of 1884. By December of the next year the court had indicted eighty more and convicted twenty-three. Seventeen of those indicted promised to abandon polygamy and obey the law in the future, thereby avoiding punishment (p. 110). The court convicted many leaders of the Church for cohabitation. "From the president down through the apostles and the Presiding Bishopric during the period, no general authority was a monogamist.... The same was true of most bishops and stake presidents, as well as, for all practical purposes, their counselors" (Arrington and Bitton, p. 204). Thus, as law professor Edwin Firmage notes, "the conviction and imprisonment of polygamists paralyzed Mormon society by removing its leadership" (Firmage, p. 168).

16. Ibid., p. 402.

17. The Edmunds-Tucker Act included provisions designed to effectively destroy the Church as a political and economic entity. It dissolved the Church as

a legal entity, requiring it to forfeit all property in excess of $50,000, and it closed the Perpetual Emigration Fund. It also disbanded the Nauvoo Legion, stipulated that legal wives could testify against their husbands, abolished women's suffrage, instituted a test oath for public service and voting that disqualified any supporter of polygamy, and made judicial and school appointments federal prerogatives. Allen and Leonard, pp. 406–7.

18. Allen and Leonard, p. 411. Idaho's territorial legislature had passed a bill that disfranchised practically all Mormons by asking them to sign an affidavit stating that they did not believe in nor belong to a church that believed in plural marriage. If they did not sign the loyalty oath they lost their voting privileges. In 1888, several Idaho Mormons had their names removed from the records of the Church so that they could vote. The constitutionality of the Idaho test oath was upheld in 1890.

19. Ibid., p. 414.

20. D. Michael Quinn, "LDS Church Authority and New Plural Marriages, 1890–1904," *Dialogue: A Journal of Mormon Thought* 18(Spring 1985): 9–105.

21. Official Declaration 1, *Doctrine and Covenants.*

22. This is'the thesis of Michael Quinn's article "LDS Church Authority."

23. Byron Harvey Allred, *A Leaf in Review* (Caldwell, Idaho: The Caxton Printers, Ltd., 1933), p. 199.

24. Ibid.

25. Ibid.

26. Nineteenth-century Mormons commonly referred to non-Mormons as Gentiles.

27. Allen and Leonard, p. 443.

28. James R. Clark, ed. *Messages of the First Presidency*, Vol. 4 (Salt Lake City: Bookcraft, 1965–75), p. 151.

29. Ibid.

30. Quinn, "LDS Church Authority," p. 100.

31. *The Trial for the Membership of John W. Taylor and Mathaias* [sic] *F. Cowley* (West Jordan, Utah., n.d.), p. 10. The most significant treatment of this episode is Victor W. Jorgensen and B. Carmon Hardy, "The Taylor-Cowley Affair and the Watershed of Mormon History," *Utah Historical Quarterly* 48(Winter 1980):4–36. Although Taylor and Cowley were respected by the fundamentalists, they both refused to join the movement and continued in mainstream Mormonism. Both would have their membership in the Church restored, Taylor posthumously. Samuel Woolley Taylor details his father's rejection of fundamentalism in his book *Family Kingdom* (Salt Lake City: Western Epics, 1974), pp. 273–79.

32. Quinn, "LDS Church Authority," pp. 102–3.

33. Ibid., p. 99. For example, Quinn suggests that the motion to accept the declaration for a sustaining vote was seconded by "Seymour B. Young (who had performed two plural marriages in Mexico under Joseph F. Smith's direction), Anthony W. Ivins (who had performed dozens of plural marriages in Mexico by First Presidency authorization), Angus M. Cannon (who had assented to the First Presidency's suggestion in 1894 that his daughter marry polygamously

Apostle Abraham H. Cannon and who knew that his three sons married polygamously in Salt Lake City in 1900 and 1901), and Moses W. Taylor (brother of post-1890 polygamists John W. Taylor and Frank Y. Taylor).... It is not surprising that some Latter-day Saints interpreted the covert message of 6 April 1904 as applying to future polygamous marriages, the reverse of the document's overt statements, and therefore regarded the Second Manifesto as no more restrictive of new polygamy than the first." Quinn has thoroughly documented post-Manifesto marriage in his important article. He describes the two decades after the Manifesto as a period of ambiguity when Church leaders continued to perform and approve new plural marriages both in the United States and in Mormon colonies in Mexico and Canada.

34. Clark, 4:218. The *Salt Lake Tribune* published numerous exposés about the continued practice of plural marriage after the Manifesto, particularly between 1901 and 1910. The *Tribune* published the names of more than two hundred men who were continuing in the practice, including Joseph W. Musser. See *Salt Lake Tribune* "Always More to Add," 14 November 1909; "Increase of Polygamists," 5 December 1909; "Musser Disfellowshipped," 14 December 1909; and "The List and the Manifesto," 8 October 1910. See also O.N. Malmquist, *The First 100 Years: A History of the Salt Lake Tribune* (Salt Lake City: Utah Historical Society, 1971), pp. 217–58.

35. Ibid.

36. 6 April 1904; 30 January 1908; 15 December 1906; 26 March 1907; 5 October 1910; 6 February 1911; 9 April 1911; 15 October 1911; 31 January 1914.

37. *Joseph W. Musser Journal*, p. 64. This published version of Musser's journal is a compilation of excerpts, dating from the late 1890s to the 1940s, taken from his original journal. Although it contains no publication information, copies are available from Pioneer Publishers, Salt Lake City. Copy in possession of the author. The original journals are located in the Church Archives, Church of Jesus Christ of Latter-day Saints, Salt Lake City, Utah. Unfortunately, these are no longer being made available to researchers.

38. *Salt Lake Tribune*, 10 October 1910.

39. "An Open Letter to J. Reuben Clark," *Truth* 5(August 1939):49.

40. This is well documented in numerous cases of surveillance in the Attorney Generals' Files, Utah State Archives. Copy in the possession of Sam Barlow.

41. *Conference Reports* (Salt Lake City: Church of Jesus Christ of Latter-day Saints, 1911), p. 17.

42. Ibid.

43. Ibid., p. 19.

44. Ibid.

45. Ibid.

46. Grant pled guilty to a charge of unlawful cohabitation in 1899. See "Heber J. Grant Appears in Court," *Deseret News*, 8 September 1899; and "Confession By Grant," *Salt Lake Tribune*, 9 September 1899.

47. Clark, 5:194.

48. Ibid., 5:242.

49. Ibid., 4:194; 3 October 1926, and 4 April 1931.

50. Anthony W. Ivins became second counselor in the First Presidency in 1921 after fourteen years as an apostle.

51. The record of forty polygamous marriages performed by Ivins between 1897 and 1904 in Mexico is one of the most important sources documenting post-Manifesto polygamy. Ivins's son Antoine gave the Ivins Record Book of Marriages to the LDS Church after his father's death. Before it was released to the Church, Stanley Ivins, another son, copied five typewritten pages from the record. This list can be found in a folder entitled "Polygamy B.F. Johnson Letter," Stanley Snow Ivins MSS, 8/10, Utah State Historical Society, and Anthony W. Ivins Collection, 16/7. Ivins's ambiguity on the issue of secret plural marriages is evident in his refusal to go to Washington to "perjure" himself before the Smoot hearings. H. Grant Ivins, "Polygamy in Mexico," Typescript, Marriott Library, p. 5.

52. "An Open Letter to J. Reuben Clark," p. 49.

53. Clark, 5:292.

54. Anthony W. Ivins carefully recorded post-Manifesto marriages in his journals. Although the references are frequently obtuse, the Ivins diaries, journals, and correspondence are one of the best monitors of plural marriage in the two decades after the 1890 Manifesto. The collection is located at the Utah State Historical Society, Salt Lake City, Utah.

55. Clark, 5:293.

56. Ibid.

57. Ibid.

58. Van Wagoner, *Mormon Polygamy*, pp. 15–58.

59. D. Michael Quinn, *J. Reuben Clark, Jr.: The Church Years* (Salt Lake City: Bookcraft, 1983), pp. 180–81. Woolley was, in fact, a key figure in the origins of fundamentalism. His son, Lorin C. Woolley, Clark's cousin, was the first leader of the polygamists separated from the Church by excommunication.

60. Ibid.

61. Ibid.

62. *Utah House Journal*, 14 March 1935.

63. *Joseph W. Musser Journal*, p. 17.

CHAPTER 2

1. It was recorded in Abraham H. Cannon's journal, 29 March 1892. Nineteen years later, during his 1911 excommunication trial, John W. Taylor claimed that several individuals, including Joseph Fielding Smith, made copies of the document (Van Wagoner, *Mormon Polygamy*, p. 183). Quinn documents the existence of such a manuscript in the Joseph Fielding Smith Papers, Church Historical Department Archives, entitled, "REVELATION to President John Taylor, September 27, 1886, copied from the original manuscript by Joseph F. Smith, Jr., August 3, 1909." Quinn also finds a "dramatic change" in John Taylor's "personal circumstances and resistance to federal laws" after that point. His last child had been born in 1881, and he had not cohabited with any of his plural wives after the Edmunds Act of 1882. However, within three months of receiving this 1886 revelation, he married twenty-six-year-old

Josephine Roueche on 19 December 1886 in a ceremony witnessed by George Q. Cannon. He died at her father's home, still in hiding, seven months later (Quinn, "LDS Church Authority," pp. 29–31).

2. The 1929 Musser version was later published in Joseph W. Musser, ed., *The New and Everlasting Covenant of Marriage an Interpretation of Celestial Marriage, Plural Marriage* (Salt Lake City: Truth Publishing Co., 1934).

3. Van Wagoner, *Mormon Polygamy*, p. 184. See also Max Anderson, *The Polygamy Story: Fiction and Fact* (Salt Lake City: Publishers Press, 1979).

4. Despite the publication of his 1912 account of the alleged Centerville visit to John Taylor, the Church called Woolley to the office of a Patriarch in June 1913. However, within a few months the Church excommunicated him for performing additional plural marriages. See "Excommunication of John W. Woolley," *Semi-Weekly Tribune*, 3 April 1914; and "Excommunication," *Deseret News*, 31 March 1914. The 1929 version of the Lorin C. Woolley story was printed in Joseph W. Musser and J. Leslie Broadbent, *Supplement to the New and Everlasting Covenant of Marriage* (Salt Lake City: Truth Publishing Co., 1934). These items were first recorded in Joseph Musser's Book of Rembrance, 7 August 1922, pp. 6, 8.

5. Allred, *A Leaf in Review*, p. 8.

6. Ibid.

7. *Joseph W. Musser Journal*, p. 2.

8. Ibid., p. 3.

9. Ibid.

10. Ibid., p. 8.

11. Ibid., p. 3.

12. Ibid., p. 8.

13. Ibid.

14. Ibid., p. 32.

15. Ibid.

16. Ibid.

17. Ibid., p. 9.

18. Ibid.

19. Ibid., p. 73.

20. Ibid.

21. *Salt Lake Tribune*, 14 December 1909. Amos Musser died that same year.

22. *Joseph W. Musser Journal*, p. 66.

23. Ibid., p. 11.

24. *Deseret News*, 23 March 1921.

25. *Joseph W. Musser Journal*, p. 34.

26. Members of the Church of Jesus Christ of Latter-day Saints are asked to contribute ten percent of their income to the Church. In addition to tithing, members contribute "fast offerings" to provide for the poor and needy.

27. *Musser Journal*, p. 44.

28. Ibid.

29. See Bruce R. McConkie, *Mormon Doctrine* 2d ed. (Salt Lake City:

Bookcraft, 1974). Temple garments are special underclothing that Mormons begin wearing after they participate in the temple endowment. They are a symbol of cleanliness, perfection, and salvation.

30. *Joseph W. Musser Journal*, p. 12.

31. Ibid.

32. Each member of the priesthood council received a similar ordination which expanded upon their original high priest ordinations and appointed them to the office of Apostle and Patriarch.

33. *Joseph W. Musser Journal*, p. 11.

34. Anderson, p. 146.

35. Leroy S. Johnson, *Sermons*, 7 vols. (Hildale, Utah: Twin City Courier Press, 1984), 4:1504.

36. Ibid., p. 1268.

37. Ibid., pp. 1606–7.

38. Johnson, 1:14–18; 3:950; 4:1479.

39. Ibid., 1:173.

40. Ibid., 4:1491.

41. Ibid., 1:210.

42. Ibid., 5:28.

43. Ibid., 1:15–16.

44. Larry M. Logue, *Sermon in the Desert: Belief and Behavior in Early St. George, Utah* (Urbana and Chicago: University of Illinois Press, 1988).

45. Johnson, 6:108–9.

46. Ibid., 5:254.

47. Ibid., 3:881.

48. Ibid., 1:317.

49. Ibid., p. 234.

50. Ibid., pp. 211–12.

51. Ibid., 4:1243–44. President Grant spoke in Kanab and Orderville during a visit to the southern Utah stakes of the Church. He spoke in Kanab at a Zion Stake Conference on 14 September 1931.

52. "Multiple Wives: Arizona Prisoner Defends His Conduct on Religious Grounds," *Literary Digest* 22(1 August 1936):9–10.

53. John Yates Barlow was born 4 March 1874 at Panaca, Nevada. He married four women: Ida May Chritchlow in 1897, Susanna Stevens Taggart on 24 September 1902, Ada Marriott on 18 February 1918, and Martha (Mattie) Jessop on 10 September 1923. For further biographical information about John Y. Barlow and his father Israel Barlow, see "Aged Patriarch of LDS Church Is Excommunicated," *Salt Lake Tribune*, 18 May 1921; and "The Tribune Thrice Sustained," *Salt Lake Tribune*, 29 September 1910. See also "Northwestern States Mission," *Liahona: The Elder's Journal*, 18 June 1918, pp. 813–15, and "Manuscript History of the Northwestern States Mission," entries for 12 April 1918, 12 May 1918, 31 January 1919, 6 February 1919, and 4 March 1919. Originals in the LDS Archives.

54. Reprinted in "Refuge of Lies," *Truth* 1(February 1936):121.

55. Ibid.

56. Anthony W. Ivins to Rulon C. Allred, 3 July 1933, Anthony W. Ivins Collection, Special Collections, Harold B. Lee Library, Brigham Young University, Provo, Utah.

57. Rulon C. Allred to Anthony W. Ivins, 20 October 1933, Anthony W. Ivins collection, Special Collections, Harold B. Lee Library, Brigham Young University, Provo, Utah.

58. Ibid.

59. Ibid.

60. Autobiographical essay, n.p., n.d. Katherine Allred State papers, Anthony W. Ivins Collection, Special Collections, Harold B. Lee Library, Brigham Young University, Provo, Utah.

61. Ibid.

62. Katherine S. Allred, diary entries, Katherine S. Allred Collection, part of the Anthony W. Ivins Collection, Special Collections, Harold B. Lee Library, Brigham Young University.

63. Katherine S. Allred to Anthony W. Ivins, 20 January 1934, Anthony W. Ivins Collection, Special Collections, Harold B. Lee Library, Brigham Young University, Provo, Utah.

64. Ibid.

65. Ibid.

66. Johnson, 1:212.

67. Ibid., 2:533.

68. Ibid., 4:1535.

69. Ibid., 4:1307.

70. *Joseph W. Musser Journal*, p. 43.

71. Ibid., p. 41.

72. Traditionally, Mormon missionaries had traveled without financial support from home, without "purse or scrip." Relying on faith, they were forced to make do with what they could get donated to them along the way. With the newer system, missionaries received financial support and assistance from their loved ones at home.

73. *Joseph W. Musser Journal*, p. 47.

74. Ibid., p. 11.

75. Ibid., p. 12.

76. Ibid., p. 43.

77. Ibid., p. 38.

78. Ibid., p. 46.

79. Ibid., p. 69.

80. Ibid., p. 37.

81. Ibid.

CHAPTER 3

1. Leroy S. Johnson, *Sermons*, 3:854–55.

2. Rufus Kay Wylls, *Arizona: the History of a Frontier State* (Phoenix: Hobson and Herr, 1950), p. 53.

3. William Bailey Maxwell's ranch at the mouth of Short Creek canyon for

a time was a stopping place for travelers. Maxwell was himself a polygamist and had three wives and twenty-seven children. The site of their homestead was later called Maxwell Canyon.

4. Wylls, p. 53.

5. The best study of the development of this area is Charles S. Peterson, *Take Up Your Mission: Mormon Colonizing Along the Little Colorado River, 1870–1900* (Tucson: University of Arizona Press, 1973), pp. 75–77.

6. Ibid.

7. Edward Leo Lyman, *Political Deliverance: The Mormon Quest for Utah Statehood* (Urbana and Chicago: University of Illinois, 1986), p. 142.

8. Johnson, 5:254.

9. Ibid., 1:327.

10. Bert M. Fireman, *Arizona Historic Land* (New York: Alfred Knopf, 1982), p. 89.

11. Malcolm L. Comeaux, *Arizona: a Geography* (Phoenix: Westview Press, 1961), p. 117.

12. *Journal of Discourses* 16:143.

13. Jacob Marinus Lauritzen was born 8 September 1869 in Aalborg, Denmark. After converting to the Mormon Church his parents sent nine-year-old Jacob and his younger brother, seven-year-old John, to America. Jacob married Annie Pratt Gardner, a granddaughter of Parley P. Pratt, on 19 June 1889.

14. Elizabeth Lauritzen, "Hidden Flowers: The Life, Letters, and Poetry of Jacob Marinus Laurizten and his wife Annie Pratt Gardner" (Genealogical Library of the Church of Jesus Christ of Latter-day Saints, compiled in 1968), p. 61.

15. Ibid.

16. Roman Malach, "Short Creek-Colorado City, on the Arizona Strip," unpublished history of Mohave County, 1982, p. 1.

17. Lauritzen, p. 64.

18. Malach, p. 2.

19. Lauritzen, p. 64.

20. Malach, p. 2.

21. Lauritzen, p. 65.

22. Isaac VanWagoner Carling, Jr. was born 21 September 1872 at Fillmore, Utah. He married Elizabeth Johnson on 1 March 1892. Frank Colvin was born 29 August 1846 at Council Bluffs, Potawatomie County, Iowa.

23. The children included Orlin, Verna, Charlotte, and Urban Colvin and Dolphy, Lyle, Glen, and Zelpha Johnson.

24. The Black children included Warren, Millard, Leonard, Edna and Wilma. Six younger children would later attend the Short Creek school: Lewis, Clifford, Ester, George, Marvin and Shirling. The children of the Carlings, Johnsons, Colvins and Blacks would figure prominently in the development of Short Creek over the next several decades and would be key players in the drama of the two raids on the polygamists during the 1940s and 1950s.

25. In this series of meetings after work at the Baldwin factory Carling became acquainted with John W. Woolley, Lorin C. Woolley, John Y. Barlow,

Joseph Musser, Leslie Broadbent, Daniel R. Bateman, and Joseph Smith Jessop. This was one of the earliest connections between the settlers of Short Creek and the key fundamentalist leadership in Salt Lake City.

    26. Lauritzen, p. 68.
    27. Ibid., p. 69.

CHAPTER 4

    1. Leroy S. Johnson, 3:844.
    2. Roman Malach, p. 5.
    3. Ibid. See also *Book of Mormon*, 3 Nephi 11:1.
    4. Malach, p. 5.
    5. Johnson, 3:844.
    6. Ibid., 4:1456.
    7. Malach, p. 5.
    8. Short Creek Branch Records, 1934–35, Church Archives, Church of Jesus Christ of Latter-day Saints, Salt Lake City, Utah.
    9. Johnson, 6:344–46.
    10. *Joseph W. Musser Journal*, p. 75.
    11. *Los Angeles Herald-Express*, 26 August 1935. The *Express* did a series of articles about the fledgling community that it described in the 26 August article as being "out in the middle of nowhere." See also articles of 27–31 August 1935.
    12. Lauritzen, p. 103.
    13. Ibid.
    14. Ibid., p. 4.
    15. "Multiple Wives: Arizona Prisoner Defends His Conduct on Religious Grounds," *Literary Digest* 22(1 August 1936):9–10.
    16. Ibid.
    17. "Short Creek Embroglio," *Truth* 1(October 1935):51.
    18. Heber J. Grant, *General Conference Reports*, April 1931.
    19. *Mohave County Miner*, 9 August 1935.
    20. Lauritzen, p. 104.
    21. *Mohave County Miner*, 23 August 1935.
    22. *Los Angeles Examiner*, 29 August 1935.
    23. Ibid.
    24. Lauritzen, p. 105.
    25. *Mohave County Miner*, 6 September 1935.
    26. Ibid., 13 September 1935.
    27. *Arizona Republic*, 7 September 1935.
    28. *Mohave County Miner*, 13 September 1935.
    29. Ibid.
    30. Ibid.
    31. *Arizona Republic*, 20 September 1935.
    32. Lauritzen, p. 106.
    33. The 1935 Kingman polygamy trials created a media circus and were described in numerous accounts including the *Arizona Republic*, "Polygamy Case Set For Today," 6 September 1935; "Justice Holds Plural Wives Charge In-

valid," 7 September 1935; "Polygamists' Trial Opens Tomorrow," 8 December 1935; "Woman's Trial Is Postponed," 9 December 1935; "Polygamist's Trial Opens At Kingman," 10 December 1935; "Polygamy is Convicted," 12 December 1935; "Polygamy Verdict Is 'Guilty,'" 13 December 1935; "18 Months Meted For Polygamy," 14 December 1935; and "Salt Creek Polygamy Colony to 'Carry On,'" 15 December 1935. See also "Polygamy Again Causes Half-Amused, Half-Bitter Arizona-Utah," *Washington Post*, 29 September 1935; "3 Polygamist Suspects Face Arizona Trial," *Los Angeles Examiner*, 12 October 1935; "Multiple Wives: Arizona Prisoner Defends His Conduct on Religious Grounds," *Literary Digest*, 1 August 1936, pp. 9–10; and "Polygamy: Court Says Religious Freedom Includes but One Wife," *Newsweek*, 21 December 1935, p. 12.

34. "Refuge of Lies," *Truth* 1(February 1936):121.
35. "Heber J. Grant to Rejoice," *Truth* 1(January 1936):102.
36. Johnson, 6:342–43.
37. Ibid.
38. The eighteen included Leonard Black, Vera Colvin Black, J. Warren Black, Ruth Walker Black, Millard Black, Eda Johnson Black, Elva Walker Carling, Charlotte Colvin, Elizabeth Johnson Colvin, Henry E. Covington, Viva Jones Covington, Charles C. Cox, Retta Stocks Cox, Leroy S. Johnson, Josephine Ford Johnson, Lola Johnson, Melvin E. Johnson, and Karl J. Olds. Records of the Rockville Ward, Zion Park Stake, 1935. Originals in the Church Archives, Church of Jesus Christ of Latter-day Saints, Salt Lake City, Utah.
39. Johnson, 6:343.
40. Ibid., 1:233.
41. "Refuge of Lies," p. 121.
42. Johnson, 1:342.
43. Ibid., 3:5.
44. *Los Angeles Examiner*, 12 October 1935.
45. *Mohave County Miner*, 11 October 1935.
46. Ibid.
47. Ibid.
48. "Polygamy and the Press," *Truth* 1(November 1935):76.
49. Ibid.
50. Lauritzen, p. 106.
51. Ibid., p. 103.
52. "Polygamy and the Press," p. 76.
53. "Short Creek Embroglio," *Truth* 1(October 1935):51.
54. *Kansas City Times*, 11 November 1935.
55. Ibid.
56. *Washington Post*, 29 September 1935.
57. *Mohave County Miner*, 13 December 1935.
58. Ibid.
59. "Polygamy and the Press," p. 76.
60. *Mohave County Miner*, 10 January 1936.
61. "Multiple Wives," *Literary Digest*, (1 August 1936):10.
62. Ibid., p. 5.

CHAPTER 5

1. Quinn, *J. Reuben Clark, Jr.*, p. 185.

2. "Who are the Real Conspirators," *Truth* 10(November 1944):41.

3. "True Christianity," *Truth* 5(August 1939):50.

4. *Church Bulletin* No. 223, as quoted in Quinn, *J. Reuben Clark, Jr.*, p. 185.

5. Letter from the Hawthorne Ward Bishopric (Fred E.H. Curtis, bishop, John L. Riley, first counselor, and Ernest Blakemore, second counselor) to J. Reuben Clark, Jr., 1939, Attorney Generals' Files, Utah State Archives; copy in the possession of Sam Barlow.

6. Excommunication court proceedings conducted for Rulon Jeffs by LDS Church officials, 1939; copy in the possession of Sam Barlow.

7. Ibid.

8. Ibid.

9. "1940 Darter's Free Lectures," leaflet; copy in the possession of Sam Barlow.

10. Joseph Wirthlin to Bishop F. E. Curtis, 12 June 1940; see also Fred Curtis to J. Reuben Clark, Jr., 10 November 1938. This extensive collection of correspondence between local ecclesiastical leaders and Clark and also the office of the Presiding Bishopric covers a time period between 1938 and 1944. The originals are located in the Attorney Generals' Files at the Utah State Archives. Copies are in the possession of Sam Barlow.

11. "Joseph W. Musser Journal," 21 September 1939. Church Archives, Church of Jesus Christ of Latter-day Saints, Salt Lake City, Utah.

12. *Truth* 2(July 1936):12.

13. The 1944 raids received remarkable media attention both in and out of the state of Utah, and was featured in news stories throughout the country. See "Forty-six Seized in Three-State Polygamy Drive," *Salt Lake Tribune*, 8 March 1944; "Religion: Fundamentalist," *Time*, 20 March 1944, p. 55; "Religion: Fundamentalist Polygamists," *Newsweek*, 20 March 1944, p. 86; "Utah Polygamy Trials: Federal State Authorities Arrest 50 men and women," *Life*, 3 April 1944, pp. 38–39; and "Polygamy: Utah Jails 15 Fundamentalists," *Life*, 3 July 1944, pp. 22–23, among numerous others. Also see bibliography for additional listings.

14. *Deseret News*, 7 March 1944.

15. Rulon Allred's first wife, Katherine, divorced him after he first became converted to the idea of beginning a plural family. According to his daughter Dorothy Solomon, he would consider this the single greatest tragedy of his life. His plural wives included Myrtle Lloyd, Leona Jeffs (the sister of Rulon Jeffs), Athline Mills, Ruth Barlow and twin sisters Mable and Melba Finlayson. Dorothy Solomon's book *In My Father's House* (New York: Franklin Watts, 1984) poignantly chronicles her polygamist family's story.

16. Samuel W. Taylor, "I Have Six Wives," *True* (November 1953): 22–23.

17. Ibid. See also *Salt Lake Telegram*, 7 March 1944.

18. *Salt Lake Telegram*, 13 March 1944.

19. *Joseph W. Musser Journal,* p. 60.

20. "Musser, Arrest, and Imprisonment," *Truth* 20(August 1954):33–34.

21. *Deseret News,* 7 March 1944.

22. "The Honor Roll of 1945," *Truth* 11(June 1945):27.

23. *Salt Lake Tribune,* 9 March 1944.

24. *Salt Lake Telegram,* 7 March 1944.

25. *Deseret News,* 9 March 1944.

26. Rhea Kunz was a fiesty leader among fundamentalist women. Clearly a faithful and committed member of the group, she later became an acknowledged spiritual leader of the fundamentalists. In 1944 she was the plural wife of Morris Quincy Kunz, a man she later divorced. She was one of Kunz's four wives, who also included Ellen May Holladay, Olive Allred, and Rachel Alveda Jessop. Rhea and Olive were the sisters of polygamists Rulon and Owen Allred.

27. *Deseret News,* 9 March 1944.

28. Ibid., 8 March 1944.

29. *Salt Lake Telegram,* 10 March 1944.

30. *Salt Lake Tribune,* 9 March 1944.

31. Ibid., 8 March 1944.

32. These included Edmund F. Barlow, Joseph W. Musser, Morris Quincy Kunz, David Brigham Darger, Ianthus Windford Barlow, Albert Edmund Barlow, Oswald Brainich, Rulon C. Allred, Lewis C. Allred, John Y. Barlow, Joseph Lyman Jessop, Louis Kelsch, Heber Kimball Cleveland, Albert Edmund Barlow, Rulon T. Jeffs, Guy K. Musser, Robert Leslie Shrewsbury, H.C. Smith, Jr., Alma A. Timpson, Marie Beth Barlow Cleveland, Rhea Allred Kunz, Myrtle Lloyd Allred, Ruth Barlow, Melba and Mabel Finlayson, Mary Mills, Leona Jeffs, Juanita Barlow, Jean Barlow, John Gerhardt Butcherits, and Jonathon Marlon Hammon.

33. *Salt Lake Telegram,* 8 March 1944.

34. *Deseret News,* 8 March 1944.

35. *Salt Lake Telegram,* 13 March 1944.

36. 46 Federal Supplement. Also see No. 334, Title 18, U.S.C.A. (No. 211 Criminal Code).

37. *United States* v. *Barlow et al.,* 56 F.S. 795–98.

38. "Who Are the Real Conspirators," *Truth* 10(November 1944):141.

39. *New York Sunday News,* 20 August 1944.

40. *United States* v. *William Chatwin, Charles F. Zitting, Edna Christensen; and Chatwin* v. *United States,* 326 US 455, 66 S.Ct. 233, 90 L. Ed. 198 (11946).

41. *Deseret News,* 7 June 1944.

42. Ibid.

43. *Cleveland* v. *United States* (32 U.S. 1 [1945]). See also *Salt Lake Telegram,* 2 January 1946.

44. Ibid.

45. Theral Roy Dockstader's four wives, Rose, Lee Jean, Leah and Anne, lived in different residences in both Salt Lake City and Short Creek. The confusion caused in transporting those wives back and forth across state lines created

the legal conditions that allowed the state to charge Dockstader with Mann Act violations.

46. *Deseret News*, 20 March 1944.

47. *United States v. Cleveland* (56 F. Supp. 890 h [D Utah 1944]), p. 894.

48. *Salt Lake Tribune*, 5 January 1945.

49. Assistant Solicitor General Judson (no first name is included in the United States Supplement) on the original argument, and Robert M. Hitchcock on the reargument. With Mr. Judson on the brief were W. Marvin Smith, Robert S. Erdahl, and Beatrice Rosenberg.

50. *Cleveland v. United States*, (329 U.S. 1 [1945]).

51. Ibid.

52. Evidence of cohabitation gathered by the state included birth certificates, school census records and surveillance reports. The births of the children of Alma Timpson's two wives, Marjorie Wooley and Guinevere Cawley, were documented with birth certificates and school records. Testimony of Esther Robinson, Marjorie's next-door neighbor for eight years at Wilmington Avenue in Salt Lake City, helped create a profile of a polygamous lifestyle.

53. E.G. Valens, "15 of Polygamy Sect Convicted: Plan to Test Law," Heber Cleveland Scrapbook; photocopy in the possession of the author.

54. Sec. 103–51–2, U.C.A. 1943.

55. *Deseret News*, 15 May 1944.

56. Ibid.

57. *State v. Barlow et al.*, (153 p. 2d 647).

58. *State v. Musser et al.*, 175 Pacific Reporter 2d Series, 729.

59. *Salt Lake Telegram*, 11 March 1944.

60. Claude Barnes's brief as reprinted in "The Conspiracy Cases," *Truth* 12(February 1947)9:227.

61. "The Conspiracy Cases," *Truth* 12(February 1947):235.

62. Ibid.

63. "Who Are the Real Conspirators," *Truth* 10(November 1944):141.

64. *Deseret News*, 25 May 1944.

65. *Salt Lake Telegram*, 26 May 1944.

66. "Removal of Judge Van Cott in Polygamy Case Asked," Heber Cleveland Scrapbook; photocopy in the possession of the author.

67. *Deseret News*, 19 September 1944.

68. *Salt Lake Telegram*, 19 September 1944.

69. Ibid., 25 September 1944.

70. *Salt Lake Tribune*, 25 September 1944.

71. "To Whom it May Concern," *Truth* 20(March 1950):337.

72. *Salt Lake Telegram*, 25 September 1944.

73. Ibid.

74. *Salt Lake Tribune*, 7 October 1944.

75. Ibid.

76. Ibid.

77. *Salt Lake Tribune*, 29 September 1944, p. 17.

78. *State v. Musser et al.*, 175 Pacific Reporter, 2d Series.

79. "The Last Chapter of the 1944 Church Crusade is Now Written," *Truth* 16(March 1950):187.

CHAPTER 6

1. See *Salt Lake Telegram*, 10 November 1944; *Salt Lake Tribune*, 11 November 1944 for reference to the letter. Reprinted in "The Conspiracy Cases," *Truth* 12(February 1947):246. Petersen's letter became part of the court files. Utah Attorney Generals' Files; copy in the possession of Sam Barlow.

2. *Salt Lake Tribune*, 14 September 1944.

3. Ibid., 25 September 1944.

4. Ibid.

5. *Salt Lake Tribune*, 16 May 1945.

6. *Joseph W. Musser Journal*, p. 15.

7. *Salt Lake Tribune*, 5 October 1945.

8. "Statement by the Editor J.W. Musser," *Truth* 11(March 1946):218.

9. *Joseph W. Musser Journal*, p. 19.

10. *Salt Lake Tribune*, 27 November 1945.

11. "Letter to Governor," *Truth* 13(March 1948):256.

12. Ibid.

13. Leroy S. Johnson, *Sermons*, 3:1386.

14. Ibid., 7:332.

15. "Collection of Fundamentalist Quotes," p. 12, assembled by Sam Barlow; photocopy in the possession of the author.

16. United Effort Plan Bill of Incorporation, 9 November 1942.

17. Utah Code Ann. Sec. 68–3–1 [1953 as amended].

18. United Effort Plan Declaration of Trust.

19. Warranty Deed, W.E. Johnson and Viola Johnson, 19 May 1944; copy in the possession of Sam Barlow.

20. Elizabeth Lauritzen, *Hidden Flowers*, p. 7.

21. For a description of nineteenth-century cooperation see Leonard Arrington, *Great Basin Kingdom: An Economic History of the Latter-day Saints, 1830–1900* (Lincoln: University of Nebraska Press, 1966), pp. 293–352; and Arrington, Dean May and Feramorz Fox, *Building the City of God* (Salt Lake City: Deseret Book, 1976).

22. *Short Creek Historical Calendar* (Hildale, Utah: Twin City Courier, Inc., 1992).

23. Joseph Smith Jessop was born on 25 January 1869 at Millville, Utah. He married Martha Moore Yeates in 1889 and Annie Marriott on 28 December 1928. Martha was the mother of Martha (Mattie) Jessop, the wife of John Yates Barlow.

24. Lauritzen, p. 136.

CHAPTER 7

1. Senate Committee of Judiciary to Study Juvenile Delinquency, Plural Marriage, 84th Cong., 2d Sess., 1955 (Washington, D.C.: Government Printing Office, 1955), p. 6.

2. Senate committee of Judiciary, 1955, p. 32. The fundamentalists questioned Nyborg's motivation in testifying, asserting that much of her testimony deviated from the truth.

3. Sharil Jessop Blackmore, "Woman to Woman," interview with Pat Mitchell on KTLA, 6 March 1984, Los Angeles, California. Sharil added additional information to this story in conversations with her daughter, Angela Hill, and the author, 7 March 1984.

4. See the appendix for a summary of the data.

5. A family unit was created by a marriage between a fundamentalist man and each of his separate wives. The offspring of each separate marriage added to each discreet unit.

6. Senate committee of Judiciary, p. 14.

7. Ibid., p. 20.

8. Leroy S. Johnson, 3:101.

9. Ibid., 2:422.

10. "The Inalienable Rights of Women," *Truth* 14(October 1948):134.

11. Ibid.

12. "Rules of Family Conduct," *Truth* 10(October 1944):113.

13. Ibid., p. 14.

14. Johnson, 3:807–9.

15. "Propriety in Dress," *Truth* 12(June 1946):19.

16. Edson Jessop with Maurine Whipple, "Why I Have Five Wives: A Mormon Fundamentalist Tells His Story," *Colliers* (13 November 1953):30.

17. Johnson, 2:763.

18. Ibid., 5:14.

19. Ibid., 6:231.

20. See Linda P. Wilcox, "Mormon Motherhood: Official Images," in *Sisters in Spirit*, Maureen Ursenbach Beecher and Lavina Fielding Anderson, editors (Urbana and Chicago: University of Illinois Press, 1987).

21. "Mrs. A. and B.," oral interview with Martha S. Bradley, 22 May 1986, Salt Lake City, Utah. Because of the sensitive nature of the issue of polygamy in modern-day Utah and the legal implications of public testimony, these two sister wives have asked to remain anonymous but wanted their interview to be part of the story.

22. "Rights of Women," p. 182.

23. The son of Church Apostle John W. Taylor, a man excommunicated for his continued belief in and practice of polygamy, Samuel W. Taylor's lifetime fascination with polygamy has produced numerous articles and books on the subject. His father's biography, *Family Kingdom* (New York: McGraw Hill, 1951) details John W. Taylor's experience with polygamy. For Samuel W. Taylor's article, "I Have Six Wives," Taylor lived with the Allred family for a few weeks to gather information and conduct interviews.

24. Samuel W. Taylor, "I Have Six Wives," *True* (November 1953):76.

25. In fact, according to Carmon Hardy in his book, *Solemn Covenant* (Urbana: University of Illinois Press, 1992), this was considered by nineteenth-century Mormon polygamists to be a particular benefit of polygamy, for it al-

lowed husbands to turn to their non-pregnant wives during times of pregnancy. He writes: "From the 1840s until the early twentieth century, Mormon authorities repeatedly warned against sexual relations when mothers were carrying and nursing children. Women free from the embraces of their husbands during pregnancy were known from science, it was said, to produce healthier and stronger offspring.... As an unnamed Mormon correspondent told E. N. Jencks, if a man desired additional women, let him marry them. But, he said, let him then 'observe, and have no commerce during gestation. Then we shall have a race...not, as now, too frequently born with unbridled lusts engendered, while in a pre-natal state, by the excesses of their parents'" (p. 90).

26. "Rights of Women," p. 102.
27. Ibid., p. 182.
28. Ibid.
29. Ibid., p. 185.
30. Ibid.
31. "Continence During Gestations," *Truth* 8(January 1942):187.
32. "A First Wife Speaks," *Truth* 10(March 1944):130.
33. Ibid.
34. Ibid.
35. "The Inalienable Right to Motherhood," *Truth* 14(October 1948): 275.
36. Ibid.
37. "Rights of Women," p. 184.
38. "A Polygamous Wife Speaks," *Truth* 10(June 1944):26.
39. Rhea Kunz quoted in "Expressions of a Plural Wife," *Truth* 10(January 1945):69.
40. "Rights of Women," p. 134.
41. Ibid., p. 102.
42. "Rules of Family Conduct," p. 113.
43. "Mrs. C.," oral interview by Martha S. Bradley, 26 July 1986, Short Creek, Arizona.
44. Jessop and Whipple, 1953, p. 29.
45. Ibid., p. 27.
46. Mrs. C., 1986.
47. Jessop and Whipple, 1953, p. 30.
48. Group oral interview with Martha S. Bradley, 5 November 1988, Short Creek, Arizona.
49. Jessop and Whipple, 1953, p. 29.
50. "A Polygamous Wife Speaks," p. 26.
51. Taylor, "I Have Six Wives," p. 78.
52. *In Re State in Interest of Black* (283 P. 2d 887).

CHAPTER 8

1. Radio address, 26 July 1953, KTAR Radio, Phoenix, Arizona. The full text of this address can be found in the appendix.
2. "Amateur Governor," 1951, p. 27. Copy obtained from Howard Pyle in

possession of the author. A copy is also in the "Howard Pyle Collection," Luhr Reading Room, Hayden Library, Arizona State University, Tempe, Arizona.

3. Barry M. Goldwater with Jack Casserly, *Goldwater* (New York: Doubleday, 1988), p. 93.

4. Cited in James M. Perry, *Barry Goldwater* (Silver Springs, Maryland: Newsbook, 1964), p. 43.

5. Kay F. Jones, "Ana Frohmiller, Watchdog of the Arizona Treasury," *Journal of Arizona History* 25(Winter 1984):349–68.

6. "Howard Pyle Collection," Arizona State University.

7. *Arizona Republic*, 31 October 1950.

8. "Howard Pyle," Howard Pyle Collection, Hayden Library, Luhr Reading Room, Arizona State University.

9. Dr. Robert Gryder, "John Howard Pyle," in *The Arizona Governors, 1912–1990* (Phoenix: Heritage Publishers Inc., 1989).

10. Barry Goldwater to Howard Pyle, 18 February 1952, "Howard Pyle Collection," Arizona State University.

11. Goldwater refers to the text of this speech as his campaign kick-off remarks in a letter to Pyle dated 29 January 1953. "Howard Pyle Collection," Arizona State University.

12. Cited in Michael Fessier, Jr., "Jessica's Story," *New West* (31 December 1979):33.

13. Goldwater with Casserly, p. 93.

14. *Arizona Daily Star*, 21 November 1953.

15. Louis J. Barlow to the State Board of Education, 16 May 1954, Public Welfare Collection, Arizona Department of Library, Archives and Public Records, Archives Division, Arizona State Capitol, Phoenix, Arizona.

16. Fessier, p. 32.

17. *Arizona Daily Star*, 8 November 1953.

18. Faulkner's testimony was given before the U.S. Senate Committee to Investigate Juvenile Delinquency on Thursday, 28 April 1955. Senate committee of Judiciary, p. 19.

19. From the first the United Effort Plan paid taxes and never existed under tax-exempt status.

20. Senate committee of Judiciary, p. 19.

21. Ibid. Faulkner made similar remarks as early as November 1953. See Wiley S. Maloney, "Arizona Raids Short Creek? Why?" *Colliers* (13 November 1953):30.

22. *Arizona Daily Star*, 8 November 1953. This was corroborated by Arizona State Legislator Polly Rosenbaum in an oral interview with Martha S. Bradley on 19 September 1991 at Phoenix, Arizona.

23. Howard Pyle, oral interview with Martha S. Bradley, 14 March 1984, Phoenix, Arizona.

24. Ibid.

25. Ibid.

26. Ibid.

27. Ibid.

28. Ibid.

29. Ibid.

30. J. Bracken Lee, oral interview with Martha S. Bradley, 3 October 1991, Salt Lake City, Utah.

31. Fred Wilson to Clinton Vernon, 26 February 1952, Attorney Generals' Files, Utah State Archives; copy in the possession of Sam Barlow.

32. Ibid.

33. Ibid.

34. Senate committee of Judiciary, p. 19.

35. *Journal of the House*, Arizona State Legislature, 1952, p. 258.

36. Ibid., p. 464.

37. Democrat Fred O. Wilson was Arizona Attorney General between November 1949 and November 1953. Republican Ross F. Jones was Attorney General between 1953 and 1955.

38. *Laws of Arizona*, 1952, p. 120.

39. Howard Pyle, text of radio address, 26 July 1953, KTAR, Phoenix, Arizona. Printed in *Arizona Republic*, 27 July 1953.

40. Ibid.

41. Maloney, p. 19.

42. Pyle interview, 1984.

43. Maloney, p. 20.

44. In a letter dated 28 June 1952, V. Pershing Nelson reported to Clinton Vernon on local efforts at gathering birth certificates to be used as proof of cohabitation. Attorney Generals' Files, Utah State Archives; copy in the possession of Sam Barlow.

45. Clinton Vernon to Scott Matheson, 11 July 1952, Attorney Generals' Files, Utah State Archives; copy in the possession of Sam Barlow.

46. Scott M. Matheson to Clinton D. Vernon, 15 December 1952, Attorney Generals' Files, Utah State Archives, copy in the possession of Sam Barlow.

47. Ibid.

48. E.R. Callister to Paul LaPrade, 26 January 1953, Attorney Generals' Files, Utah State Archives; copy in the possession of Sam Barlow.

49. Ross Jones to E.R. Callister, 3 February 1953, Attorney Generals' Files, Utah State Archives; copy in the possession of Sam Barlow.

50. Ogden Kraut, oral interview with Martha Bradley, 14 March 1990, Salt Lake City, Utah.

51. Pyle interview, 1984.

52. Ibid. While Governor Pyle was remarkably candid about his role in the 1953 raid, it is more difficult to determine the Church's participation in the plan. There are two tantalizing files in the Church Archives of the LDS Church earmarked: "Short Creek 1953," and "The Church and the Fundamentalists." Both files could potentially be of considerable interest for this study but both are restricted from researchers. One can only speculate that Mark E. Petersen, David O. McKay and Spencer W. Kimball (three fundamentalist specialists among the general authorities) were apprised of the situation because of their

particular interest and expertise. It is also interesting to note that Pyle's correspondence for the three months before and after the raid has been removed from the governor's files at the Arizona State Archives.

53. Howard Pyle, "Crimes Against the State," transcript of a speech, n.d. Howard Pyle Collection.

54. Lee, 1991.

55. Paul LaPrade to E.R. Callister, 23 April 1953, Attorney Generals' Files, Utah State Archives; copy in the possession of Sam Barlow.

56. Paul LaPrade to E.R. Callister, 8 May 1953, Attorney Generals' Files, Utah State Archives; copy in the possession of Sam Barlow.

57. Paul LaPrade to E.R. Callister, 11 May 1953, Attorney Generals' Files, Utah State Archives; copy in the possession of Sam Barlow.

58. Walter L. Budge, Utah Assistant Attorney General, suggested that family Bibles might provide evidence that could establish cohabitation. Walter L. Budge to Ross Jones, 13 May 1953, Attorney Generals' Files, Utah State Archives; copy in the possession of Sam Barlow.

59. Paul LaPrade to Walter L. Budge, 17 June 1953, Attorney Generals' Files, Utah State Archives; copy in the possession of Sam Barlow.

CHAPTER 9

1. The names of the highway patrolmen involved in the raid were later published in the *Arizona State Highway Album* (Tucson: State of Arizona, 1982).

2. Ibid.

3. Trudy Camping, oral interview with Martha S. Bradley, 20 September 1991, Phoenix, Arizona.

4. "Arizona, the Great Love-nest Raid," *Time*, 3 August 1953, p. 16.

5. Camping, 1991.

6. David Broadbent had three plural wives in 1953: twenty-three-year-old Viola Johnson Broadbent; fifteen-year-old Fawn Stubbs; and fifteen-year-old Rula Kunz.

7. Dan Barlow was married to Elnora Black, twenty years old; Edith Black, fifteen years old; and Lorna Allred, fifteen years old.

8. *Salt Lake Tribune*, 29 July 1953. The polygamists shared this story with the author in a series of group and individual interviews in Colorado City between 1986–1992.

9. Leota Dockstader Jessop was the fifth wife of Edson P. Jessop. She was thirty-three years old at the time of the raid.

10. "Citizens Affadavits," *Truth* 19(May 1954):353–74.

11. Ibid.

12. Superior Court of Arizona, Mohave County, Arrest Warrants, 26 July 1953, Kingman County Courthouse. Photocopy in the possession of the author.

13. Ibid.

14. *Arizona Daily Star*, 27 July 1953.

15. *Mohave County Miner*, 30 July 1953.

16. Edson Jessop with Maurine Whipple, "Why I Have Five Wives: A Mormon Fundamentalist Tells His Story," *Colliers* (13 November 1953):30.

Edson Jessop's five wives included twenty-eight-year-old Margaret Lucille Hunter; twenty-six-year-old Evelyn Camilla Fisher; twenty-seven-year-old Irene Nielson; thirty-year-old Lulu Alyne Bistline; and thirty-three-year-old Leota Dockstader.

17. *Salt Lake Tribune*, 29 July 1953.

18. Ibid.

19. *Arizona Daily Star*, 29 July 1953.

20. *Arizona Republic*, 28 July 1953.

21. *Salt Lake Tribune*, 1 August 1953.

22. Ibid.

23. *Salt Lake Tribune*, 28 July 1953.

24. *Arizona Daily Star*, 30 July 1953.

25. Ibid., 31 July 1953.

26. Ibid., 2 August 1953.

27. Ibid., 8 November 1953.

28. Ibid.

29. Trudy Camping, 1991.

30. Jessop and Whipple, p. 30.

31. Group interview with Martha S. Bradley, 5 November 1988, Colorado City City Hall, Colorado City, Arizona.

32. Ibid.

33. Superior Court, Mohave County, Search Warrants, 27 July 1953, Kingman County Courthouse. Photocopy in the possession of the author.

34. *Salt Lake Tribune*, 27 July 1953.

35. Ibid.

36. Ibid.

37. Ibid.

38. *Arizona Daily Star*, 27 July 1953.

39. Ibid.

40. Ibid.

41. "Citizens Affadavits," p. 77.

42. *Salt Lake Tribune*, 27 July 1953.

43. *Kane County Standard*, 31 July 1953.

44. Leroy Johnson's wives in 1953 included Josephine Ford Johnson, sixty years old; Mae Bateman Barlow, fifty-five years old; Gwendolyn Balmforth, twenty-four years old; Sara Elizabeth Barlow, twenty-nine years old; Wilma Black, forty-four years old; and Mildred Barlow, twenty years old. Group interview with Martha S. Bradley, 5 November 1988, Leroy S. Johnson Meetinghouse, Colorado City, Arizona.

45. Martha S. Bradley, "The Women of Fundamentalism: Short Creek, 1953," *Dialogue* 23(Summer 1990):31–32.

46. Group interview 1988.

47. *Salt Lake Tribune*, 2 August 1953.

48. *Arizona Republic*, 3 August 1953.

49. *Arizona Daily Star*, 12 August 1953.

50. The *Salt Lake Tribune*, 30 July 1953, and the *Deseret News*, 30 July

1953, reported the release of the mothers. The women arrested were Dorothy Norval Jessop, Emma Norval Jessop, Beth Jessop, May Johnson Jessop and Colleen Cooke.

51. *Salt Lake Tribune*, 31 July 1953.

52. *Arizona Republic*, 2 August 1953.

53. *Salt Lake Tribune*, 7 August 1953.

54. Ibid., 8 August 1953.

55. *Arizona Republic*, 2 August 1953.

56. *Arizona Daily Star*, 14 August 1953.

57. *Salt Lake Tribune*, 14 August 1953.

58. Ibid., 14 August 1953.

59. *Arizona Daily Star*, 19 August 1953, and 20 August 1953.

60. Superior Court, Mohave County, Notice of Bail, 27 July 1953, Kingman County Courthouse. Photocopy in the possession of the author.

61. *Arizona Republic*, 3 August 1953.

62. Ibid., 4 August 1953.

63. Ibid.

64. *Arizona Daily Star*, 3 August 1953. See also *Arizona Republic*, 3 August 1953.

65. Christina Small reponded to Elnora Barlow's request for aid in a letter dated 27 October 1953, Attorney Generals' Files, Utah State Archives. Copy in the possession of Sam Barlow.

66. Senate committee of Judiciary.

67. Marjorie Price, oral interview with Martha S. Bradley, 21 September 1991, Phoenix, Arizona. After acting as a foster mother to this polygamous family, sometime later Delas White and her husband Coy left Glendale and moved to Short Creek, where they became fundamentalists.

68. Blackmore, 1984.

69. Group interview 1988.

70. Bradley, "The Women of Fundamentalism," p. 33.

71. Ibid., p. 34.

72. Ibid.

73. Group interview 1988.

74. Bradley, "Women of Fundamentalism," p. 34.

75. James Baldwin (Casework Supervisor, Maricopa County Department of Public Welfare) to Owen Allred, 10 September 1953, Attorney Generals' Files, Utah State Archives. Copy in the possession of Sam Barlow.

76. "August Report from Welfare Department," 1954, Attorney Generals' Files, Utah State Archives. Copy in the possession of Sam Barlow.

CHAPTER 10

1. Leroy S. Johnson, *Sermons*, 3:1391.

2. Ibid., 1:227.

3. Ibid., 3:1082.

4. *Deseret News*, 27 July 1953.

5. Howard Pyle to Barry Goldwater, 31 July 1953, "Howard Pyle Collection," Arizona State University.

6. *Arizona Republic*, 27 July 1953.

7. Ibid., 6 October 1985.

8. "The Hazards of Public Life," "Howard Pyle Collection," Arizona State University.

9. Ibid.

10. Robert Gryder, "John Howard Pyle," in *The Arizona Governors, 1912–1990* (Phoenix: Heritage Publishers Inc., 1989).

11. *Southern Utah News and Kane County Standard*, 3 December 1953.

12. *Arizona Republic*, 30 August 1953.

13. *Arizona Daily Star*, 3 August 1953.

14. Ibid., 6 August 1953.

15. Ibid., 11 August 1953.

16. Ibid.

17. *Arizona Daily Star*, 6 August 1953.

18. Ibid., 15 August 1953.

19. Ibid.

20. Ibid., 30 July 1953.

21. Leo Reeve, oral interview with Martha S. Bradley, 14 October 1991, Hurricane, Utah.

22. Ibid.

23. *Arizona Daily Star*, 10 November 1953.

24. Ibid., 29 December 1953.

25. Jim Smith, address before the Arizona State Senate, 31 March 1954; photocopy in the possession of the author.

26. Ibid.

27. Ibid.

28. Leroy S. Johnson to a Mr. Cartwright, 6 August 1953, Attorney Generals' Files, Utah State Archives. Copy in the possession of Sam Barlow.

29. *Arizona Daily Star*, 12 September 1953.

30. Ibid., 4 August 1953.

31. Judge Robert S. Tuller, Superior Court of Arizona, Mohave County, Court Brief, 7 December 1953. Photocopy in the possession of the author.

32. Lorna Lockwood to H. L. Smith, 16 September 1964; photocopy in the possession of the author.

33. *Mohave County Miner*, 6 August 1953.

34. *Salt Lake Tribune*, 23 August 1953.

35. "In the Superior Court of the State of Arizona for the County of Mohave," No. J-498, Order-Juvenile, 29 July 1953; copy in the Attorney Generals' Files, Utah State Archives. Photocopy in the possession of Sam Barlow.

36. Order of the Superior Court of the State of Arizona in and for the County of Maricopa, March 3, 1955, Judge Henry S. Stevens.

37. *Arizona Daily Star*, 28 August 1953.

38. Ibid., 29 August 1953.

39. Ibid., 23 September 1953.

40. Louis J. Barlow to State Board of Education, Public Instruction Collection, Arizona Department of Library, Archives, and Public Records, Archives Division, Arizona State Capitol, Phoenix, Arizona.

41. Judge Robert S. Tuller, Superior Court of Arizona, County of Mohave, Court Brief, 7 December 1953; originals in the Kingman County Courthouse. Photocopy in the possession of the author.

42. Ibid.

43. *Arizona Daily Star*, 8 December 1953.

44. Tuller, 7 December 1953.

CHAPTER 11

1. In the Matter of the Revocation of Teacher's Certificates of Clyde Mackert, Louis J. Barlow and Jerold Williams, Findings and Order, 20 February 1954, Public Instruction Collection, Arizona Department of Library, Archives, and Public Records, Archives Division, Arizona State Capitol, Phoenix, Arizona.

2. Howard Pyle to Clyde Chapman Mackert, Public Instruction Collection, Arizona Department of Library, Archives, and Public Records, Archives Division, Arizona State Capitol, Phoenix, Arizona.

3. Louis J. Barlow to the State Board of Education, 16 May 1954; photocopy in the possession of the author.

4. *Mohave County Miner*, 5 May 1955.

5. Barlow, 16 May 1954.

6. Jerold Roy Williams to State Board of Education, 27 May 1954, Public Instruction Collection, Arizona Department of Library, Archives, and Public Records, Archives Division, Arizona State Capitol, Phoenix, Arizona.

7. Ibid.

8. A series of letters between Pyle/Barlow/Williams and the Board of Education are housed in the Public Instruction Collection, Arizona Department of Library, Archives, and Public Records, Archives Division, Arizona State Capitol, Phoenix, Arizona.

9. Robert W. Pickrell to State Board of Education, 30 April 1954, Public Instruction Collection, Arizona Department of Library, Archives, and Public Records, Archives Division, Arizona State Capitol, Phoenix, Arizona.

10. *Clyde Mackert, Louis J. Barlow, and Jerold Williams* v. *Arizona State Board of Education, Howard Pyle, Chairman, F.J. Benedict, R.E. Booth, Bessie Kidd Best, Grady Gammage, Richard A. Harvill, L.A. Eastburn, M.L. Brooks, members*. Copy in Public Instruction Collection, Arizona Department of Library, Archives, and Public Records, Archives Division, Arizona State Capitol, Phoenix, Arizona.

11. In the Matter of the Revocation of Teacher's Certificates of Clyde Mackert, Louis J. Barlow and Jerold Williams, Findings and Order, 31 July 1954.

12. Ibid.

13. Senate committee of Judiciary.

14. *Arizona Republic*, 3 May 1955.

15. Senate committee of Judiciary.

16. Ibid.

17. LaVar Rockwood to Martha S. Bradley, 23 April 1990.

18. Ibid.

19. Ibid.

20. Senate committee of Judiciary, p. 114.

21. This correspondence is included in the Attorney Generals' Files, Utah State Archives; copy in the possession of Sam Barlow. Ken Driggs in his article, "Who Shall Raise the Children? Vera Black and the Rights of Polygamous Utah Parents" *Utah Historical Quarterly* 60(Winter 1992)1:27–46, goes so far as to suggest that the outcome was determined before the evidence was even heard, p. 34.

22. Paul LaPrade to David Anderson, 9 September 1953, Attorney Generals' Files, Utah State Archives; copy in the possession of Sam Barlow.

23. David Anderson to Ross F. Jones, 11 September 1953, Attorney Generals' Files, Utah State Archives; copy in the possession of Sam Barlow.

24. David Anderson to John Farr Larson, 23 October 1953, Attorney Generals' Files, Utah State Archives; copy in the possession of Sam Barlow.

25. Ibid.

26. Ibid.

27. Ibid.

28. H.C. Shoemaker to Judge Anderson, 29 October 1953; Attorney Generals' Files, Utah State Archives; copy in the possession of Sam Barlow.

29. Unsigned memo, 9 November 1953, Attorney Generals' Files, Utah State Archives; copy in the possession of Sam Barlow.

30. Fundamentalists ordered to appear before the court included Joseph and Clea Black, Marion Broadbent Barlow, Louis J. and Isabell Johnson, Adaire Stubbs Barlow, David R. and Arleen Jessop Bateman, Leonard and Vera Johnson Black, George Lynn and Beth Black Cooke, Jack W. and Caroline Cope Zitting, Eva Jessop, Lola Jessop Cooke, Carl and Louise Jessop Holm, Joseph S. and Annie M. Jessop, Virgil Y. and Mae Jessop, LeRoy Sunderland and Wilma Black Johnson, Warren E. and Jeannine Stubbs, Clela S. Cooke Johnson, Clyde Chapman, Dona May Kunz, Mildred Eads Mackert, Lawrence Ritchie and Genevieve Pratt Stubbs. Attorney Generals' Files, Utah State Archives; copy in the possession of Sam Barlow.

31. David Anderson to H.C. Shoemaker, 9 December 1953, Attorney Generals' Files, Utah State Archives; copy in the possession of Sam Barlow.

32. Anderson to LaPrade, 15 November 1953, Attorney Generals' Files; copy in the possession of Sam Barlow.

33. H. C. Shoemaker to the parents of Short Creek, Utah, 28 January 1954, Attorney Generals' Files, Utah State Archives; copy in the possession of Sam Barlow.

34. The Utah Attorney General's office conducted an investigation into whether Knowlton was himself a polygamist during 1954. During these hearings Knowlton was negotiating with a man named Wayne Pearson for the purchase of a large parcel of land in Monteview, Idaho. Attorney Generals' Files, Utah State Archives; copy in the possession of Sam Barlow. Although the state's findings were inconclusive, the fundamentalists remember Knowlton as a polygamist.

35. Senate committee of Judiciary, p. 115.

36. The *Salt Lake Tribune* covered every step of the legal process. See

"Custody Trial Readied for Cult Children," 1 August 1953; "Counsel Seeks New Decision in Child Case," 16 June 1955; "High Court Backs Utah Rule on Children in Sect Squabble," 13 December 1955; Joe Fitzpatrick, "State Moves For Custody of Polygamy Cult's Tots," 17 December 1955; "State Welfare Plans Care of Cult Children," 31 December 1955; "Officials to Take Custody of 8 Cult Children Today," 10 January 1956; D.C. Dix, "Officers Spurn Force, Fail To Take Cultist Children," 11 January 1956; "Mother of Eight Gives Up Family in Cult Dispute," 13 January 1956; "Judge Agenda To Include Cult Children," 24 January 1956; "State Seeks Custody of 8th Cultist Child," 10 February 1956; "Cult Mother of 8 Pleads for Family," 1 May 1956; "Motion Filed for Dismissal of Cult Child Custody Plea," 8 May 1956; "Tuesday Hearing Scheduled on Child Custody Petition," 14 May 1956; "Court Rejects Cult Mother Custody Plea," 16 May 1956; "State to Return Children of Cult Mother," 12 June 1956; "Cult Mom's Reason Told for Assent to Sign Pledge," 13 June 1956; and "Mrs. Black Takes Family, Fulfills Dream," 14 June 1956.

37. *In Re Black*, 283 P. 2d Series, p. 896. The Utah Supreme Court has a file on the Blacks' petition for a writ of certiorari to the United States Supreme Court. This record includes 149 pages of assorted legal documents as well as the transcripts of the juvenile court proceedings.

38. Senate committee of Judiciary, p. 116.

39. Section 55–1–16, Utah Code Annotated, 1953.

40. Certiorari File, pp. 118–19.

41. Ibid. Leonard Black's testimony is found on pp. 3–50.

42. "Hearing for Children of Vera Johnson and Leonard Black, in the Juvenile Court, St. George, Utah, March 20, 1954," Attorney Generals' Files, Utah State Archives; copy in the possession of Sam Barlow.

43. Ibid.

44. Certiorari File, pp. 79–89.

45. Ibid., pp. 91–92.

46. Ibid., pp. 95–109.

47. Ibid.

48. Ibid., pp. 120–23.

49. Ibid.

50. The court issued nineteen findings of fact established in the hearing. Finding 12 held "that Leonard and Vera Johnson Black and the majority of the adult residents of Short Creek are and have been members of an organized religious group. That the members of this religious group entertain a religious belief in substance and effect that there is a law of God requiring men to take and live with more than one wife and that failure to do so constitutes a breach of religious duties." Finding 14 accused the Blacks of encouraging their children to become polygamists when they were old enough to marry. Finding 17 described the Black home as an immoral environment for the rearing of children, justified the transfer of custody and control over these children to the state. Certiorari File, pp. 120–23.

51. Levi Peterson, *Juanita Brooks: Mormon Woman Historian* (Salt Lake City: University of Utah Press), p. 246.

52. *Black* v. *Anderson*, 277 P. 2d 975 (Utah 1954).

53. The concept of *parens patriea* was most recently defined by two court cases, *State of West Virginia* v. *Chas. Psizer and Company*, C.A. New York, 440 Federal 2nd, and *Gibbs* v. *Tittelman*, D.C. Penn., 369 Federal Supplement 38. It is the idea of the state as sovereign guardian of persons under legal disability, such as juveniles or the insane, and in child custody cases when acting on behalf of the state to protect the interests of the child. It is the principle that the state must care for those who cannot care for themselves, including minors who lack proper care and custody from their parents.

54. *In Re Black.*

55. Worthen's opinion is in *In Re Black*, 283 P. 2d at 914.

56. Ibid.

57. Ibid.

58. The court order made and entered on the 11th day of May 1954.

59. John Farr Larson to Vera Black, letter dated 3 December 1956.

60. *Black* v. *Utah*, 350 U.S. 923, 76 S. Ct. 211, 100 I., Ed. 807 (1955).

61. Letter to the editor from Norman C. Pierce, *Salt Lake Tribune*, 21 December 1955.

62. Maurine Whipple Collection, 1956, Special Collections, Harold B. Lee Library, Brigham Young University, Provo, Utah.

63. Ibid.

64. Ibid.

65. Ibid.

66. Ibid.

67. Ibid.

68. Ibid.

69. Juanita Brooks to Elsa Harris, 17 January 1956, reproduced in *Truth* 21(March 1956):13.

70. Peterson, p. 248.

71. *Salt Lake Tribune*, 11 January 1956. See also *Salt Lake Tribune*, 13 January 1956, and *Time*, 23 January 1956.

72. *Salt Lake Tribune*, 26 January 1956.

73. Ibid., 8 March 1956.

74. Ibid.

75. Ibid., 12 June 1956.

CHAPTER 12

1. Paul Van Dam comments, in "A Matter of Principle"; video produced by KUED television, Ken Verdoia, producer, University of Utah, Salt Lake City.

2. Thomas K. Martin, Tim B. Heaton, and Stephen J. Bahr, *Utah in Demographic Perspective* (Salt Lake City: Signature Books, 1986), pp. 183–85.

3. Ibid.

4. Ibid.

5. Seymour Parker, Janet Smith, and Joseph Ginat, "Father Absence and Cross-Sex Identity: The Puberty Rites Controversy Revisited," *American Ethnologist* 2(November 1975):687–706.

6. Ibid.

7. *My Kingdom Shall Roll Forth* (Salt Lake City: Church of Jesus Christ of Latter-day Saints, 1979).

APPENDIX A

1. This list was compiled through the combined efforts of the Utah and Arizona Attorney Generals' offices, and was based on birth certificates and school census records, and merit certificates. Some dates and ages were not verifiable, so that information has been left blank. Original information is available in the Utah Attorney Generals' Files, Utah State Archives, Salt Lake City.

2. Gerald's age was listed variously as either 9 or 12 at the time of the raid.

3. Jay Jessop was killed in the Kaibab Forest in 1946. Lulu and Leota then married Edson P. Jessop.

APPENDIX B

1. Howard Pyle Collection, Luhr Reading Room, Hayden Library, Arizona State University, Tempe, Arizona.

Bibliography

Books and Articles

Alexander, Thomas G. "Charles S. Zane, Apostle of the New Era," *Utah Historical Quarterly* 34(Fall 1966):290–314.

Allen, James B., and Glen M. Leonard. *The Story of the Latter-day Saints*. Salt Lake City: Deseret Book Company and the Historical Department of The Church of Jesus Christ of Latter-day Saints, 1976.

Allred, Byron Harvey. *A Leaf in Review*. Salt Lake City: Caxton Publishers, 1933.

Anderson, Jerry. "Polygamy in Utah." *Utah Law Review* 5(Spring 1957):381.

Anderson, Max. *The Polygamy Story: Fiction or Fact*. Salt Lake City: Publishers Press, 1979.

Arizona State Highway Album. Tucson: State of Arizona, 1982.

"Arizona, the Great Love-nest Raid." *Time*, 3 August 1953, 16.

Arrington, Leonard J. *Brigham Young: American Moses*. New York: Alfred A. Knopf, 1985.

———. *Great Basin Kingdom: An Economic History of the Latter-day Saints, 1830–1900*. Lincoln: University of Nebraska Press, 1966.

Arrington, Leonard J., and Davis Bitton. *The Mormon Experience: A History of the Latter-day Saints*. New York: Alfred A. Knopf, 1979.

Arrington, Leonard J., Dean May, and Feramorz Fox. *Building the City of God*. Salt Lake City: Deseret Book, 1976.

Baird, Mark J., and Rhea A. Kunz. *Reminiscences of John W. Woolley and Lorin C. Woolley*. 4 vols. Draper, Utah: N.p, n.d.

Barlow, Sam, comp. "A Collection of Fundamentalist Quotes." Colorado City, Ariz. Photocopy.

Barnes, Sisley. "The Short Creek Incident." *Liberty* 74(July/August 1979):7–9.

Beecher, Maureen Ursenbach, and Lavina Fielding Anderson. *Sisters in Spirit*. Urbana and Chicago: University of Illinois Press, 1987.

Bennion, Lowell C. "The Geography of Polygamy Among the Mormons in 1880." Paper presented at the Mormon History Association Conference, May 1984, Provo, Utah.

Bitton, Davis. "Mormon Polygamy: A Review Article." *Journal of Mormon History* 4(1977):106–11.

Bradlee, Ben, Jr., and Dale Van Atta. *Prophet of Blood—The Untold Story of Ervil LeBaron and the Lambs of God*. New York: G.P. Putnam's Sons, 1981.

Bradley, Martha S. "'Hide and Seek': Children on the Underground." *Utah Historical Quarterly* 51(Spring 1984):133–53.

———. "The Women of Fundamentalism: Short Creek, 1953." *Dialogue* 23(Summer 1990):14–37.

Brooks, Juanita. "A Close-up of Polygamy." *Harper's Magazine*, February 1934, 299–307.

Cannon, Abraham H. Journal. Special Collections, Harold B. Lee Library. Brigham Young University, Provo, Utah.

Cannon, Kenneth, II. "Beyond the Manifesto: Polygamous Cohabitation Among LDS General Authorities after 1890." *Utah Historical Quarterly* 46(Winter 1978):24–36.

Carey, J. "Untold Story of Short Creek." *American Mercury* 78 (May 1954):119–23.

Clark, James R., ed. *Messages of the First Presidency*. 6 vols. Salt Lake City: Bookcraft, 1965–75.

Clayton, James L. "The Supreme Court, Polygamy and the Enforcement of Morals in Nineteenth Century America: An Analysis of Reynolds v. United States." *Dialogue* 12(Winter 1979):46–61.

Cleveland, Heber. "Heber Cleveland Scrapbook." Photocopy.

Comeaux, Malcolm L. *Arizona: A Geography*. Phoenix: Westview Press, 1981.

Conference Reports. Salt Lake City: Church of Jesus Christ of Latter-day Saints, 1904, 1911.

Driggs, Ken. "Who Shall Raise the Children? Vera Black and the Rights of Polygamous Utah Parents," *Utah Historical Quarterly* 60(Winter 1992):27–46.

———. "Twentieth-Century Polygamy and Fundamentalist Mormons in Southern Utah." *Dialogue* 24(Winter 1991):44–58.

Embry, Jessie. *Mormon Polygamous Families.* Salt Lake City: University of Utah Press, 1987.

Fessier, Michael, Jr. "Jessica's Story." *New West* (31 December 1979):33.

Fireman, Bert M. *Arizona Historic Land.* New York: Alfred A. Knopf, 1982.

Firmage, Edwin Brown, and Richard Collin Mangrum. *Zion in the Courts: A Legal History of the Church of Jesus Christ of Latter-day Saints, 1830–1900.* Urbana and Chicago: University of Illinois Press, 1988.

Flanders, Robert B. *Nauvoo: Kingdom on the Mississippi.* Urbana: University of Illinois Press, 1965.

Foster, Lawrence. *Religion and Sexuality: Three American Communal Experiments of the Nineteenth Century.* New York: Oxford University Press, 1981.

"Fundamentalist Polygamist." *Newsweek,* March 20, 1944, 86.

Ginat, Joseph, Seymour Parker, and Janet Smith. "Father Absence and Cross-Sex Identity: The Puberty Rites Controversy Revisted." *American Ethnologist* 2(November 1975):687–706.

Goff, John S. *Biographical Dictionary.* Cave Creek, Ariz.: Black Mountain Press, 1983.

Goldwater, Barry, with Jack Casserly. *Goldwater.* New York: Doubleday, 1988.

——. *With No Apologies.* New York: William Morrow and Co., 1979.

Gryder, Robert. *The Arizona Governors, 1912–1990.* Phoenix: Heritage Publishers Inc., 1989.

Hardy, Carmon. *Solemn Covenant.* Urbana and Chicago: University of Illinois Press, 1992.

Higham, John. *Strangers in the Land.* New Brunswick, N.J.: Rutgers University Press, 1957.

Hill, Marvin S. *Quest for Refuge.* Salt Lake City: Signature Books, 1989.

Hilton, Jerold A. "Polygamy in Utah and the Surrounding Area Since the Manifesto of 1890." M.A. thesis, Brigham Young University, 1959.

Ivins, Anthony W. *Anthony W. Ivins Collection.* Utah State Historical Society Library. Salt Lake City, Utah.

Ivins, H. Grant. "Polygamy in Mexico." Marriott Library, University of Utah, Salt Lake City. Typescript.

Ivins, Stanley. "Notes on Mormon Polygamy." *Western Humanities Review* 10(Summer 1956):229–39.

Jensen, Kimberly James. "Between Two Fires: Women on the 'Underground' of Mormon Polygamy." M.A. thesis, Brigham Young University, 1981.

Jessee, Dean C. "A Comparative Study and Evaluation of the Latter-day Saint Fundamentalist Views Pertaining to the Practice of Plural Marriage." M.A. thesis, Brigham Young University, 1963.

Jessop, Edson, with Maurine Whipple. "Why I Have Five Wives: A Mormon Fundamentalist Tells His Story." *Colliers*, 13 November 1953, 27–30.

Johnson, Leroy S. *Sermons*. 6 vols. Hildale, Utah: Twin City Courier Press, 1984.

Jones, Kay F. "Ana Frohmiller, Watchdog of the Arizona Treasury." *Journal of Arizona History* 25(Winter 1984):349–68.

Jones, Marcus F. "The Present Situation in Utah as the Result of Statehood." *Kinsman*, 5 February 1898.

Jorgensen, Victor W., and Carmon B. Hardy. "The Taylor-Cowley Affair and the Watershed of Mormon History." *Utah Historical Quarterly* 48(Winter 1980):4–36.

Journal of Discourses. 26 vols. Liverpool and London: Latter-day Saint Book Depot, 1854–86.

Kraut, Ogden. *Polygamy in the Bible*. Salt Lake City: Kraut's Pioneer Press, 1983.

Kunz, Rhea. *Voices of Women Approbating Celestial or Plural Marriage*. Draper, Utah: Review and Preview Publishers, n.d.

Larson, Gustive O. *The Americanization of Utah for Statehood*. San Marino, Calif.: The Huntington Library, 1971.

Lauritzen, Elizabeth. "Hidden Flowers: The Life, Letters, and Poetry of Jacob Marinus Laurizten and his wife Annie Pratt Gardner." Genealogical Library, The Church of Jesus Christ of Latter-day Saints, Salt Lake City. Typescript.

Life. 3 April 1944; 4 April 1944; 3 July 1944; 24 July 1944; 14 September 1953.

Linford, Orma. "The Mormons and the Law: The Polygamy Cases." *Utah Law Review* 9(Winter 1964/Summer 1965):308–70, 543–91.

Lockwood, Lorna. Letter to H. L. Smith, 16 September 1964. Photocopy.

Logue, Larry M. *A Sermon in the Desert: Belief and Behavior in Early St. George, Utah*. Urbana and Chicago: University of Illinois Press, 1988.

Lyman, Edward Leo. *Political Deliverance: Mormon Quest for Utah Statehood*. Urbana and Chicago: University of Illinois Press, 1986.

McClintock, James H. *Mormon Settlement in Arizona*. 1921. Reprint. Tucson: University of Arizona Press, 1985.

McConkie, Bruce R. *Mormon Doctrine.* 2d ed. Salt Lake City: Book-craft, 1974.

McFarland, Ernest W. *The Autobiography of Ernest W. McFarland.* N. p. 1979.

Malach, Roman. "Short Creek-Colorado City, on the Arizona Strip." Unpublished history of Mohave County, 1982.

Maloney, Wiley S. "Arizona Raid Short Creek? Why?" *Colliers,* 13 November 1953, 30–31.

———. "Short Creek Story." *The American West,* September 1953, 16–32.

Malmquist, O.N. *The First 100 Years: A History of the* Salt Lake Tribune. Salt Lake City: Utah Historical Society, 1971.

Martin, Thomas K., Tim B. Heaton, and Stephen J. Bahr. *Utah in Demographic Perspective.* Salt Lake City: Signature Books, 1986.

"A Matter of Principle." Video produced by KUED television. Ken Verdoia, producer. University of Utah. Salt Lake City, Utah.

Miller, David E., and Della S. Miller. *Nauvoo: The City of Joseph.* Santa Barbara: Calif.: Peregrine Press, 1974.

"Multiple Wives: Arizona Prisoner Defends His Conduct on Religious Grounds." *Literary Digest* 22(1 August 1936):9–10.

Musser, Joseph W. *Celestial or Plural Marriage.* Salt Lake City: Truth Publishing Co., 1944.

———. *Joseph W. Musser Journal.* N.p., n.d. These published excerpts are available from Pioneer Publishers, Salt Lake City.

———. Journal. Historical Department Archives. Church of Jesus Christ of Latter-day Saints. Salt Lake City, Utah.

———. *The New and Everlasting Covenant of Marriage an Interpretation of Celestial Marriage, Plural Marriage.* Salt Lake City: Truth Publishing Co., 1934.

Musser, Joseph W. and J. Leslie Broadbent. *Supplement to the New and Everlasting Covenant of Marriage.* Salt Lake City: Truth Publishing Co., 1934.

My Kingdom Shall Roll Forth. Salt Lake City: Church of Jesus Christ of Latter-day Saints, 1979.

Newell, Linda King and Valeen Tippetts Avery. *Mormon Enigma: Emma Hale Smith.* New York: Doubleday and Co., 1984.

Parkinson, Preston Woolley. *The Utah Woolley Family.* Salt Lake City: Deseret Press, 1973.

Penrose, Charles W. Address in *Conference Reports,* Spring 1918. Salt Lake City: Church of Jesus Christ of Latter-day Saints.

Perry, James M. *Barry Goldwater: A New Look at a Presidential Candidate.* Silver Springs, Maryland: Newsbook, 1964.

Peterson, Charles S. *Take Up Your Mission: Mormon Colonizing Along the Little Colorado River, 1870–1900.* Tucson: University of Arizona Press, 1973.

Peterson, Levi. *Juanita Brooks: Mormon Woman Historian.* Salt Lake City: University of Utah Press, 1988.

"Proposed Policy on Plural Marriage." American Civil Liberties Union. September 10, 1990.

Pyle, Howard. "Crimes against the State." Transcript of a speech, n.d. Howard Pyle Collection.

———. Howard Pyle Collection. Department of Archives and Manuscripts. Hayden Library. Arizona State University. Tempe, Arizona.

———. Papers. Archives Division. Arizona State Capitol. Phoenix, Arizona.

———. "Laws are Not Enough." Speech delivered 1 February 1954. In *Vital Speeches.* Vol. 4, 236. Phoenix: City News Publishing Co., 1954.

———. Text of radio address delivered 26 July 1953 on KTAR Radio, Phoenix, Arizona. Printed in *Arizona Republic*, 27 July 1953.

Quinn, D. Michael. *J. Reuben Clark, Jr.: The Church Years.* Salt Lake City: Bookcraft, 1983.

———. "LDS Church Authority and New Plural Marriages, 1890–1904." *Dialogue* 18(Spring 1985):9–105.

Rockwood, LaVar. Letter to the author, 23 April 1990.

Reimann, Paul E. *Plural Marriage Limited.* Salt Lake City: Utah Printing Co., 1974.

Rich, Russell. *Those Who Would Be Leaders.* Provo, Utah: Brigham Young University Press, 1959.

Short Creek Branch of the Church of Jesus Christ of Latter-day Saints, Records, 1934–1935. Church Archives. Church of Jesus Christ of Latter-day Saints. Salt Lake City, Utah.

Short Creek Historical Calendar. Hildale, Utah: Twin City Courier Inc., 1992.

Smith, Jim. Address before the Arizona State Senate, 31 March 1954. Photocopy.

Solomon, Dorothy Allred. *In My Father's House.* New York: Franklin Watts, 1984.

———. "A Very Different Kind of Family." *Good Housekeeping*, April 1979.

Taylor, Samuel W. *Family Kingdom.* New York: McGraw Hill, 1951.

———. "I Have Six Wives." *True*, November 1953.

Trimble, Marshall. *Arizona: A Panoramic History of a Frontier State.* New York: Doubleday and Co., 1977.

Truth magazine. "The Conspiracy Cases," 12(February 1947); "Continence During Gestation," 7(January 1942); "Expressions of a Plural Wife," 10(January 1945); " A First Wife Speaks," 10(March 1944); "Heber J. Grant to Rejoice," 1(January 1, 1936); "The Inalienable Right to Motherhood," 10(March 1945); "The Inalienable Rights of Women," 14(October 1948); "The Last Chapter of the 1944 Church Crusade is now Written," 16(March 1950); "Letter to Governor," 13(March 1948); "A Polygamous Wife Speaks," 10(June 1944); "Polygamy and the Press," 1(November 1, 1935); "Propriety in Dress," 12(February 1947); "Refuge of Lies," 1(February 1, 1936); "Rules of Family Conduct," 10(October 1944); "Short Creek Embroglio," 1(October 1, 1935); "True Christianity," 5(August 1939); "Who Are the Real Conspirators," 10(November 1944): 141.

Van Wagoner, Richard S. *Mormon Polygamy: A History.* Salt Lake City: Signature Books, 1986.

——. "Mormon Polyandry in Nauvoo." *Dialogue* 18(Fall 1985):67–83.

Whipple, Maurine. Maurine Whipple Collection. Special Collections, Harold B. Lee Library, Brigham Young University. Provo, Utah.

Wood, Rob and Dean Smith. *Barry Goldwater.* New York: Avon Books, 1961.

Wylls, Rufus Kay. *Arizona: The History of a Frontier State.* Phoenix: Hobson and Herr, 1950.

Wyatt, Clair L. *Some That Trouble You: Subcultures in Mormonism.* Salt Lake City: Bookcraft, 1974.

Zion Park Stake, Manuscript History. Church Archives. Church of Jesus Christ of Latter-day Saints. Salt Lake City, Utah.

Public Documents

Arizona. Analysis of Appropriation No. 1–1–06–000–1300, December 31, 1953. Archives Division. Arizona State Capitol. Phoenix, Ariz.

Arizona. State Legislature. *Journal of the House.* Phoenix, 1935–53.

Arizona. Public Instruction Files. Archives Division. Arizona State Capitol. Phoenix, Ariz.

Arizona. Revolving Fund. Archives Division. Arizona State Capitol. Phoenix, Ariz.

Proceedings...in the Matter of the Protests against the Right of Honorable Reed Smoot, a Senator from the State of Utah to Hold his Seat. 4 vols. 1904–1906.

Special Census of Colorado City. Mohave County, Arizona. 10 April 1986.

"Summary of Special Activities." Colorado City Unified School District #14. 29 November 1988.

"Summary of Visitors to the School." Colorado City Unified School District #14. 29 November 1988.

United Effort Plan Bill of Incorporation. 9 November 1942. Short Creek, Arizona.

U.S. Congress. Senate. Committee of Judiciary to Study Juvenile Delinquency, Plural Marriage. 84th Cong., 2d Sess., 1955. Washington, D.C.: Government Printing Office, 1955.

U.S. Congress. House. *The Morrill Act.* 37th Cong., 2d sess., 1862. H. Doc. 78.

Utah. Attorney Generals' Files. Utah State Archives. Salt Lake City, Utah.

Utah. Biennial Report of the Attorney General to the Governor of the State of Utah, 1896–present.

Utah. State Legislature. *Journal of the House.* Salt Lake City, 1896–present.

Newspapers

The American Weekly Review. Philadelphia. 28 May 1944.

Arizona Republic. Phoenix. 28 July 1953 to 6 October 1985, selected.

Arizona Daily Star. Phoenix. 27 July 1953 to 10 July 1959, selected.

Daily Herald. Provo, Utah. 8 March 1944.

Deseret News. Salt Lake City. 7 March 1944 to 30 July 1953, selected.

Erie Pennsylvania Daily Times. 30 April 1944.

Kansas City Times. 11 November 1935.

Los Angeles Examiner. 23 March 1944. 29 August 1935.

Los Angeles Herald-Express. 26 August 1935 to 12 October 1935, selected.

Mohave County Miner. Kingman, Arizona. 9 August 1935 to 9 May 1957, selected.

New York Sunday News. 20 August 1944.

New York Times. 27 July 1953, "Arizona Raids Polygamous Cult: Seeks to Wipe Out Its Community," by Gladwin Hill.

Phoenix Gazette. 3 May 1957; 5 May 1974, "Hazards of Public Life,

Ex-Governor Recalls Career," by Glen Law; 20 August 1980, "50–Year Affair with Politics Not Over for Ex-governor," by Lori Grezesiek.

Salt Lake Telegram. 7 March 1944 to 26 December 1946, selected.

Salt Lake Tribune. 8 March 1944 to 2 December 1954, selected.

San Francisco Examiner. 21 March 1944 to 2 October 1944, selected.
    Southern Utah News and Kane County Standard. Kanab, Utah. 31 July 1953. 3 December 1953.

Tempe Daily News. 25 April 1977. "Ex-Governor is Citizen of the Year."

Times-Herald. Los Angeles. 16 April 1944.

Washington Post. 29 September 1935.

Oral Interviews

All interviews were conducted by the author at Colorado City, Arizona, unless otherwise noted. Audio tapes of all interviews are in her possession.

Barlow, Alwin. Interview with author. 26 July 1987, 5 November 1988.

Barlow, Dan. Interview with author. 26 July 1986, 4–5 November 1988.

Barlow, Louis. Interview with author. 25 April 1992.

———. Interview on KSUB radio, August 1953. Cedar City, Utah.

Barlow, Sam. Interview with author. 5 November 1988. Further consultations with author from 1991 to 1992.

Barlow, Veda. Interview with author. 4 November 1988.

Blackmore, Sharil Jessop. Interview with author. Los Angeles, California, 6 March 1984.

———."Woman to Woman." Interview with Pat Mitchell on KTLA television. Los Angeles, California, 6 March 1984.

Broadbent, Viola. Interview with author. 26 July 1986.

Mrs. C. Interview with author. 26 July 1986.

Camping, Trudy. Interview with author. Phoenix, 20 September 1991.

Darger, Colleen Barlow. Interview with author. 4 November 1988.

Darger, Mary. Interview with author. 4 November 1988.

Janice T. Interview with author. 26 July 1986.

Jessop, Margaret Hunter. Interview with author. 5 November 1988.

Jessop, Lydia Johnson. Interview with author. 4 November 1988.

Johnson, Gwen Balmforth. Interviews with author. 4–5 November 1988, November 1991.

Johnson, Mildred Barlow. Interview with author. 4 November 1988.

Kraut, Ogden. Interview with author. Salt Lake City, 14 March 1990.

Kunz, Rhea. Interview with author. Salt Lake City, 27 August 1987.

Lee, J. Bracken. Interview with author. Salt Lake City, 3 October 1991.

Price, Marge. Interview with author. Phoenix, 20 September 1991.

Pyle, Howard. Interview with author. Phoenix, 14 March 1984.

Reeve, Leo. Interview with author. Hurricane, Utah, 14 October 1991.

Rosenbaum, Polly. Interview with author. Phoenix, 19 September 1991.

Survivors of the 1953 raid, group interviews with author. 26 July 1986, 4–5 November 1988.

Mrs. S. W. and Mrs. C. W. Interview with author. Salt Lake City, 22 May 1986.

Index